Women Pioneers in Continental European Methodism, 1869–1939

Despite the fact that women are often mentioned as having played instrumental roles in the establishment of Methodism on the Continent of Europe, very little detail concerning the women has ever been provided to add texture to this historical tapestry. This book of essays redresses this by launching a new and wider investigation into the story of pioneering Methodist women in Europe.

By bringing to light an alternative set of historical narratives, this edited volume gives voice to a broad range of religious issues and concerns during the critical period in European history between 1869 and 1939. Covering a range of nations in Continental Europe, some important interpretive themes are suggested, such as the capacity of women to network, their ability to engage in God's work, and their skill at navigating difficult cultural boundaries.

This ground-breaking study will be of significant interest to scholars of Methodism, but also to students and academics working in history, religious studies, and gender.

Paul W. Chilcote is Professor of Theology at Asbury Theological Seminary in Orlando, Florida. He has published 25 books, many of them on the history of Methodism and women's studies, including *She Offered Them Christ* and *The Methodist Defense of Women in Ministry*.

Ulrike Schuler is Professor of Church History, Methodism, and Ecumenical Studies at United Methodist-related Reutlingen School of Theology in Germany. She has published widely on Methodism in Europe and has served as Chair of the European Methodist Historical Society and President of the World Methodist Historical Society.

Routledge Methodist Studies

Series Editor: William Gibson, Director of the Oxford Centre for Methodism and Church History, Oxford Brookes University, UK

Editorial Board:

Ted A. Campbell, Professor of Church History, Perkins School of Theology, Southern Methodist University, USA

David N. Hempton, Dean, Harvard Divinity School, Harvard University, USA

Priscilla Pope-Levison, Associate Dean, Perkins School of Theology, Southern Methodist University, USA

Martin Wellings, Superintendent Minister of Oxford Methodist Circuit and Past President of the World Methodist Historical Society, UK.

Karen B. Westerfield Tucker, Professor of Worship, Boston University, USA

Methodism remains one of the largest denominations in the USA and is growing in South America, Africa, and Asia (especially in Korea and China). This series spans Methodist history and theology, exploring its success as a movement historically and in its global expansion. Books in the series will look particularly at features within Methodism which attract wide interest, including: the unique position of the Wesleys; the prominent role of women and minorities in Methodism; the interaction between Methodism and politics; the "Methodist conscience" and its motivation for temperance and pacifist movements; the wide range of Pentecostal, holiness and evangelical movements; and the interaction of Methodism with different cultures.

Image, Identity and John Wesley
A Study in Portraiture
Peter S. Forsaith

Methodist Heritage and Identity
Brian E. Beck

John Wesley and the Education of Children
Gender, Class and Piety
Linda A. Ryan

John Wesley, Practical Divinity and the Defence of Literature
Emma Salgård Cunha

Women Pioneers in Continental European Methodism, 1869–1939
Edited by Paul W. Chilcote and Ulrike Schuler

For more information about this series, please visit: www.routledge.com/religion/series/AMETHOD

Women Pioneers in Continental European Methodism, 1869–1939

Edited by Paul W. Chilcote
and Ulrike Schuler

 Routledge
Taylor & Francis Group

LONDON AND NEW YORK

First published 2019
by Routledge
2 Park Square, Milton Park, Abingdon, Oxon OX14 4RN

and by Routledge
711 Third Avenue, New York, NY 10017

Routledge is an imprint of the Taylor & Francis Group, an informa business

British Library Cataloguing-in-Publication Data
A catalogue record for this book is available from the British Library

Library of Congress Cataloging-in-Publication Data
Names: Chilcote, Paul Wesley, 1954– editor.
Title: Women pioneers in Continental European Methodism, 1869–1939 / edited by Paul W. Chilcote and Ulrike Schuler.
Description: New York : Routledge, 2018. | Series: Routledge Methodist studies series | Includes bibliographical references and index.
Identifiers: LCCN 2018024293 | ISBN 9781138633049 (hardback : alk. paper) | ISBN 9781315207926 (ebook)
Subjects: LCSH: Women in the Methodist Church—Europe—History. | Methodist women—Europe—Biography. | Methodism.
Classification: LCC BX8345.7 .W665 2018 | DDC 287.082/094—dc23
LC record available at https://lccn.loc.gov/2018024293

ISBN: 978-1-138-63304-9 (hbk)
ISBN: 978-1-315-20792-6 (ebk)

Typeset in Sabon
by Apex CoVantage, LLC

In honor of those women
whose stories have been reclaimed in this volume,
and in memory of all those nameless women,
whose lost history may never be uncovered,
but are also known by God

Contents

Maps and figures

Maps

Maps are reproduced here with the permission of Westermann Gruppe, Braunschweig, appearing originally in color in the *Diercke International Atlas* (pages 36.1, 36.2, 36.3) and reformatted in black and white specifically for this volume by Westermann.

Figures

Each chapter and part of the book is introduced by a photograph as follows:

Contributors

Andrea Annese is postdoctoral researcher in the history of Christianity at Sapienza University of Rome. He has published on Christian origins and on the history of Protestantism in Italy, including a book on the history and theology of Italian Methodism from 1861 to 1946.

Mareike Bloedt is a Methodist probationary minister in Stuttgart, having completed graduate studies at the Theologische Hochschule Reutlingen. Her research interests include the rise and development of the deaconess movement in Europe.

Christina Cekov studied German and German literature in Skopje, the Republic of Macedonia. She has responsibility for women's work and Christian literature in The United Methodist Church of Macedonia and devotes energy to the rediscovery of women pioneers in this context.

Paul W. Chilcote is Professor of Theology at Asbury Theological Seminary in Orlando, Florida. He has published 25 books, many of them on the history of Methodism and women's studies, including *She Offered Them Christ* and *The Methodist Defense of Women in Ministry*.

Margit Herfarth teaches church history and Old Testament at Wichern-Kolleg in Berlin, a school for deacons. She studied at the universities of Muenster, Greifswald, Tübingen, and Heidelberg, earning her PhD in 2013 from the University of Heidelberg.

Jacqui Horton is an ordained minister in the Methodist Church in Britain, currently serving a circuit in south Norfolk. She has a strong interest in both local and Methodist history and serves as Vice-President of the East Anglia Branch of the Wesley Historical Society.

S T Kimbrough, Jr. serves as Research Fellow at Duke Divinity School in his retirement. His role in the renaissance of Methodism in Eurasia led to the publication of his heralded *Methodism in Russia & the Baltic States*, as well as the definitive biography of *Anna Eklund*.

Lars-Erik Nordby is currently Director of the deaconess-related Bethany Foundation in Oslo. He served previously as Rector of The United

Methodist Seminary in Oslo and provided significant ecumenical leadership, primarily as co-chair of the dialogue with the Church of Norway.

Ulrike Schuler is Professor of Church History, Methodism, and Ecumenical Studies at United Methodist-related Reutlingen School of Theology in Germany. She has published widely on Methodism in Europe and has served as Chair of the European Methodist Historical Society and President of the World Methodist Historical Society.

Thor Bernhard Tobiassen serves as Director of the Methodist Church's Archives in Oslo in his retirement. Educated for the ministry at the Norwegian School of Theology in Oslo and the Methodist seminary in Bergen, he has served as chaplain at the Bethany Foundation in Bergen.

Michael Wetzel, Methodist archivist and historian, serves as Chair of the European Methodist Historical Society and as Co-chair of its World Methodist counterpart. Having completed his PhD in 2003, his historical interests have carried him to Zimbabwe as well as throughout Europe.

Foreword

When we as Methodists in Europe explain who we are, of course, we tell the stories of the beginning of the Wesleyan movement in England in the eighteenth century. We speak of John and Charles Wesley, their commitment to mission, evangelism, and social action, and their emphasis on spreading holiness over the land. In Continental Europe we often celebrate the fact that we are part of a worldwide web of Methodist conferences. We also mention that our history is linked to migration; migration from Europe to the USA and also to England and back to Continental Europe. Newcomers to the USA from Germany, for example, found Christ in Methodist congregations. Some of them migrated back to Continental Europe in order to share this lively faith in their home countries. Others encouraged their conferences and boards in the USA or England to send missionaries to Europe.

The mission field was different from other places on the earth. Missionaries came to a Christianized continent. Protestant, Roman Catholic, or Orthodox Churches were well-established. Some were State Churches; others had strong links with the political powers. The Methodists came in order to revitalize those existing churches; nevertheless, over the years, Methodist Churches came into being. Methodism in Europe has not had the chance to become a big denomination. Yet we are a vital part of the Christian family in our small and diverse continent, engaged in lively ecumenical relationships for the sake of the mission "so that the world may believe" (John 17:21).

We Methodists seek to explore our church history. Because we are rather small conferences, there are not many books available in order to learn about the details of the mission work. Therefore, I am very grateful to Paul Chilcote and Ulrike Schuler for their efforts in collecting, writing, and publishing essays about the Methodist mission in Continental Europe. And I am even more appreciative that they focused on the impact of women in early Methodism here. Although I am a United Methodist female bishop from Germany, I did not know until recently that female pioneers were deeply involved in the Methodist mission in Europe. As is often the case, women are rarely mentioned when we speak about our history. I am well aware that women have always been the majority in the pews. I also know that they have been influential in ministries with children in their families and in the congregations and that they bore witness to God's love by serving needy people in their communities. I valued the impact of the deaconesses in my country and beyond. But until recently I had no idea that women served at the forefront in the Methodist mission work in several Methodist countries.

It was at a conference in Ruse, Bulgaria, September 9–12, 2015, organized by the European Section of the World Methodist Historical Society and co-funded by the General Commission on Archives and History of The United Methodist Church, that I heard of the Bible Women in Bulgaria, Macedonia, and Italy and of other pioneering women like Anna Eklund, a deaconess who served in Russia under very difficult political and economic circumstances from 1907 to 1930. I discovered hidden treasures and I was not the only participant who learned new things. I am very grateful to Ulrike Schuler and Paul Chilcote for their efforts, not only to encourage the presenters at the conference in Ruse to work on their manuscripts, but also to add other essays and to order and publish the material. Now the hidden treasures are accessible to anyone who is able to read this volume in the English language. This book not only uncovers unknown female pioneers, it also generates curiosity and will lead, hopefully, to further explorations related to the impact of women in the Methodist movement in Europe and other parts of the world. I am sure there are many other female pioneers whose stories need to be told and whose witness needs to be shared and celebrated.

Sharing our history and the witness of our foremothers and forefathers not only gives us a better understanding of who we are. It also provides instruction in terms of who God is calling us to be today. We desperately need pioneers in mission in the twenty-first century. We are called to go into unchartered territory, even in the regions where we are at home. Many people are longing for a meaningful life in Europe and elsewhere. At least in Western Europe, many of those who are seeking would never go to church. Some of them are in families that have not been part of any faith community for two or three generations. We need mission-minded Christians who take a risk and reach out to their neighbors, sharing their faith with them and trusting that Christ is already there. May the readers of this volume take inspiration from the stories of these pioneering women and move forward in their partnership with God's mission in the twenty-first century.

Rosemarie Wenner, Retired United Methodist Bishop, Germany
First female Methodist bishop in Europe, 2005–2017
President, United Methodist Council of Bishops, 2012–2014

Preface

Dr. Schuler developed the idea for this book originally in response to some research she had undertaken at the Methodist Archives at Drew University, Madison, New Jersey, under the auspices of the Bell Research Scholarship program administered by the School of Theology there. Given Dr. Chilcote's interests in and publications about women in Methodism, she turned to him to inquire about the possibility of entering into a collaborative project together. We both agreed to the merits of the effort to uncover some of the lost stories of Methodist women in Europe. As we began to work together in this general direction and think about publication, given the status of scholarship and the lack of resources, we first contemplated an article on a fairly rudimentary level. But the more we invested time and energy into unearthing the materials needed for this minimalist agenda, the more interesting documentation fell into our hands. We forged ahead on our plan for an article, but one article soon became two. First we published an historical essay related to Methodist Bible Women in Bulgaria and Italy. We followed up with a sequel related to Methodist women missionaries in that same context. Both these articles, in revised form, appear in this volume.

Conversations with colleague historians, in particular, led to the vision of a book that might help break ground in this unexplored terrain. We did not feel that this was something we could accomplish alone and began to think about like-minded colleagues who could assist us in the task. Dr. Schuler delivered a paper related to our work at the Oxford Institute of Methodist Theological Studies in August 2013, and then we presented our research together at two conferences with the hopes of engendering some interest in this topic and to celebrate our discoveries. The Methodist Theological School in Ohio and the Women's Division of the General Board of Global Ministries of The United Methodist Church co-sponsored a conference on Methodist Women's History, "Voices Lost and Found," in Delaware, Ohio, May 28–30, 2015, in which we participated and shared our vision. Just several months later, September 9–13, the World Methodist Historical Society – European Section sponsored a conference on the topic, "Mission Empowered by Methodist Women," in Ruse, Bulgaria, supported by the General Commission on Archives and History (GCAH) of The United

Methodist Church as well. This event aligned perfectly with our vision – the conference examined the pioneering role of European women in the establishment of Methodism on the continent – and we participated, in part, with hopes of identifying potential contributors to this project. More than 50 participants from Bulgaria, Czech Republic, Denmark, Germany, Hungary, Italy, Macedonia, Norway, Russia, Slovakia, Switzerland, the UK, and the USA gathered with all the United Methodist bishops who served in Europe, Dr. Patrick Streiff (Switzerland, Central and Southern Europe Episcopal Area), Dr. Eduard Khegay (Russia, Eurasia Episcopal Area), Christian Alsted (Denmark, Nordic, and Baltic Episcopal Area), Rosemarie Wenner (Germany, Germany Episcopal Area), and Dr. Walter Klaiber (retired) to explore this topic.

In a subsequent news release related to the conference, Dr. Fred Day, the General Commission on Archives General Secretary, reflected on the importance of this event:

> This conference was another opportunity for our Commission to do what we do across the UMC worldwide: to remember and offer resources about how the seeds of the past yield the harvest of the future. We are keepers and interpreters of the stories and experiences that shape the UMC's ethos and DNA. Insights from the challenging frontiers where these European and later American women broke new ground have much to teach us for ministry and mission now and into the future. Women traversed insurmountable geographical and cultural obstacles. They were leaders with little more than an abiding passion for sharing God's love with people hungry for hope. They crossed borders and boundaries that turned others away.

At this event we engaged in conversation with a number of scholars whom we felt could make a contribution to this volume. This volume reflects this collaboration.

We are fully aware that this collection of historical essays only scratches the surface. It is our fervent hope that many will receive this volume as a challenge to explore the vast array of issues related to Methodist women in continental Europe. We are convinced that the story of the pioneer women is important and that the history of the Methodist people is incomplete without them. So we invite others to fill in the gaps, fill out the portraits, and fill up the pages of a new wave of women's studies related to these women; also, feel free to correct our errors and mistaken impressions. So much of this exciting story still needs to be uncovered!

Ulrike Schuler and Paul W. Chilcote, Holy Week 2018

Acknowledgements

Our debts are great to many people who both helped inspire this volume and who provided assistance to us in all that has led to the completion of this project. First and foremost, we appreciate all those women who found a spiritual home in Methodism and helped plant this heritage of faith across continental Europe.

We express our gratitude to a number of institutions for their support and encouragement along the way: the General Commission on Archives and History of The United Methodist Church for a Women's History Writing Grant that helped support our research and for their sponsorship of the Women's History Conference in Ruse, Bulgaria, that brought various scholars and practitioners around tables to discuss important topics related to this theme; Oxford Brookes University for a Visiting Fellow Grant; the Methodist Archives at Drew University for professional support in locating and deciphering resources; the Methodist Theological School in Ohio for hosting and the Women's Division of the General Board of Global Ministries of The United Methodist Church for co-sponsoring a conference on Methodist women's history in which we presented some of our initial findings; Sarum College for providing hospitality on the fringes of an unrelated conference we both attended that permitted us to put some finishing touches on the volume; and Ashland Theological Seminary, Asbury Theological Seminary, and Theologische Hochschule Reutlingen, the institutions that employed us throughout the course of this project, promoted our scholarship for the life of the church and academy, and afforded time for us to pursue these endeavors.

We are grateful to the editors of *Methodist History* who gave their permission for us to reprint two articles previously published in that journal, but altered somewhat substantially in form: "Methodist Bible Women in Bulgaria and Italy," *Methodist History* 52, 2 (2014): 94–113; and "Methodist Women Missionaries in Bulgaria and Italy," *Methodist History* 55, 1–2 (October 2016 & January 2017): 108–127. Thanks as well to the following institutions and individuals who permitted the use of the images related to women throughout the volume: United Methodist Church Archives, Vienna, Austria; United Church of Canada Archives, Toronto; United Methodist

Church Archives – GCAH, Madison, New Jersey; Archives, Theologische Hochschule Reutlingen; S T Kimbrough, Jr.; and Christina Cekov; and to Bildungshaus Schulbuchverlage Westermann Schroedel Diesterweg Schöningh Winklers GmbH for the preparation of maps to enhance this volume.

Personal relationships, as the women explored in this volume knew so well, shape us into the people we are. We appreciate so many who have encouraged our work, provided us resources, guided our steps in the process, and have helped us shape a volume, that we believe is now worthy of serious study. First and foremost, to our contributors, we offer our hearty thanks. It has been a joy to work with these wonderful colleagues: Andrea Annese, Mareike Bloedt, Christina Cekov, Margit Herfarth, Jacqui Horton, S T Kimbrough, Jr., Lars-Erik Nordby, Thor Bernhard Tobiassen, and Michael Wetzel. We trust that this finished product of great labor puts a smile on their faces. We appreciate the support of the very fine editorial and production team at the Taylor & Francis Group, particularly Joshua Wells and Jack Boothroyd, and those who oversee the Routledge Methodist Studies Series in which this volume appears, including the series editor, Bill Gibson, and our colleagues on the board, many of whom we consider to be dear friends, Ted A. Campbell, David N. Hempton, Priscilla Pope-Levison, Martin Wellings, and Karen B. Westerfield Tucker. In addition to these, we express our gratitude, in particular, to Rebekah Chilcote, Fred Day, Karyn Douglas, Ulrike Knöller, Judit Lakatos, Frances Lyons, Dale Patterson, Dana Robert, and Bob Williams, for the various ways in which they have contributed to this volume. We were particularly delighted when Rosemarie Wenner, retired United Methodist bishop and former President of the United Methodist Council of Bishops, agreed to provide a Foreword for this volume. We express our appreciation to her for the generosity of her time and her gracious response to this book. Finally, to our spouses, Janet Chilcote and Michael Schuler, for their incalculable support in all our endeavors.

Europe before World War One (1914)

1830 Year of acquisition   ——— National border   ● Capital

············· Internal border

0   200   400   600   800   1000 km

© Westermann

Map 1

Europe after World War One (1920/21)

1908 Year of independence —————— National border • Capital

-------- Internal border

0   200   400   600   800   1000 km

Map 2

Europe before World War Two (1939)

Dictatorship (year of establishment)
1922 Fascist
1928 Authoritarian military
1917 Communist

——— National border
------- Internal border

● Capital

0 200 400 600 800 1000 km

Map 3

Uncovering the story of women pioneers in European Methodism

An introduction

Paul W. Chilcote and Ulrike Schuler

Baroness Amelie von Langenau, Deaconesses, & Children

Women figured prominently in the foundation and expansion of Methodism in continental Europe. Historians of the past, however, constrained by the exclusionary conventions of their age, failed to identify these women fully and document their role and influence within the life of the movement. While they frequently acknowledge that women played instrumental roles in the establishment of Methodism on the continent, they provided very little detail concerning the women to add texture to this historical tapestry. In this volume of collected essays we initiate an effort to remedy this neglect, therefore, discuss the rightful place of women in early European Methodism, identify particularly significant women, and locate the women pioneers in a more fully developed historiography of Methodism.

This volume gives voice to a broad range of religious issues and concerns during the critical period in European history between 1869 and 1939. We make an effort here to break new ground in research related to women and their imprint on the establishment of Methodism in Europe. The research reflected in this collection of essays suggests some important interpretive themes, such as the ability of women to network effectively, their capacity to engage in God's work without the need of applause, their skill in navigating difficult cultural and national boundaries, and perhaps even the indispensable nature of their ministry. In spite of the fact that the women discussed in this book were all products of their age, shaped by attitudes that were simultaneously constraining and liberating, their pioneering efforts illustrate the powerful connection between women and mission, and potentially help to define more fully these kinds of relationships for the future.

The purpose of this volume is to examine the role and influence of these women pioneers, to tell the story of their loves and labors, and through this documentation and interpretation to open more questions for further study than this volume, in itself, can resolve. To introduce the following chapters properly, it will be helpful to discuss the general historical context and the origins of Methodism in Europe, the parameters of this volume and how they were determined, the role of women in European Methodist missions, the various categories of women pioneers, and some of the conclusions that can be drawn with regard to their legacy.

The European context of church and state: 1869–1939

An examination of Christianity in Europe presents a serious challenge because the continent is enormously diverse.[1] Although it is the world's second smallest continent with a population of about 700 million in a relatively small area, Europe includes today 48 nations, 23 official languages, more than 100 spoken languages, and innumerable dialects. The geographic area called "Europe" has changed over the centuries and is not clearly defined. The following true story told in a radio broadcasting interview by an old farmer, illustrates this reality: "I was born as a subject of the Austrian emperor and Hungarian king, went to school in Czechoslovakia, that I finished in Slovakia. I was farmer in Hungary and served in the Red Army Faction of the Soviet Union. Today I am retired in the Ukraine. Beside my military service I have never left my home village."[2] Currently, most historians view Europe as the coalescence of those states identifying themselves with the historical and cultural traditions rooted in Greece and Rome.

Europe has played an important role in the history of the Christian church – its organization, theology, and doctrine. Three of the basic family streams within Christianity – Roman Catholicism, Eastern Orthodoxy, and Protestantism (Lutheran and Reformed) – were born and developed in the geographic and cultural boundaries of Europe. Beginning in the nineteenth century, the call for the abolition of established state churches as well as freedom of faith, conscience, and creed led to a variety of constitutional systems in European countries. For example, in France and Portugal this movement led to the complete separation of state and church (laicism). Germany, Italy, and Spain developed a kind of partnership or cooperation in public affairs with a system of agreements with churches (a concordat with the Roman Catholic Church or with Protestant churches). Norway, Denmark, and England embraced a "unity system" in which the head of state is also the head of the church. Several other developments were especially important for the unfolding of Christianity in the modern era: the continuing legacy of the Protestant reformations of the sixteenth century, the Enlightenment, the rise of Pietism, and the industrial revolution. In light of these developments within the European context, Methodist missions "reintroduced" Christianity to the "cradle of the Reformation" – trying to support renewal and reform, and dedicated to continuing the reformation that continental Pietism had advocated. This complex matrix of history and culture shaped the women who pioneered Methodism and influenced the nature of their mission.

The origins of Methodism in Europe

The origins of Methodism in Europe extend from the late eighteenth to the middle of the nineteenth century.[3] Like new communities of faith in the apostolic age, Methodism sprang up in continental Europe initially by word of mouth, through the personal sharing of stories of faith among migrants, sailors, and travelers.[4] Those who had encountered British and American Methodists, and had been transformed by their message, eagerly talked about the gospel that had revolutionized their lives. As others were drawn by this faith-sharing, small informal Methodist gatherings were sometimes formed until denominational officials offered formal support and supervised further organization. In these developments, the phase of informal connections and relationships gave way to the more organized and formal relationships of the burgeoning missionary movement.

The primary driving force behind all this labor was the desire "to spread scriptural holiness over the land."[5] With the main Methodist mission policy oriented around reaching the "heathen," in the minds of many it made sense to focus attention on Asia and Africa. When requests began to pour in from the European continent for British and American missionary support, the response of mission agencies was initially hesitant and even dismissive given the fact that many of these countries were deeply rooted in the Protestant heritage.[6] When the mission boards began to deploy missionaries to these regions of Europe, their primary strategy revolved around an effort to renew Protestant state churches, often through an awakening or rediscovery of Pietist roots and practices in those traditions.[7] So missionaries employed typical Methodist practices such as Bible study, prayer meetings, hymn singing, shared experiences of faith, personal spirituality, assemblies outside the context of worship, and encouraged personal faith decisions as platforms for renewal. Ministers of state churches often welcomed the missionaries openly. But once the indigenous clergy began to sense differences in theology and perspective, ecclesiastical tradition, and liturgical practice, however, this hospitality soon dissipated. Outright resistance and antagonism sometimes displaced an earlier spirit of tolerance and acceptance.[8]

In those nations of Europe where Catholicism and Orthodoxy dominated, the situation was very different from that of the Protestant arenas. These two religious traditions, in particular, tended to pervade community and family life – Christianity and life were much more symbiotic and organic in these areas and directly tied to nationality. Moreover, most of the people in cohesive Roman Catholic and Eastern Orthodox contexts were illiterate, not even allowed to own or read the Bible in their own language.[9] They perceived no need for renewal or change in their lives in terms of religious vision or practice. In Roman Catholic countries Methodism encountered immediate, strong, and aggressive opposition in its attempt to break the Catholic stronghold and to bring the Reformation to completion.[10] Eastern Orthodoxy presented this and other, more complex, challenges. In Bulgaria, for example, the Ottoman Sultan officially sanctioned an autonomous Bulgarian Orthodox Church in 1849, but he also invited other confessions to engage in evangelistic work.[11] While Methodism's first expressed mission effort in 1857 was to enliven the Orthodox Church, the Islamic government's motivation was much more to destabilize the Orthodox Church as well as to provide for Christian plurality.[12] That situation provoked strong Orthodox resistance that precluded the idea of cooperation with other churches. Reflecting on this particular dynamic, Christina Cekov has argued that the aim of the mission was, quite simply, "to reintroduce the Bible to Biblelands."[13]

While strategies for mission reflected these various contexts, differences can also be discerned among the various mission boards as well. Leaders of these multiple Methodist bodies in Britain and the USA established mission strategies, approaches, and protocols on the basis of their own unique perspectives. The approach of British Methodists, shaped dramatically by the three-self policy of Henry Venn (advancing a self-governing, self-supporting, self-propagating vision for a "native" church), sought to establish indigenous autonomy as quickly as possible in the mission context. Mission promoted by the Methodist Episcopal Church (MEC) in the USA tended to create an international connectional structure by integrating mission fields while permitting them increasing administrative and financial autonomy. Initially they founded "Mission Conferences," therefore, with the understanding that they would evolve into proper "Annual Conferences." In 1884, however, the MEC established "Central Conferences" to respond, on the one hand, to its international expansion and a growing self-understanding as an international church, and to counteract world-wide national tendencies aiming for autonomy at the turn of the twentieth century, on the other.

In this regard, a European Central Conference of the MEC was founded in 1911, with William Burt as its first bishop based in Zürich, joined the following year by Bishop John Nuelsen. In 1920 the MEC General Conference decided to divide the European Central Conference into three. The Evangelical Association (EA) had a similar structural arrangement, organizing a parallel Central Conference for Europe in 1922. It included all the EA's European missions in Germany and Switzerland, dividing it into three annual conferences: North German, South German, and Switzerland. Although the name was changed in the USA in 1922 to the Evangelical Church due to a union, no such union was needed in Europe. The church maintained the title *Evangelische Gemeinschaft*.

Almost all the Methodist mission activity in Europe was linked, primarily, with the issue of migration. Emigration to the USA from many European nations played an increasing role in these new developments, with immigrants consistently expressing concern about the moral and religious poverty of their homelands and the need for Christian renewal. The organization of Methodist Foreign Language Annual Conferences in the USA of the MEC as well as the EA and the Church of the United Brethren in Christ (UB) provided a natural bridge between the continents. These Conferences, in particular, initiated new missions, provided financial support, and nurtured personal contacts among family and friends. They also helped foster deeper understanding of the cultural differences, approaches, and contextual dynamics. These Conferences produced periodicals for members in their congregations as well as in the respective countries of origin.[14]

Numerically, the greatest success of Methodist mission occurred in the Protestant German-speaking countries and Scandinavia. But Methodist congregations were organized all over Europe. Typically, the organizational strategy, following the patterns described above, included forming classes, Sunday schools, translating, and publishing Methodist hymnbooks and *Disciplines*, and establishing periodicals.[15] Later, in some places they established publishing houses,[16] pastoral training institutions (seminaries) for Methodist preachers,[17] and deaconess "mother houses."[18] Nursing care facilities, hospitals, children's schools, and other social institutions followed.[19] Through all these efforts, the primary Methodist objective of spreading social holiness across the continent particularly included the support of the poor in rural and urban areas with educational and other social service ministries, and it was in these areas that women tended to flourish.

Parameters of this volume

Defining the parameters of this volume proved to be an arduous task. In the end, the natural process that unfolded reflected a basic funnel approach, starting initially as broadly as possible, but narrowing increasingly with the identification and examination of the records of the respective Methodist institutions. We also had to bear in mind the resources at hand and the scholars who have been engaged in research related to this arena of study. Above all, three essential questions guided our deliberations with regard to the parameters of the study: 1) Who were the women pioneers and with which Methodist traditions were they affiliated? 2) Where were Methodist women deployed in Europe? and 3) When did they engage in their pioneering work?

Who? The most critical and initial concern, then, revolved around the question, How do we identify the women who functioned as pioneers in the development of Methodism in Europe? In consultation with other colleagues and staff members at the Methodist Archives at Drew University, with regard to mission work emanating from the USA, most recommended ferreting through the records of the Methodist mission agencies, particularly the various women's foreign missionary societies, and their respective publications. The wives of male missionaries entered the field of mission under the auspices of the primary denominational mission boards and were not registered autonomously. The publications and records of women's societies provided a more highly textured portrait of the work of women whom they sent and supervised. Identifying indigenous women presented the greatest challenges and, perhaps, yielded the best fruit. Excavations in this arena entailed the highest levels of collaboration, with dependence on local scholars who possessed the indispensable cultural and linguistic capacity.

Where? Working through these materials, questions about Methodist outreach to Europe revolved quite simply around the issue of where Methodist leaders decided to deploy missionaries. Given the fact that some of the mission agencies focused their energy in arenas other than Europe made some decisions easy, as a brief survey of these Methodist mission organizations reveals. Various Methodist mission boards emerged in the early nineteenth century,[20] with parallel women's societies established independently of these agencies during the second half of the century.[21] The Wesleyan Methodists in Great Britain were the first to launch their formal mission work in 1813.[22]

The British Woman Missionary Society was part of the Wesleyan Methodist Church (WMC) and not an agency independent of the conference. Despite the fact that British Methodist mission work was concomitant with that of American counterparts, basic research related to women in British Methodist missions remains in a very nascent stage of development. We came to the conclusion early in this process that the unique relationship of the Wesleyan Methodists in Britain to their native Church of England – a relationship still in flux in the early nineteenth century – necessitated a separate examination of their mission work in Europe outside the scope of this volume, disentangled also from the web of American influences. Despite few opportunities to access vital records of the MWC in the UK or to coordinate efforts with British colleagues, however, we do share some insights in this book related to that side of the Methodist family, and a chapter devoted to a Wesleyan Methodist missionary, with the hope that others will take up the call for further research in that arena.[23]

Methodists in the USA, of course, developed their own mission agencies: the Missionary Society of the MEC in 1819, the *Missionsgesellschaft* (mission agency) of the EA in 1838, and the Home, Frontier, and Foreign Missionary Society of the UB in 1853. Women concerned about "woman's work for woman" founded the Woman's Foreign Missionary Society (WFMS) as a sending agency independent of the MEC mission board in 1869.[24] Women in other Methodist denominations followed their lead in fairly quick succession. The UB established their Woman's Missionary Association in 1873, with their German-speaking EA counterpart launching a *Frauen-Missionsgesellschaft* (Women's Missionary Society) in 1884. Neither of these organizations, however, employed female missionaries in Europe; rather, the work of women developed organically in German-speaking areas with partnerships among women who felt a personal call to serve.[25] Some of these women were deployed to Asian contexts, primarily India, China, and Japan, and the African continent, beginning in Liberia and Sierra Leone. In 1878 the Methodist Episcopal Church, South (MECS) founded its own Woman's Foreign Missionary Society (WFMSS), later to become the Women's Missionary Council in 1910, deploying women in 1920 to three European nations: Belgium, Czechoslovakia, and Poland.

All these churches and mission organizations that figured prominently in the transplantation of Methodism to continental Europe knew about and acknowledged each other. Moreover, they supported one another, informed each other about their activities, and even negotiated their areas of mission through comity agreements so as to avoid competition. In 1882, for example, at a *Vereinigte Versammlung* (Associated Assembly), delegates of the WMC, the MEC, and the EA adopted a principle of the newly organized Ecumenical Methodist Conference.[26] They expressed their intention to work together in "the spirit of brotherhood" with mutual respect, and explicitly committed themselves to avoid mission activities in the same geographical areas.[27] No summarization of this mission to Europe has superseded that of Bishop Paul N. Garber in *The Methodists of Continental Europe* where he drew these terse conclusions:

1   European immigrants converted abroad were primarily responsible for founding the church in Germany, Sweden, Denmark, Norway, and Finland. As Bishop John L. Nuelsen has stated: "Historically speaking, European Methodism is a reflex of European immigration to America, and, in a less degree, to England."

2   The European Methodists have always been missionary in theory and practice. From Germany, Methodism was carried to Switzerland, Russia, Austria, Hungary and Yugoslavia. In like manner the Finnish Methodists exerted missionary efforts in Russia.

3   There have always been countries in Europe which, because of the weakness of native Protestantism, have been considered as special fields of Protestant missionary activity. It was thus that Methodism entered Bulgaria, Italy, Spain . . . and France.

4   Methodism in Belgium, Czechoslovakia, and Poland is the result of Southern Methodist relief activity after World War One. It was felt that real reconstruction in these countries involved a spiritual ministry as well as material assistance.[28]

Given our discoveries about the "where" question, therefore, this volume includes information and reflections on the pioneering activities of Methodist women in the following arenas of mission in Europe: Austria, Belgium, Bulgaria, Czechoslovakia, Denmark, Finland, Germany, Italy, Macedonia, Norway, Poland, Russia, and Sweden.[29] Any sense of balance or symmetry among these various regions remains elusive. The general historical contours of Methodism are unique to each setting. The portrait of the church may be fully developed in one setting and based upon a plethora of sources, but in another context it is constrained by limited material and a dearth of scholarship. Methodist influence was deep and widespread in one country, but fragmentary and episodic in a different context. And this is to say nothing of the status of scholarship related to the Methodist women in these areas. Those countries we have excluded, but where Methodist was undertaken, are France, Hungary, Portugal, Spain, and Yugoslavia.[30] Methodism in these countries has not been considered for lack of resources, for lack of scholars who have facility in the languages relevant to the context, or for lack of evidence of women's involvement. To put this more positively, those nations included in this study met most of these criteria.

When? All studies of this nature require clear parameters with regard to timeframe. Several factors played into the determination of these demarcations. The launch of the WFMS in 1869 functions as an obvious starting date for the volume. The onset of World War One in 1914 initially seemed to be an appropriate and natural terminal point for the study. Activities related to the mission effort appeared, at first, to confirm this conjecture. To illustrate, the WFMS deployed no new missionaries to Italy between 1902 and 1918, nor to Bulgaria between 1906 and 1926. But this terminus would have eliminated some of the important pioneering work of women that came later, particularly that of the WFMSS after World War One. While pioneering work ended in Italy by the turn of the century, at that same time it was only beginning in places like Poland. Given the renewed efforts related to mission immediately following the war, it seemed reasonable to include the interwar period and terminate the study with the onset of World War Two.

Several advantages to a terminus of 1939 emerged. This year not only marked the beginning of World War Two, it also witnessed the reunification of the MEC, MECS, and Methodist Protestant Church to form The Methodist Church, and stands as a benchmark, therefore, well-known in Methodist historiography. Obviously, the war effectively mitigated against pioneering efforts across most of Europe. By this time, in some regions of Europe, the pioneering phase had ended, leading to an era of consolidation and institutionalization, especially beyond 1945. So during the 70-year period, 1869–1939, women helped to establish Methodism in various European contexts. Given the fact that real life seldom falls neatly into any timeframe, it has been important, in several instances, to view these dates as general parameters rather than clear-cut boundaries that cannot be transgressed.

Categories of Methodist women pioneers

During the first half of the nineteenth century, Protestant women became increasingly interested in mission as they learned about the terrible plight of women and children around the globe from women who were beginning to enter the mission force. The exclusively female missionary societies had begun as small prayer group meetings focused on the burgeoning missionary activity of the church, but rapidly expanded into powerful networks of women activated for mission in the world. In the USA, for example, the effects of the Civil War (1861–1865) forced immense changes related to the traditional roles of women in society as they assumed responsibilities in domains previously dominated by men. Similar circumstances obtained in European countries where wars or revolutions led to political upheaval or, as a consequence of the industrial revolution, to economic changes. All these forces led to social modification. These kinds of changes fueled the organization of women's missionary societies as well as professional education for women.

In most histories of Methodist mission in Europe, previous scholars devoted very little attention, if any, to the role and influence of women in any of these developments although they sometimes mentioned the "immense role" of women.[31] Similarly, the unnamed wives of male missionaries received a slight nod under the rubric of "Mrs. So-and-so," but hardly any serious labor was devoted to examining the pioneering work of women.[32] To state the obvious, women were there. But this volume goes beyond that simplistic observation to make the claim that women played an important role far beyond that which has been fully recognized or documented. As is the case in many other arenas, this "lost history" begs to be discovered. The important first step in this process of recovery, most certainly, is the identification of important Methodist women pioneers and missionaries in Europe, determining their roles and the influence they exerted on others as they sought to be faithful to their vision of mission. In the establishment of Methodism in Europe, women served as missionary wives, Bible Women, deaconesses, missionaries, and some individuals stood out with regard to their singular influence on the life of the movement.[33]

Missionary wives

Dana Robert has provided helpful analysis with regard to the role of missionary wives in the nineteenth century.[34] In the early decades of that century, the wives of missionaries engaged in benevolent activities, often pushing back the boundaries of acceptable behavior for women in the public sphere. These women obtained a high degree of education, something frequently distinguishing them from others throughout the period under discussion in this volume. Indeed, good education had been "the hallmark of the American missionary wife from the beginning."[35] Perhaps more importantly, being married to a missionary meant that women were in a position to lead prayer meetings, visit the sick, engage in evangelistic activities, exhort and even, perhaps, preach. In other words, it made it possible for some to function as ministers, to engage in a vocation to which they may have even felt called, but had no way to fulfill under "normal" circumstances. More than anything else, these women sought to be "useful." "The actual conditions of missionary life," as Robert concludes, however, "quickly turned motivation for usefulness into the realities of self-sacrifice."[36]

It should not be surprising that the work of missionary wives focused primarily on women, children, and concerns about education and the implementation of educational programing. They often discovered, however, that navigating the primitive conditions of their mission context and dealing with the day-to-day activities related to a growing family sapped their energy and diverted their efforts. Emily Vernon, wife of the first MEC missionary to Italy, Leroy M. Vernon, orchestrated the first educational activities of the young mission in her own home! She may have been the first Methodist to inaugurate the work of Bible Women in Italy (Chapter 4). But so little is known about her actual work due to the dearth of resources. Quite a number of other missionary wives appear in this volume, but a lack of resources makes it difficult to paint a full portrait of their work. Mary Ellen Piggott, who also served in Italy but under the auspices of the WMC, stands out as an exception here, owing to her detailed journal. But even here, while the sketch of her life provided here (Chapter 10) affords substantial biographical information, it is difficult to identify the specific missional practices in which she engaged alongside her family responsibilities. The legacy of the missionary wife in European Methodism remains one of the untold stories; much work remains to be done in this rich but largely uncharted terrain.

Bible Women

One impetus for this volume emerged from the editors' work on and discoveries about Bible Women in Bulgaria and Italy (Chapter 1). The WFMS hired these indigenous women to do evangelistic work, primarily, and to function very much like the deaconesses of the early church. Trained for this ministry in an ad hoc manner initially, training schools, directed by missionary wives or other women missionaries, displaced personal mentoring. Given their knowledge of language, customs, and context, it made sense for these indigenous women to become the "face" of the mission, leaving oversight and missional visioning to the expatriate missionaries. So while they functioned primarily as evangelists, the Bible Women also devoted time and energy to teaching and discipling, distributing Christian literature, and providing health care services to the needy. Questions remain with regard to the role of Bible Women in other European contexts and how their roles evolved in relation to the growing missionary community.

Deaconesses

The Methodist deaconess movement emerged as an extremely important influence with regard to the mission of the Methodist churches in the last quarter of the nineteenth century. Emanating from *Mutterhäusern* (mother houses) which were centers of missionary training and spiritual nurture, deaconesses (women who personally experienced God's call to ministry in the church) became nurses, midwives (a few physicians), or social workers who were also sent for mission work in and outside their homeland. The deaconess movement spread from Germany to Great Britain, Scandinavia, the USA, and other countries. Two essays in this volume (Chapters 2 and 3) deal directly with the rise of the office of deaconess within the various Methodist traditions. They detail the work of these women and the way in which this movement affected the development of the church on both sides of the Atlantic Ocean. But the Methodist deaconess, in fact, pervades this volume. No history of Methodism in continental Europe can be written without a clear acknowledgment of their presence and witness.

Women missionaries

Alongside the missionary wives and the Bible Women, no group of early Methodist pioneers stands out with greater distinction than women missionaries. The evidence demonstrates that they were extremely intelligent and deeply committed to Christ, but also captive in many ways to the currents of culture that shaped their age. In many of the European contexts under study here, these highly educated and deeply pious women moved into positions of leadership and supervision, consolidating the efforts of their sisters in the faith. Their story is very complex and interwoven with the contexts in which they served, the changing landscape of mission theory at the turn of the century, and their own personal sense of calling to ministry. Many of these almost exclusively single women entered the field of mission with hopes of changing the world, elevating women across the European sphere, and initiating this transformation by means of education for all. But the ways in which they were changed by their experience are as fascinating as the changes they sought to implement. Several chapters here examine the role of women missionaries across Europe, in Germany and Switzerland (Chapter 5), in Bulgaria and Italy (Chapter 4), in Belgium, Czechoslovakia, and Poland (Chapter 6), and in the portrayal of individuals (Chapters 7–10). Many more questions remain concerning them than have been answered in these initial explorations.

Distinguished individuals

It became clear to us quite early on in this project that a number of women stood out with regard to the individual contributions they made to this pioneering work of the various Methodist churches and women's organizations. Some were quite well-known but remained largely unacknowledged. On the other hand, individuals surfaced about whom we wished we knew much more. They deserved at least a biographical sketch that acknowledged their contribution, despite the dearth of resources or lack of scholarly attention. Part II of this volume includes portraits and sketches of these women, the details concerning which are discussed below in connection with the organization of the material.

Primary conclusions

Through this process of tracking emergent Methodist mission in various European contexts, and identifying the women who pioneered in this arena, we arrived at a number of conclusions related to the roles of women: the importance of indigenous women, the ability of women to navigate difficult contextual dynamics, the significance of the women's missionary societies, the influence of a shifting missiological terrain, the ecumenical nature of the women's endeavors, the competency of women to network among themselves and other women and children, the authentic witness of women through personal and incarnational evangelism, and the significance of female philanthropy.

Indigenous women

One observation that merits much more research and reflection relates to the complex relationship obtaining between indigenous women and their expatriate missionary counterparts. Our preliminary examination of the interface of these two groups of women has enhanced our appreciation for the work of the indigenous women. Their experience tends to reveal a typical pattern of growing expatriate control and subsequent domination. As the scales of power shifted in the direction of the missionaries, indigenous women fall increasingly under their shadow and do not re-emerge until a "native ministry" is fully developed. The Bible Women represent this indigenous element in concrete fashion and to state our observation succinctly, echoing Ruth Tucker's settled opinion, "without Bible Women, female missionaries would have been at a loss."[37]

Contextual dynamics

Context determines everything. In areas in which Orthodoxy dominated, for example, the Methodist mission was viewed as a foreign sectarian movement with unsolicited intruders during a period of unprecedented national and ethnic resurgence. In a context in which Methodist women were suspected occasionally as being spies who had been indoctrinated in their ways, this mistrust impeded their mission. This was equally true, of course, in areas dominated by Roman Catholicism. This dynamic made the work of the indigenous Bible Women all the more critical. Being "inside" these issues by virtue of heritage and birth, but also "outside" them by virtue of gender, status, and role (with little standing within the corridors of power), gave these women a unique space to inhabit in the missionary movement. They were able to go about their business, as it were, inconspicuous and unobtrusive; they understood the political landscape, but had the ability to rise above it by remaining "low." In nations steeped in the heritage of Protestant Christianity, the missionary endeavors of Methodist women could easily be interpreted as presumptive and even arrogant. On the other hand, these women draw upon the heritage of Pietism and the movements of awakening in the nineteenth century to build bridges connecting them to these foundations. The soil was already prepared, so to speak, for the women to enrich and enhance the practice of the Christian faith already well-rooted in the lives of the native peoples. Even so, they met with a lot of distrust because Methodism was viewed by many as a sect at this time.

Women's missionary societies

Once women's missionary societies were formed in the various Methodist denominations during the last quarter of the nineteenth century, they became a template for women's development and empowerment in the European context. One might even describe these groups for fellowship and service as the heartbeat of the Methodist congregations that were established. More often than not the women missionaries considered the formation of these groups to be their first order of business. They inherited a structure for this from the WFMS and WFMSS, as well as other mission organizations in which women had a central role (see Chapter 5). To illustrate, in the nation's evangelized by the MECS, namely, Belgium, Czechoslovakia, and Poland, the new missionaries were instructed to organize the indigenous women into these structures as quickly as possible (see Chapter 6). These societies functioned on several levels: 1) they provided a direct connection between women in Europe and women in the USA; 2) they afforded women missionaries a community of support for the difficult work in which they were engaged; 3) they bonded expatriate missionaries with indigenous women; and 4) they empowered indigenous women so that they could take the reins of leadership in the nascent churches as quickly as possible. Local women's societies functioned as the dynamos of mission. They supported the mission work of the church financially, informed their congregations about the activities of their missionaries, recruited new missionaries and volunteers for home and foreign mission, and prayed incessantly for those they had sent.

Shifting missiological terrain

With regard to the whole area of mission theology and practice during this period, much needs to be said with regard to women in terms of our conclusions. In an incisive analysis of the way in which the WFMS created a sphere for single women, Rosemary Skinner Keller observed:

> The W.F.M.S. was created not only to liberate women in non-Christian lands from the bondage and subordination to which custom and religion had subjected them, but to provide outlets for the energy, ability, and leadership of American women in missionary societies, since such avenues were closed to them in the existing structures of the church. . . . they were highly cultured and well-trained women, who needed a sphere in which to express their own commitment to the church and to develop leadership ability.[38]

Keller's statement about women in the USA applies equally to European Methodist women, and the deployment of women of this disposition and caliber before the turn of the century, illustrates at least three significant shifts in mission theory and practice at that time.[39] Moreover, the experience of women in the Methodist mission community reflects trends that would reshape mission in the early twentieth century.

First, female mission societies began to deploy single women to augment the labor of missionary wives. This shift was dramatic and pervasive. It reflects the same change that Christ-An Bennett noted with regard to British Wesleyan Methodist mission in other spheres during this same period: "As their families and their husbands' work expanded," she notes, "these missionaries' wives began to feel torn between their commitment to their families and their commitment to their out-of-home ministries. They found they could no longer do justice to their home role while they carried on their missionary ministries."[40] Single women were needed to sustain and expand the ministries of missionary wives whose domestic responsibilities consumed increasing amounts of their time and energy. "By 1890," as Dana Robert has noted, "the infusion of single women meant that women constituted 60 percent of the American mission force."[41] While the concept of "woman's work for woman" had guided the work of missionary wives early in the nineteenth century, new attitudes about mission established a new trajectory for this work. "For 'heathen' women," Robert argues, "evangelization was intertwined with 'civilization,' with being elevated by Christianity into social equality with western women and into positions of respect in their own societies."[42] In Bulgaria, women equated being Protestant with no longer being illiterate; Methodism and education went hand in hand. This change of goal, embraced by the new generation of single women missionaries, interfaced seamlessly with a second shift in method.

Secondly, the focus of the WFMS missionaries shifted from evangelistic to educational endeavors. In the earliest stages of their activity, the missionaries viewed these practices in a symbiotic fashion. Evangelism was distinct but not separate from education. But with the arrival of the single women in a second wave of mission activity, the energy that had been poured into the preparation of indigenous Bible Women for evangelistic ministries was diverted to the education of girls and women for other purposes. "Most importantly for the overall mission of the church," as Dana Robert has observed with regard to the motivation of this new class of missionaries, their hope was that "the education of women would subvert the very foundations of 'heathen' society and would catalyze the profound social changes needed to accompany broad conversion to Christianity."[43] Our research with regard to the European context of mission substantiates Roberts' earlier analysis. An effort to transform the culture through education began to supplant a strategy that had elevated the importance of individual conversion. Certainly, this change of method or strategy interfaced directly with changing attitudes about culture and the purpose of mission.

So thirdly, a close examination of late nineteenth century developments reflects a growing sense of cultural imperialism and a concomitant distrust of indigeneity.[44] "Many missionary women," Robert has also demonstrated definitively, "also shared the crusading optimism and sense of superiority of their fellow citizens during the height of western imperialism from approximately 1885 to the end of the First World War."[45] In his well-known exploration of mission history, Rufus Anderson (1796–1880), a near contemporary to all these events, actually drew attention to the monumental change of attitude associated with this shift that some were beginning to make toward the end of this life. Earlier mission strategy stressed the establishment of native churches under indigenous control (the three-self policy) and trusted the power of the Christian faith to transform individual lives, thereby avoiding the dangers of cultural imperialism.[46] Ann White has argued further that when these new women in mission placed a philosophy of social transformation at the center of their missional vision, they "became as vulnerable as the rest of the American missionary enterprise to charges of cultural imperialism."[47] These trends exerted a profound influence upon the vision and practice of WFMS missionaries, a consequence in large measure due to their training.

Ecumenical endeavors

We remain fascinated by the ecumenical character of the pioneering work of women, from the outset of mission activity to the end of the period under study. The close connection and cooperation, for example, between the American Board of Commissioners for Foreign Mission (ABCFM) and WFMS – both Protestant movements in non-Protestant contexts – surfaced repeatedly.[48] The education of women for mission, perhaps, illustrates this ecumenical dimension of the work most dramatically. In several regions of Europe, women received their initial training in mission schools of the ABCFM, supported and worked alongside the wives of MEC missionaries, and engaged in work among girls, in particular, without regard to comity agreements or denominational boundaries. With regard to developments related to the deaconess movement, the interface of Lutheran and Methodist traditions provides a stunning paradigm of ecumenical cooperation in mission.

Networking with women

Methodist women pioneers, whether Bible Women, deaconesses, or missionaries, had immediate access to women and children. They met women at the market place, visited them in their homes, worked with their children, and connected with them as mothers (at least the missionary wives and Bible Women). Like ancient Christian women, they sought to meet both the physical and spiritual needs of others. This dynamic and organic networking also meant that women had to be flexible and grasp opportunities as they emerged and as situations changed; they had to be nimble and walk through open doors as they were opened to them. In most of the European contexts, women were the primary bearers of religious meaning and had the responsibility to transmit these values to their children. Whenever Methodist women connected to women and children in meaningful ways, therefore, their influence was multiplied. The WFMS slogan, "mission of woman for woman," perfectly characterizes the networking function of the pioneering women.

Authentic witness

We move seamlessly from this conception of networking to the authenticity of the missional practice of evangelism among many of these women, particularly those in the earlier generations of missionary service. Methodism, as already noted, sprang up in Europe initially by word of mouth. Those who had been transformed by the Methodist message eagerly talked about the gospel that had revolutionized their lives. They openly shared their stories of faith. The concept of faith-sharing among the women tended to be much more organic, directly connected to the lives of the women and children they sought to serve. They lived their lives with authenticity and integrity before others. While they functioned primarily as women who simply bore witness to the gospel – as evangelists – they devoted much time and energy to teaching, discipling, and educating the rising generation. Without question, with the passage of time and the increasingly entrenched structures of institutional church in most of these regions, education tended to displace evangelism in this sense. But the integral connection between these two ministries was never fully lost.

Female philanthropy

Finally, an examination of some of the extraordinary women in the history of Methodism in Europe reveals a philanthropic legacy that shaped the Methodist movement profoundly. Among the various women named in this volume, two stand out in this regard. Fredrikke Nielsen, a Norwegian actress evangelist, supported the work of Methodist mission wherever her career took her (Chapter 10). Likewise, many would go so far as to say that there would be no strong presence of Methodism in Austria today, had it not been for the financial support of Baroness Amelie von Langenau (Chapter 7). Her support of the deaconess movement, as well, in different regions of Europe made education and the dissemination of the gospel across Europe by women a reality. One cannot think of Methodism in Europe apart from the contributions of countless women in Great Britain and the USA, and principally from within the women's societies, who gave sacrificially so that the ministry of women could flourish. This led European women to respond positively to God's call upon their own lives and to continue this legacy in their homelands and literally around the world. True philanthropy is always a matter of mutuality; women inspired women across all these contextual boundaries and their connection led to the flourishing of the church.

All these dimensions of Methodist women's pioneering activity require further study. It would be premature to consider our discussion of these roles as anything other than preliminary conclusions.

The organization of this volume

The essays collected in this volume fall into two primary categories represented by the two-part division. Part I explores pioneering roles among Bible Women, deaconesses, and missionaries across a wide range of European contexts. The opening chapter related to Bible Women in the non-Protestant contexts of Bulgaria and Italy demonstrates the importance of indigenous women in the earliest developments related to Methodism in those contexts (Chapter 1). The next two chapters explore the role of the deaconess movement in the shaping of women's lives for mission service and the way in which these developments established a bond between the European community and American Methodist churches and women's organizations as missionary-sending agencies of the late nineteenth century (Chapters 2 and 3). Chapter 4 provides a case study with regard to Methodist women missionaries in Bulgaria and Italy and how changing conceptions of mission and mission education effected their relationships with indigenous women. Chapter 5 examines the mission organizations developed by Methodist women in Germany and Switzerland and the women missionaries they trained and deployed. The final chapter in Part I explores women's mission activities in Belgium, Czechoslovakia, and Poland under the auspices of the MECS after World War One (chapter 6).

Part II provides portraits of individual women who figured prominently in the establishment of Methodism in their respective nations and regions. Chapter 7 examines the life of Baroness Amelie von Langenau, one of the most important pioneers of Methodism in Austria, and demonstrates how her philanthropic endeavors secured a foothold for Methodism in other regions of Europe as well. S T Kimbrough Jr. has documented the life of Anna Eklund, a Methodist pioneer who lived and worked in Russia at one of the most significant periods of both Methodist and Russian history. In Chapter 8 he not only provides the basic parameters of her life and witness, but affords a unique glimpse into her life through her own letters. Chapter 9 explores the life and publications of Ines Piacentini Ferreri, an entrepreneurial "feminist" of the Methodist Church of Italy during the early decades of the twentieth century. We provide biographical sketches of Methodist women pioneers in Denmark, Finland, Italy, Norway, and Macedonia in Chapter 10.

This volume only begins to uncover the untold story of women in the history of Methodism in continental Europe. The contributors here have only scratched the surface of a lost history that is well worth discovery. Our hope is that this collection of essays will inspire others and stimulate a new generation of scholars to bring women to light who have remained in the shadows far too long.

Methodist mission in Europe

Wesleyan Methodist Church

Year Established	Nation	Means
1808	Gibraltar	British soldiers
1816	Belgium	British soldiers
1818	France	Tradesman
1826	Sweden	Manufacturer
1842	Switzerland (French)	Minister from Great Britain
1854	Spain	Missionary from Gibraltar
1859	Germany	Returning emigrants
1861	Italy	Converted Catholic priest
1870	Austria	Preacher from Germany
1871	Portugal	Lay person

Evangelical Association

Year Established	Nation	Means
1850	Germany	letter connections of emigrants with relatives and friends
1866	Switzerland	personal contacts between Germans and people in German-speaking Switzerland
1868	Alsace-Lorraine[49]	personal contacts between Germans and People in Alsace-Lorraine; relatives
1895	East Prussia[50]	personal connections from emigration
1911	Latvia	ministers from East Prussia

Methodist Episcopal Church

Year Established	Nation	Means
1849	Germany	correspondence of immigrants
1853	Norway	converted sailors Bethel Ship
1854	Sweden	converted sailors Bethel Ship
1857	Bulgaria	request of the American Board[51]
1858	Denmark	returning emigrant
1871	Italy	decision of the mission board
1880	Finland	layperson Bethel Ship
1886	Switzerland[52]	preachers from Germany
1889	Russia	contact from Finland
1899	Serbia[53]	contact with Austro-Hungarian settlers
1921	Macedonia[54]	American Board action
?	France/Alsace	contact with German-speaking people

Methodist Episcopal Church, South

Year Established	Nation	Means
1920	Belgium	American Board action
1920	Czechoslovakia	American Board action
1920	Poland	American Board action

United Brethren in Christ

The mission in Germany was opened by Georg Christian Heinrich Bischoff (1829–1885), an emigrant to the USA who was converted to the UB and was sent back to Germany as a lay preacher. His primary agenda was to learn more about the German culture so as to support people in the German-speaking Annual Conferences in the US more fully. This mission remained small and was integrated into the MEC mission in 1905.

Notes

1 This, and the subsequent segment of the introduction, depend heavily on the more extensive chapter of Ulrike Schuler, "Methodism in Northern and Continental Europe," in *T & T Clark Companion to Methodism*, ed. Charles Yrigoyen (London: Continuum, 2010), 166–187.

2 A former bishop of The United Methodist Church in Eurasia, Dr. Rüdiger Minor, told this story.

3 The historical account that follows depends largely on Patrick Ph. Streiff, *Der Methodismus in Europa im 19. und 20. Jahrhundert* (Stuttgart: EmKGM 50, 2003). Based on secondary literature, conference minutes, and mission board reports, this remarkable survey provides the essential signposts of European Methodist history, but also raises many important questions that require further study.

4 In addition to Schuler, "Methodism in Northern and Continental Europe," see the discussion of Methodism in various European spheres in Friedrich Hecker, Vilém Schneeberger, and Karl Zehrer, *Methodismus in Osteuropa: Polen – Tschechoslowakei – Ungarn* (Stuttgart: EmKGM 51, 2004); Ulrike Schuler, *Die Evangelische Gemeinschaft: Missionarische Aufbrüche in gesellschaftspolitischen Umbrüchen* (Stuttgart: EmK studien 1, 1998); Peter Stephens, *Methodism in Europe* (Peterborough: Methodist Publishing House, 1998); and Patrick Ph. Streiff, ed., *Der europäische Methodismus um die Wende vom 19. zum 20. Jahrhundert* (Stuttgart: EmKGM 52, 2005). An older study that is still of great significance is D. John Nuelsen, Theophil Mann, and J. J. Sommer, eds., *Kurzgefasste Geschichte des Methodismus* (Bremen: Verlagshaus der Methodistenkirche GmbH, 1929).

5 John Wesley used this phrase in his "Minutes of Several Conversations" to describe one important part of the mission of his new movement of spiritual renewal in the eighteenth century. See Thomas Jackson, ed., *The Works of John Wesley*, 14 vols. (London: J. Mason, 1831), 8, 299.

6 In the nineteenth century the territories in Europe were still very strictly separated according to confessions. According to the principle *cuius regio, eius religio* (whoever's region, his religion), the ruling political leader determined the religion for his dominion. This principle remained in effect from the Peace of

Augsburg (1555) to the end of World War Two although in some countries the separation of state and church was statutorily regulated earlier. As a consequence of the war, however, refugees of different confessions became increasingly mixed in the population across Europe. The dismissal of mission work in south Germany was based upon the Wesleyan Methodist argument not to work in a Protestant context (see Friedemann Burkhardt, *Christoph Gottlob Müller und die Anfänge des Methodismus in Deutschland, Arbeiten zur Geschichte des Pietismus, Bd. 43* (Göttingen: Vandenhoeck & Ruprecht, 2003)).

7 This is true of all Methodist missions working in Protestant contexts. E.g., see Friedemann Burkhardt, "Anerkennung als Gemeinschaft innerhalb der Landeskirchen," in Burkhardt, *Christoph Gottlob Müller,* 253–280.

8 With regard to these arguments, see "Reaktion landeskirchlicher Pfarrer und Consistorien auf die 'ausländischen Missionar' – Auswertung Polemischer Schriften," in Schuler, *Die Evangelische Gemeinschaft,* 141–159.

9 For Roman Catholics, this situation did not change until Vatican II (1962–1965). With regard to Orthodox Christians in Bulgaria, the Bible was first translated into the Bulgarian language through the auspices of the British and Foreign Bible Society. They first had to create a Bulgarian Grammar in 1835. The first New Testament in Slavic-Bulgarian was published in 1840. It was one of the first Methodist missionaries, Albert L. Long, who translated and published the new translation of the Bible in Bulgarian in 1871 with the assistance of two native speakers. Not acknowledged by the Orthodox Church, this translation became known as the "Protestant Bible" (see Ueli Frei, *Der Methodimus in Bulgarien, 1857–1989/90* (Frankfurt am Main: Medienwerk der evangelisch-methodistischen Kirche 2012), 67–68; 101–103).

10 Including Portugal, Spain, Austria-Hungary, France, and Italy. After the 1848 Italian Revolution, with the formation of the national Italian Union and the annexation of the Vatican State (1861), consideration was given to entering for the purpose of converting liberal Roman Catholic priests (which really happened) and introducing Methodism.

11 That was also true in Macedonia where a Congregational mission had been founded and in 1921 was ceded to the MEC (in that year Macedonia became part of Yugoslavia).

12 This is how Streiff interprets this advance; see *Der Methodismus in Europa,* 58.

13 Christina Cekov, *Bible Women in the Balkans* (Strumica: United Methodist Church in Macedonia, 2011), 4.

14 Massimo Di Gioacchino conducted research at the Methodist Archives at Drew University on the Italian Methodist Annual Conference in the US and published an essay on this topic: "Evangelizzare gli italiani, salvare l'America: l'Italian mission della Methodist Episcopal Church degli USA (1908–1916)," *Protestantesimo* 67, 4 (2012): 335–344. But much more can and needs to be done in this arena. According to maps at the Methodist Archives, foreign-language Annual Conferences – German, Swedish, Norwegian, and Danish – were still in existence in 1920, others, not yet documented, had existed before (like the Italian).

15 Examples of these include: *Der Evangelist* (MEC, Germany, 1850), *Les Archives du Méthodisme,* later *L'Evangéliste* (WMC, France, 1853), *Der Evangelische Botschafter* (EA, Germany, 1863), *Zornitza* (MEC, Bulgaria, 1864), *Lilla Sändebudet* (MEC, Sweden, 1868), *Il Corriere Evangelico* (WMC, Italy, 1870), *Missionstidende* (MEC, Denmark, 1873), *Der Heilsbote* (UB, Germany, 1883), and *Kristelig Tidende* (MEC, Norway).

16 Publishing commenced as follows: Germany (MEC, Bremen, 1850), Norway (MEC, 1867), Norway (MEC, Oslo, 1867), Germany (EA, Nürtingen, 1871), Sweden (MEC, c. 1874), and Switzerland (EA, 1895).

17 Theological education was provided, within the parameters of this study, in French-speaking Switzerland (MEC, Lausanne,1850s, with Free Reformed Church), Germany (MEC, Bremen, 1858), Germany (WMC, Waiblingen, 1864), Denmark/Norway (MEC, Oslo, 1874); Sweden, (MEC, Orebro, Stockholm, Uppsala, 1874), Germany (EA, Reutlingen, 1877), France, (WMC, Paris, 1889), Italy (MEC, Rome, 1893), Finland (MEC, Tampere, Helsinki, 1897), and for all Scandinavian countries (MEC, Goteburg, 1924).

18 Centers were founded in Germany and spread to other countries: *Bethanien-verein* in Frankfurt am Main (MEC, Germany, 1874), *Bethesdaverein für allge-meine Krankenpflege zu Elberfeld* (EA, Germany, 1886), *Martha-Maria-Verein* Nürnberg (WMC, Germany, 1889), *Sosternhjemmet Bethanien* (MEC, Norway, 1897), *Bethanienverein* (MEC, Denmark, 1895), and *Diakonissenschwestern-schaft* (MEC, Sweden, 1900).

19 There were different types of schools for girls (later for boys) in Bulgaria, Hungary, Italy, Macedonia, Portugal, Spain, Yugoslavia, and a residential school in Albania.

20 For the development and history of mission agencies in British Methodism, see George G. Findlay and W. W. Holdsworth, *The History of the Wesleyan Methodist Missionary Society*, 5 vols. (London: Epworth Press, 1921–1924). With regard to parallel developments in the USA, consult Wade Crawford Barclay and J. Tremayne Copplestone, *History of Methodist Missions*, 4 vols. (New York: Board of Missions, 1949–1973).

21 On this subject, in particular, see Francis J. Baker, *The Story of the Woman's Foreign Missionary Society of the Methodist Episcopal Church 1869–1895* (Cincinatti: Curts & Jennings/New York: Eaton & Mains, 1898); Laura Bixby, *An Outline History of the Foreign Missions of the Methodist Episcopal Church* (Syracuse: n.p., 1876); Sarah F. Butler, *History of Woman's Foreign Missionary Society, Methodist Episcopal Church, South* (Nashville: Publishing House of the MECS, 1904); Mary S. Wheeler, *First Decade of the Woman's Foreign Missionary Society, Methodist Episcopal Church* (New York: Phillips & Hunt, 1881); and Mary Isham, *Valorous Ventures: A Record of Sixty and Six Years of the Woman's Foreign Missionary Society, Methodist Episcopal Church* (Boston: WFMS, 1936). For more contemporary analyses of this movement and its effects, see Theodore L. Agnew, "Reflections on the Woman's Foreign Missionary Movement in Late 19th-century American Methodism," *Methodist History* 6, 2 (January 1968): 3–16; Patricia Hill, *The World Their Household: The American Woman's Foreign Mission Movement and Cultural Transformation* (Ann Arbor: University of Michigan Press, 1985); Dana L. Robert, "Holiness and the Missionary Vision of the Woman's Foreign Missionary Society of the Methodist Episcopal Church, 1869–1894," *Methodist History* 39, 1 (October 2000), 15–27; and Susan E. Warrick, " 'She Diligently Followed Every Good Work': Mary Mason and the New York Female Society," *Methodist History* 34, 4 (July 1996): 214–229.

22 The Wesleyan Methodists from Great Britain engaged in missions in France, Belgium, Spain, Sweden, Germany, Switzerland, Austria, Italy, and Portugal. If these missions did not unite with the Methodist Episcopal Church missions, they mainly became independent Methodist Churches. Despite the fact that Wesleyan Methodists did not take the formal title of Church until late in the nineteenth century, they are referred to as the Wesleyan Methodist Church (WMC) throughout this volume.

23 The mission records of the WMC are deposited at the archives of the SOAS (School of Oriental and African Studies) in London and can be used only with special allowances and limited support on-site.

24 It is significant to note the 150th anniversary, in 2019, of this monumental development. Dana Roberts describes this as "first gendered mission theory, and it provided a unique rationale for the mission and ministry of women in the nineteenth century" (see Dana L. Robert, ed., *Gospel Bearers – Gender Barriers: Missionary Women in the Twentieth Century* (Maryknoll: Orbis Books, 2002), 248). In the records of this organization, and in the case of other denominations as well, the formal title shifts back and forth between "Woman's" and "Women's." For simplicity sake, we refer to these organizations, in terms of formal title, as "Woman's Missionary Societies."

25 The EA developed their primary mission work in Germany and Switzerland, but later expanded their work among German-speaking people in a limited way in other European areas (Alsace-Lorraine (present day France), East Prussia (present day Poland), and Latvia).

26 The Ecumenical Methodist Conferences was founded in London in 1881. The name was formally changed in 1951 to the World Methodist Council.

27 "Protokolle der 'Vereinigte Versammlungen' (1881–85)," *Mitteilungen der Studiengemeinschaft für Geschichte des Methodismus* 2, 1–2 (1963/1964): 5–9.

28 Paul N. Garber, *The Methodists of Continental Europe* (New York: Editorial Dept., Division of Education and Cultivation, 1949), 30.

29 One of the most difficult issues in this volume has been how to navigate the nearly constant changes in the names of some of these nation states and their boundaries over the course of the roughly 70 years covered in this volume. Our policy has been to use the names of the countries as they were known between 1869 and 1939, but to provide helpful guidance to changes in the scholarly apparatus of the volume.

30 Yugoslavia consisted of Serbo-Croatia, Slovenia, and Macedonia. Chapter 10 in this volume includes material on a significant woman missionary in Macedonia. The author, Christina Cecov, has also published some articles about women pioneers in Macedonia that fall outside the timeframe of this study but should be mentioned here (all are self-published booklets on *Rösli Isler (1907–1998): Erinnerungen an die Schweizer Missionarin in Makedonien, An Extraordinary Woman: Paula Mojzes (1906–1970)*, and *Bible Women in The Balkans.*

31 One exception to this rule was the work of Francis J. Baker, *The Story of the Women's Foreign Missionary Society of the Methodist Episcopal Church 1869–1895* (Cincinnati: Curts & Jennings/New York: Eaton & Mains, 1898).

32 Among efforts to redress this imbalance in Methodist scholarship, in particular, see the work of Dana L. Robert, *American Women in Mission: A Social History of Their Thought and Practice* (Macon: Mercer University Press, 1997), 125–188 and Robert, *Gospel Bearers – Gender Barriers*, as well as Hilah F. Thomas and Rosemary Skinner Keller, eds., *Women in New Worlds: Historical Perspectives on the Wesleyan Tradition*, vol. 1 (Nashville: Abingdon Press, 1981) and Rosemary Skinner Keller, Louise L. Queen, and Hilah F. Thomas, eds., *Women in New Worlds: Historical Perspectives on the Wesleyan Tradition*, vol. 2 (Nashville: Abingdon Press, 1982). Scholars have also begun to document the beginnings of women societies in European countries. See two publications, in particular focusing only on German-speaking areas in Europe: *Mit Weisheit, Witz und Widerstand: Die Geschichte(n) von Frauen in der Evangelisch-methodistischen Kirche* (Stuttgart: Medienwerk der Evangelisch-methodistischen Kirche, 2003) and *Frauen in der Evangelisch-methodistischen Kirche Schweiz/Frankreich* (Zürich: Selbstverlag, 2000).

33 In some German-speaking contexts, deaconesses, minister's wives, and other women were designated *Gemeindeschwestern* (Community Sisters) and functioned as assistants to the pastors and engaged in community service.

34 See Dana L. Robert, "Evangelist or Homemaker? Mission Strategies of Early Nineteenth-Century Missionary Wives in Burma and Hawaii," *International Bulletin of Missionary Research* 17 (January 1993): 4–12 and Robert, "The Missionary Wife," *American Women in Mission*, 1–80.

35 Robert, *American Women in Mission*, 16.

36 Ibid., 35.

37 Ruth A. Tucker, "The Role of Bible Women in World Evangelism," *Missiology* 13, 2 (April 1985): 134.

38 Rosemary Skinner Keller, "Creating a Sphere for Women," in *Women in New Worlds*, 1: 251.

39 R. Pierce Beaver, *American Protestant Women in World Mission* (Grand Rapids: Wm. B. Eerdmans, 1969) deals with these changes in mission theory, but the most definitive study on this topic as it relates to women missionaries is Robert, *American Women in Mission*.

40 Christ-An C. Bennett, "Women's Work: The Role of Women in Wesleyan Methodist Overseas Mission in the Nineteenth Century," *Methodist History* 32, 4 (July 1994): 232. Cf. Deborah Kirkwood, "Protestant Missionary Women: Wives and Spinsters," in *Women and Missions: Past and Present Anthropological and Historical Perceptions*, ed. Fiona Bowie, Deborah Kirkwood, and Shirley Ardener (Oxford: Berg, 1993), 32.

41 Robert, *American Women in Mission*, 130. While it is not yet possible to make such a claim about women in European Methodism given the nascent stage of the scholarship, it would appear that a parallel between the USA and Europe could be drawn.

42 Ibid. This view was based in large measure "on the materialistic, albeit idealistic, belief that non-Christian religions trapped and degraded women, yet all women in the world were sisters and should support each other" (Robert, *American Women in Mission*, 134).

43 Ibid., 83.

44 Perhaps no event illustrates this watershed in mission theory during the 1880s better than the so-called Berlin conference of 1884–1885. With the intent of regulating European colonization and trade in Africa, this conference ushered in the era of a new imperialism. The General Act of the Berlin Conference, the final document produced by the European participants, formalized the "scramble for Africa." One of its primary consequences was the undoing and elimination of African autonomy and self-governance. This spirit of cultural imperialism was endemic to the age. See M. E. Chamberlain, *The Scramble for Africa* (Burnt Mill/Harlow/Essex: Longman Group Ltd., 1974).

45 Robert draws upon the work of William Hutchinson and Toben Christensen to demonstrate how "the emphasis on social change toward western norms, couched in the language of helping to bring about God's kingdom on earth, made 'Woman's Work for Woman' a partner with the myths of western superiority so prominent during the late nineteenth century" (*American Women in Mission*, 135).

46 In his two-volume *History of the Missions of the American Board of Commissioners for Foreign Missions to the Oriental Churches* (Boston: Congregational Publishing Society, 1872) Anderson promoted a theology of mission oriented around the principle of "a scriptural self-propagating Christianity." His contemporary Henry Venn, secretary of the Church Mission Society in Britain, stressed "indigenization" as well. Cf. Paul W. Harris, *Nothing but Christ: Rufus Anderson and the Ideology of Protestant Foreign Missions* (Oxford: Oxford University Press, 2000) and Wilbert R. Schenk, *Henry Venn: Missionary Statesman* (Maryknoll: Orbis Books, 1984).

47 Ann White, "Counting the Cost of Faith: America's Early Female Missionaries," *Church History* 57, 1 (March 1988): 29.

48 Founded in 1810, the ABCFM was the largest and most important of American missionary organizations throughout the course of the nineteenth century (see Anderson, *History of the American Board of Commissioners for Foreign Missions*).

49 The Alsatian people suffered living in boundary area between Germany and France that was occupied several times from both sides – always followed by the change of the main language and persecutions. From 1871 to 1918 Alsace and Lorraine were designated the administrative district of "Alsace-Lorraine" in the *Deutsches Reich* (German Empire). Today the territory is part of France.

50 East and West Prussia were the territories of the Teutonic Knights in the late medieval and reformation periods and became part of the Ducal Prussia (later the Kingdom of Prussia) in the sixteenth century. From 1871 to 1945 it was part of the German Empire, then after World War Two it fell under Polish and then Soviet control. Since 1992 the area has been part of Poland, but the most northern region belongs to Russia. The EA held revivals in this area at the beginning of the twentieth century up to the 1930s, a time during which new congregations emerged. By 1945 they had developed 42, but as a consequence of the political changes after World War Two the church buildings were occupied and the German inhabitants were banished.

51 The ABCFM was officially chartered in 1812.

52 Work under Italian-speaking foreign workers in Switzerland.

53 Serbia was part of the Ottoman Empire from 1459 to 1804. After a series of revolutions and wars, Serbia became an autonomous kingdom in 1882. At the end of World War One the Kingdoms of Serbia, Croatia, and Slovenia constituted Yugoslavia. Following World War Two, as one part of a six-part Republic of Yugoslavia, this state later came to be known as the Socialistic Republic of Serbia. It gained its independence in 1991 along with many other republics. After further wars (e.g., the Kosovo War) and federation with Montenegro, Serbia became an independent Republic in 2006.

54 Macedonia was part of the Ottoman Empire from 1371 to 1913. After the second Balkan War it was segmented into Greek, Albanian, Bulgarian, and Serbian quarters. After World War Two Macedonian was partitioned again, an action which included the violent relocation and displacement of the people. Both after World War One and during World War Two Macedonia was an occupied state under the control of Bulgaria. In 1944 it became part of Yugoslavia. In 1991 Macedonia achieved independence but with the challenge of uniting an ethnically diverse and oppressed "patchwork" society.

Sources

Agnew, Theodore L. "Reflections on the Woman's Foreign Missionary Movement in Late 19th-century American Methodism." *Methodist History* 6, 2 (January 1968): 3–16.

Anderson, Rufus. *History of the Missions of the American Board of Commissioners for Foreign Missions to the Oriental Churches.* 2 volumes. Boston: Congregational Publishing Society, 1872.

Baker, Francis J. *The Story of the Women's Foreign Missionary Society of the Methodist Episcopal Church 1869–1895.* Cincinnati: Curts & Jennings/New York: Eaton & Mains, 1898.

Barclay, Wade Crawford, and J. Tremayne Copplestone. *History of Methodist Missions*. 4 volumes. New York: Board of Missions, 1949–1973.

Beaver, R. Pierce. *American Protestant Women in World Mission*. Grand Rapids: Wm. B. Eerdmans, 1969.

Bennett, Christ-An C. "Women's Work: The Role of Women in Wesleyan Methodist Overseas Mission in the Nineteenth Century." *Methodist History* 32, 4 (July 1994): 229–236.

Bixby, Linda. *An Outline History of the Foreign Missions of the Methodist Episcopal Church*. Syracuse: np, 1876.

Burkhardt, Friedemann. *Christoph Gottlob Müller und die Anfänge des Methodismus in Deutschland. Arbeiten zur Geschichte des Pietismus, Bd. 43*. Göttingen: Vandenhoeck & Ruprecht, 2003.

Butler, Sarah F. *History of Woman's Foreign Missionary Society, Methodist Episcopal Church, South*. Nashville: Publishing House of the MECS, 1904.

Cekov, Christina. *Bible Women in the Balkans*. Strumica: United Methodist Church of Macedonia, 2011.

Cekov, Christina. "An Extraordinary Woman: Paula Mojzes (1906–1970)." Self-published, n.d.

Cekov, Christina. "Rösli Isler (1907–1998): Erinnerungen an die Schweizer Missionarin in Makedonien." Self-published, n.d.

Chamberlain, M. E. *The Scramble for Africa*. Burnt Mill/Harlow/Essex: Longman Group Ltd., 1974.

Di Gioacchino, Massimo. "Evangelizzare gli Italiani, Salvare l'America: l'Italian Mission Della Methodist Episcopal Church Degli USA (1908–1916)." *Protestantesimo* 67, 4 (2012): 335–348.

Findley, George G. and W. W. Holdsworth. *The History of the Wesleyan Methodist Missionary Society*. 5 volumes. London: Epworth Press, pp. 1921–1924.

Frauen in der Evangelisch-methodistischen Kirche Schweiz/Frankreich. Zürich: Selbstverlag, 2000.

Frei, Ueli. *Der Methodimus in Bulgarien, 1857–1989/90*. Frankfurt am Main: Medienwerk der evangelisch-methodistischen Kirche, 2012.

Garber, Paul N. *The Methodists of Continental Europe*. New York: Editorial Dept., Division of Education and Cultivation, 1949.

Harris, Paul W. *Nothing but Christ: Rufus Anderson and the Ideology of Protestant Foreign Missions*. Oxford: Oxford University Press, 2000.

Hecker, Friedrich, Vilém Schneeberger, and Karl Zehrer. *Methodismus in Osteuropa: Polen – Tschechoslowakei – Ungarn*. Stuttgart: EmKGM 51, 2004.

Hill, Patricia. *The World Their Household: The American Woman's Foreign Mission Movement and Cultural Transformation*. Ann Arbor: University of Michigan Press, 1985.

Isham, Mary. *Valorous Ventures: A Record of Sixty and Six Years of the Woman's Foreign Missionary Society, Methodist Episcopal Church*. Boston: WFMS, 1936.

Jackson, Thomas, ed. *The Works of John Wesley*. 14 volumes. London: J. Mason, 1831.

Keller, Rosemary Skinner, Louise L. Queen, and Hilah F. Thomas, eds. *Women in New Worlds: Historical Perspectives on the Wesleyan Tradition*. 2 volumes. Nashville: Abingdon Press, 1982.

Kirkwood, Deborah. "Protestant Missionary Women: Wives and Spinsters." In *Women and Missions: Past and Present Anthropological and Historical*

Perceptions. Edited by Fiona Bowie, Deborah Kirkwood, and Shirley Ardener. Oxford: Berg, 1993.

Mit Weisheit, Witz und Widerstand: Die Geschichte(n) von Frauen in der Evangelisch-methodistischen Kirche. Stuttgart: Medienwerk der Evangelisch-methodistischen Kirche, 2003.

Nuelsen, D. John, Theophil Mann, and J. J. Sommer, eds. *Kurzgefasste Geschichte des Methodismus*. Bremen: Verlagshaus der Methodistenkirche GmbH,1929.

"Protokolle der 'Vereinigte Versammlungen' (1881–85)." *Mitteilungen der Studiengemeinschaft für Geschichte des Methodismus* 2, 1–2 (1963/1964): 5–9.

Robert, Dana L. *American Women in Mission: A Social History of Their Thought and Practice*. Macon: Mercer University Press, 1997.

Robert, Dana L. "Evangelist or Homemaker? Mission Strategies of Early Nineteenth-Century Missionary Wives in Burma and Hawaii." *International Bulletin of Missionary Research* 17 (January 1993): 4–12.

Robert, Dana L. "Holiness and the Missionary Vision of the Woman's Foreign Missionary Society of the Methodist Episcopal Church, 1869–1894." *Methodist History* 39, 1 (October 2000): 15–27.

Robert, Dana L., ed. *Gospel Bearers – Gender Barriers: Missionary Women in the Twentieth Century*. Maryknoll: Orbis Books, 2002.

Schenk, Wilbert R. *Henry Venn: Missionary Statesman*. Maryknoll: Orbis Books, 1984.

Schuler, Ulrike. *Die Evangelische Gemeinschaft: Missionarische Aufbrüche in gesellschaftspolitischen Umbrüchen*. Stuttgart: EmKS 1, 1998.

Schuler, Ulrike. "Methodism in Northern and Continental Europe." In *T & T Clark Companion to Methodism*. Edited by Charles Yrigoyen, pp. 166–187. London: Continuum, 2010.

Stephens, Peter. *Methodism in Europe*. Peterborough: Methodist Publishing House, 1998.

Streiff, Patrick Ph., ed. *Der europäische Methodismus um die Wende vom 19. zum 20. Jahrhundert*. Stuttgart: EmKGM 52, 2005.

Streiff, Patrick Ph. *Der Methodismus in Europa im 19. und 20. Jahrhundert*. Stuttgart: EmKGM 50, 2003.

Thomas, Hilah F. and Rosemary Skinner Keller, eds. *Women in New Worlds: Historical Perspectives on the Wesleyan Tradition*. 1 Volume. Nashville: Abingdon Press, 1981.

Tucker, Ruth A. "The Role of Bible Women in World Evangelism." *Missiology* 13, 2 (April 1985): 133–146.

Warrick, Susan E. " 'She Diligently Followed Every Good Work': Mary Mason and the New York Female Society." *Methodist History* 34, 4 (July 1996): 214–229.

Wheeler, Mary S. *First Decade of the Woman's Foreign Missionary Society, Methodist Episcopal Church*. New York: Phillips & Hunt, 1881.

White, Ann. "Counting the Cost of Faith: America's Early Female Missionaries." *Church History* 57, 1 (March 1988): 19–30.

Part I
Bible Women, deaconesses, and missionaries

Jean Scott, Superintendent, Methodist National Training School, Toronto

1 Methodist Bible Women in Bulgaria and Italy

Paul W. Chilcote and Ulrike Schuler

Bulgarian Bible Women

When one thinks of the global character of The United Methodist Church today, the nations of Bulgaria and Italy do not immediately spring to mind as arenas in which this tradition has had a presence. Yet, the Methodist churches in these European countries have a deep and rich history, and much of it may be traced back to the influence of women. Women functioned as pioneers on multiple levels in these two settings, but we must first turn to the indigenous women of Bulgaria and Italy to identify the earliest pioneers of Methodist evangelism and mission.

Pioneering Bible Women

In Bulgaria and Italy the early evangelistic work of the Methodists was closely linked with so-called Bible Women. These women, also known as Bible Readers, were simply indigenous women hired to do evangelistic work, functioning much like the deaconesses of the early church.[1] There seems to be little question that the development of this role for women coincided directly with the rise of the various women's societies since there was no such practice prior to their birth. In Methodism, the earliest "use" of Bible Women as paid employees dates from as early as 1861, perhaps, when Mrs. T. C. Doremus sent money to Annie Gracey "for the employment of some native Christian woman as Bible reader or teacher."[2]

According to R. Pierce Beaver, "The Bible woman, catechist or evangelist, was the lowliest employee on the hierarchical ladder of the mission churches."[3] These women seemed to have been trained at first in an ad hoc manner and provided only the most rudimentary skill base for personal evangelism. Actual training schools soon displaced personal tutelage, and schools for girls, in particular, became the primary training ground for these women. The training of girls became all the more significant for the ministry of the mission since boys educated in similar schools often transferred their skills into business, industry, and government rather than finding a place in the service of the church. Used to great effect in Asian contexts, therefore, the office of Bible Woman later spread throughout the various arenas of the Woman's Foreign Missionary Society (WFMS) activity.[4] Beyond this, Dana Robert has noted the predilection of WFMS leaders to use indigenous women in simple evangelistic practices. "Bible women were both cheaper to support and more effective as evangelists than western women," she observes. "Methodist women were more likely to find themselves training Bible women than serving as evangelists themselves."[5] While they functioned primarily as evangelists, the Bible Women also devoted time and energy to teaching and discipling, distributing Christian literature, and providing health care services to the needy. Unlike other national workers, they were salaried employees of the mission station. While Frances Hiebert correctly notes that they shared in "the evangelism and Bible teaching that brought to birth the churches of the non-Western world," Methodist Bible Women in Europe also fulfilled this significant role in a Western context.[6]

It is less known that

> in 1845 women missionaries serving with the American Board of Commissioners of Foreign Mission [ABCFM] opened a Female Seminary in Constantinople (the capital of the Ottoman Empire, today Istanbul). It began with eight students, but the number quickly increased. By the 1860s Bible Women were being employed in that city by the American Bible Society.[7]

Tucker also notes that "there were training programs for Bible women at several mission stations in Turkey, including a Girl's Seminary at Aintab . . . still training women five decades later."[8] At the beginning of Methodist work with Bible Women in Bulgaria, it is difficult to distinguish between those who worked for the ABCFM and those who worked for the Methodists; it appears that the greater concern was for a common "Protestant mission." It is very difficult to document where the first Bible Women in Italy received their education. It seems that Emily Vernon, the wife of the first Methodist Episcopal Church (MEC) missionary to Italy, had her hand in this.[9] Barclay confirms that she "had been in charge of women's work in the mission [and] considered the work of the Bible women as highly important."[10]

The MEC mission board and the WFMS simply replicated the non-Western pattern in their European centers, in which the Bible Women became the "backbone of women's work in missions" through their wide-ranging ministry.[11] The evidence drawn from the Methodist work in Bulgaria and Italy confirms Tucker's settled opinion that "without Bible Women, female missionaries would have been at a loss."[12]

Bible Women in Bulgaria

The ABCFM began their work in the Ottoman Empire in 1819, having received calls from Bulgaria for support to renew the Orthodox Church.[13] While the Ottoman Empire formally authorized the practice of Islam, Christianity, and Judaism in 1839, in 1850/51 the Turkish Sultan granted a special dispensation to Protestants, permitting them to engage in mission activities in the Ottoman Empire and in the Balkans, in particular.[14] Personnel challenges led the ABCFM to request support from MEC, which appointed two missionaries to Constantinople as their base in 1857.[15] In Tulča, Frederick William Flocken, later appointed Methodist Superintendent, opened a Sunday school and day school.[16] Clara Proca was the first woman employed as a Bible Woman of the WFMS in 1874 when Methodist work began in Bulgaria.[17] She was also "one of the first scholars in the mission school in 1860."[18]

For details with regard to these developments, we must turn to the *Heathen Woman's Friend*.[19] Rev. Flocken arrived in Shumen, Bulgaria, in 1859 where he established the first Methodist work in that area.[20] As superintendent of the work in the 1870s, he submitted reports of the activities of the Bible Women to the women's periodical. In 1875, Flocken quoted from Clara Proca's quarterly report, detailing her encounter with an Armenian widow. She wrote:

> I then took out my Russian Testament and read to her of Jesus; how He loved the world, died for sinners, shed His blood for their redemption, and how He invites all sinners to come to Him. I read to her of the prodigal son, and the malefactors on the cross, and begged her to pray to Jesus, to trust in Jesus, and to hope everything from no one else but Jesus. I prayed with her, commended her to Jesus, and left her.[21]

She later reported the positive effect of her prayers. According to Flocken's report, during the previous quarter she had visited 65 families and distributed tracts throughout the neighboring areas. Her general pattern was to teach a number of the children part of the day and to visit from house to house during the course of the remaining hours.

The October 1875 issue of the *Heathen Woman's Friend* provided a biographical account of Clara and identified some of her accomplishments.[22] Born of German parents in Transylvania around 1848, she immigrated with her family to Bulgaria and enrolled in the mission school in Samokov in 1860. Four years later she was appointed assistant teacher at the school and engaged in informal evangelistic work. In 1867 she married, but when her husband's business failed two years later, he left her for America, leaving behind two children and Clara's parents under her own care. The WFMS began to fund her work in 1873, thereby providing her with a livelihood – remuneration for the meaningful work she had continued in for some years. Flocken reflected on the range of her accomplishments during the course of her formal appointment as a Bible Woman:

> She has now been almost two years in the employ of the mission, and I have many proofs that she has accomplished what no male agent could have done. She has reorganized our former Sabbath School at Tultscha, holds regular prayer-meetings with the women, visits them in their houses, reads, and instructs them in the Bible, and distributes tracts to such as can read. The women attending her meetings are Germans, Russians, Bulgarians, Wallachians, and Jews, with all of whom she can converse in their respective languages.

He also identified Magdalena Elief as a partner in this work with Clara. An excerpt from her quarterly report provides some insight into the nature of her work as well:

> In my visits from house to house I find that some of the women leave the house just as soon as I enter, and find something to do in their yards, so

as to avoid my talking to them; but a good occasion offers itself to me at the time of the birth of a child in a family, when usually the women of the whole neighborhood come together to congratulate the happy mother. On such occasions I have good opportunities to read to the women from the Bible, and to speak to them.

In 1877 Flocken reported how Magdalene Elief exhibited great courage in the face of war:

The prospect of a war with Russia and the atrocities of the Torkshave have so taken up the mind that they hardly talk of anything else. At Lone Paleanka where Magdalene Elief is at work, the native preacher has been obliged to leave his charge to attend to the war sufferers, but Magdalene keeps bravely at her Bible work through heavy persecution and difficulties.[23]

Here we have but a glimpse of the pioneering work of Bulgarian Bible Women, a small group of gifted women whose contribution should not be underestimated.

"In 1877 the WFMS increased their appropriation to provide support for four Bible women. These women worked under great difficulties and faced heavy persecution again and again."[24] The following year, Ellen Stone, a Congregationalist missionary from New England, had been sent by the ABCFM to Samokov to teach at the girls' school.[25] An important part of her ministry there was the organization and oversight of women's work and the education of Bible Women.[26] In these early years a very close connection obtained between the ABCFM and the MEC/WFMS, despite the fact that the region had been divided between them in a typical comity agreement,[27] and some of the Methodist Bible Women received their training at Samokov. In 1886, Stone formalized the basic instruction she had been providing into a four-week formal curriculum, generally taught during the summer, that included Bible study, church history, moral philosophy, and geology, as well as remedial work in reading, writing, and mathematics.[28] Despite the fact that the WFMS had employed Bible Women for some years by this time, they quickly replicated her vision, and her imprint on the lives of the later Methodist women was deep.

The 1881 report of WFMS work in Bulgaria had noted that the Society was "carrying for several years the support of two or three Bible women."[29] Well in advance of Stone's more formal provision of training, in 1881, the Methodist leadership appealed to the WFMS "to send out two ladies to establish a solid, permanent work there, manage the school and employ Bible women."[30] One of the hopes expressed by Rev. DeWitt C. Challis,[31] at that time the superintendent of the MEC mission in Bulgaria, was that the schools they were establishing would produce a generation of Bible Women who would render invaluable service to the church.[32] He and his wife,

"Mrs. Callis,"[33] opened a school for girls in their own home in Loftcha in November 1880. The following year, Challis was instructed by his board to build a school that, over the course of the following years would go through a rollercoaster of successful work, interruptions by several government-ordered closings, and relocation to Samakov. The 1882 report celebrated the fact that "already the girls have begun to read the Bible in the homes of the women. Two of them, Ceika Dematrof and Suka Petkof, have been engaged in this work during the summer vacation."[34]

The supervising pastors and missionaries, however, provided very little detail concerning the work of these women and generally excluded their names from their communications. Most of the reports to the WFMS focused on the work of the missionaries and their hired assistants. In 1884, for example, Linna Schenck, the WFMS missionary, secured Miss Stonata Atanasova, "a graduate of the Samokof school, with ten years' experience as teacher and some years residence in England, a very companionable lady."[35] She also engaged Mrs. Kassova, "an experienced Bulgarian teacher,"[36] to assist her in the work of the mission school. They provided support in the classroom and dealt with logistical matters in the institution.[37] More often than not, these women are simply referred to as the "native assistants." While these women tended to remain fixed in their institutional settings, the Bible Women expanded the influence of the mission into areas outside the reach of Methodist institutions. "The Bible women report a wonderful interest among the women in the villages," claimed the 1887 review, "and they say that there is work for twenty additional women to travel all the time."[38] The mission schools, as had been hoped, tended to fill the ranks of the Bible Women as a comment in the 1888 report infers: "The girls who graduated are all engaged in teaching and Bible work."[39]

Generally, the girls' schools functioned to recruit future evangelists on different levels – women to "infuse" Protestant influences into the Bulgarian society from the grassroots. Occasionally the hopes were fulfilled. "Four people graduated in 1886. . . . Two of these girls were engaged to marry young preachers, graduates of the Theological school at Sistov. One of them took work as a Bible woman, and another returned to the school as primary teacher."[40] Unfortunately, in the Bulgarian context, the repeated cryptic comment in the reports, "the Bible work has been faithfully done, superintended by an efficient woman," reveals little about who these women were or what they actually did.[41] Paul Mojzes, an expert on the Methodist Church in Bulgaria,[42] could only fill two pages about Bible Women, where he states that they were "the most significant torchbearers of evangelical work," that they "taught women, by reading to them and selling them Bibles."[43] He also determined that

> these women were mainly humble souls whose identity is not easy to establish. Only a few were mentioned by name . . . Missionary wives assisted the Bible women and toured the region with their husbands

but their main activity was in the locality of the station where they taught sometimes in the schools, or organized Ladies' Benevolent Societies to help destitute women . . . the women had to be cultivated more carefully, and only women, Bible women, could do this job as they so admirably did.[44]

Bible Women in Italy

The Italian context reveals a very different picture with regard to this "office" within the life of the Methodist community there. Records reveal no fewer than 29 named Bible Women between 1877 and 1892. (See the chart at the conclusion of the chapter for a full listing of the names and vital information for each of these women.) Likewise, the reports – many of which were prepared by Emily F. Vernon, the wife of the superintending pastor, Dr. Leroy M. Vernon[45] – provide a full portrait of these women and their activities. In 1877, the General Executive Committee of the WFMS appropriated funds for "five Bible readers, to be stationed where the mission should most need their services."[46] Mrs. Aurelia Conversi and Mrs. Carolina were immediately appointed to Rome and Venice respectively. The tenure of several women in this service stands out: Camilla Stazi (14 years), Miss Monta (11 years), and Mrs. Campani (eight years), all of whom ministered in the city of Milan, soon to become a major center of Methodist influence. Despite the fact that Camilla Mattioli married a Methodist preacher in 1881, Rev. S. Stazi, she spent all but two of her years as a Bible Woman in her native Milan. Many of the Bible Women, in fact, were Methodist preachers' wives, some of their husbands being former priests of the Roman Catholic Church. Whereas it is quite difficult to determine the length of service of these women, due to the lack of precise records, from the information available it appears that the Italian Bible Women functioned in this role on average about four years.

Emily Vernon's very first report of Mrs. Conversi's work in Rome provides both a biographically informed snapshot of her spirituality and a detailed description of her work:

> Mrs. Conversi has been employed as Bible reader under the auspices of your Society since August 1st, 1877, and gives her entire time to such duties. Her labors are varied. She daily visits the homes and haunts of the people, carrying always a small quantity of testaments and tracts, adroitly seizing every occasion and opportunity to teach the one great truth so grateful to every human heart, the full, free, unmerited love of Christ. She rarely fails of getting a hearing, and winning over the roughest characters to respectful attention.
>
> Her personal experience of the saving power of the truth in Christ makes her ever welcome among the sick and afflicted, where she goes with words of cheer, and comfort and prayer. She visits the cafés, drinking places, etc.; and her journal, which she brings as a monthly report, is

full of conversations and disputations at different times and places, with various persons. She conquers in so far that they generally acknowledge she is right.[47]

Quoting a letter of Dr. Vernon, the report concluded:

There is a broad margin here where only ladies can work – at least, judiciously and with security, and I believe your labors would reach rich realms and interests intangible to us; would carry fuller spirituality and faith into the houses, the sheltered quarters of our work in this mission of truth and grace in the land of hearty loud song.[48]

In these early years, the annual reports of the work in Italy give large place to the activities of the Bible Women, often quoting copiously from their own journals and letters. In fact, the work of these women dominates the reports. In 1880 Emily Vernon expressed her high esteem for these women and their peculiar role in the expanding work of the mission: "We feel that the work of these Bible Women is highly important, and that, urgently and faithfully prosecuted, it may be eminently useful and successful."[49] Two years later she provides an account of the work of the six women then in their employ. An excerpt of the report reveals both the tensions and the strategies at play:

We have been making some changes among our workers. Mrs. Conversi and Mrs. Folchi have been dismissed. Miss Quercia and Miss Benincasa have been employed in their places. Both of them are well educated, energetic and earnest Christians. They will be able to reach a good class of people. Miss Quercia has already found access to families of good position. She is very courageous in presenting religious truth to them. The leaven of truth must work, as we hope, and pray, till all Italy is renovated.[50]

We are left to speculate about the dismissal of the earliest Bible Women. Perhaps the growing responsibilities of parenthood deflected energy from the mission. Perhaps their passion for the work had dissipated over the course of several years. Perhaps their theological perspective did not align with that of the mission leadership.[51] Perhaps they were not in a position to reach into the strata of the society that a newly emergent strategy required. The shift in Vernon's approach to the work – engaging women in the upper echelons of society through the work of the Bible Women, with its implied "trickle down" strategy – is reflected elsewhere in the report. Camilla Stazi, for example, began to give "gratuitous lessons in music in some of the better families for sake of getting an influence over them for good." The following comment reflects her preference for unmarried or childless Bible Women: "She is married, but has no children, and will be able to give herself wholly to the work."[52] She concluded her report with a note of triumphalism: "There ought to be . . . at least a hundred women at work in the different towns and cities before the ringing of the Christmas bells of 1883." The following year Vernon's husband appealed to the WFMS to send a superintendent for the work of the women, a task that had become too burdensome for his wife.[53] He identifies two issues that mitigated against their success: 1) Women who are "incapable and untrustworthy" for the work, and 2) Catholic prejudice. "It is a new husbandry to which they are called," he wrote, "and *amid a sea of difficulties and a tangle of obstacles*, such as your banner-bearers *nowhere* else encounter. *Mark that.*"[54]

The ranks of the Bible Women grew through the coming years. In 1885 the Vernons attached their hopes, in particular, on Mrs. Conte, a teacher and the wife of one of their indigenous preachers just moved to Naples. His glowing report of her work reflects both their strategy and the extent of Conte's ministry:

> She is an experienced teacher, and being convinced that the best way to reach the mother is through the child, she opened a day school for gratuitous instruction, which met with great success, the number increasing so rapidly that she was obliged to refuse further admissions – at one time she had as many as eighty-seven. In order to have a more direct influence over the women she formed an evening adult class; ten women joined, four of whom are now members of our church, and two probationers. She also conducts a Sunday afternoon Bible Class, besides being the head and heart of the Sunday school. Making the acquaintance of a rich and prominent family of the neighboring town of Malfi, through her influence two young sisters have been won to Christ, and the brother has become a firm friend, though not an adherent of the cause. The Bible women use tracts, bibles, testaments, and religious books in their work, distributing or selling them as they can, though there are few who wish to buy.[55]

That same year the WFMS appointed their first missionary to Italy, Emma Hall, but the work was being done largely by the 12 Bible Women, employed in as many cities. The Vernons appealed for support for 15 Bible Women, but a less than veiled critique of their work also indicated the need for some changes:

> The Bible women are, of course, unacquainted with the system and methods used in our American evangelistic work and are slow to make improvements upon the most simple plans. Many of them are the wives of pastors, and are very busy mothers; others have embraced Christianity but recently and have so much to learn, hence the great necessity of someone to visit them, oversee their work, make suggestions, and modify and enlarge the plans.[56]

The year 1888 proved to be momentous for the Methodist mission in Italy.[57] A new generation of missionaries, spearheaded by William Burt, severely criticized the supervision of the mission, particularly shocked by the prevalence of smoking and drinking among the indigenous clergy.[58] Under pressure and having served for 17 years in Italy, Dr. Vernon tendered his resignation. Burt replaced Vernon as Presiding Elder over all of Italy, reappraised the mission, and inaugurated what might be properly described as a purge. While the ranks of the Bible Women had remained fairly stable up to this point, under the new policies, and with many of the Bible Women being wives of former Roman Catholic priests, disintegration was inevitable. By 1890 only six Bible Women remained.[59] Despite their shrinking numbers, the women continued their work with indefatigable energy. Miss Monta, of Turin, the senior Bible Woman of the group, managed no less than 869 visits during 1891.[60] Of the three women remaining in 1893, Miss Biondi deserves special attention. Having labored at that time for seven years, she had been converted, in fact, while attending a holiness meeting of Phoebe Palmer[61] in New York.[62] She returned to Italy "full of zeal for the conversion of her country women."[63] She reported twice daily meetings in her home and a total of 692 visits for 1892. In the successive reports of the WFMS work in Italy, the voices of American missionaries displace those of the Italian Bible Women who simply disappear.

Through this process of tracking emergent Methodist mission in Bulgaria and Italy, and identifying the Bible Women and their primary roles, we arrived at a number of conclusions related to this significant group of pioneer women. 1) Ruth Tucker articulated our most important conclusion in a terse statement: "without Bible Women, female missionaries would have been at a loss."[64] 2) In both Bulgaria and Italy, these women were able to "go about their business," as it were, inconspicuous and unobtrusive; they understood the political landscape, but had the ability to rise above it. 3) Bible Women occupied a crucial ecumenical terrain that positioned them in places where they could build bridges. 4) They engaged in dynamic and organic networking, particularly with other women who bore the primary responsibility of transmitting religious values to their children. 5) Bible Women bore an authentic witness to the gospel through personal testimony and relational evangelism. Not only did they read the Bible to any who would listen, they lived the gospel in ways that won the hearts and souls of many.

Methodist Bible Women in Bulgaria 1873–1882

Name	Post	Events	Status
Clara Proca	Loftcha	born (b) 1848? appointed (a) 1873	
Magdalena Elief	Lom Palank	a 1874?	
Ceika Dematrof	Loftcha	a 1882	student at school
Suka Petkof	Loftcha	a 1882	student at school

Methodist Bible Women in Italy 1877–1892

Name	Post	Events	Status
Mrs. Aurelia Conversi	Rome	appointed (a) 1877 died (d) 1881	
Mrs. Carolina	Venice	a 1877 retired (r) 1881?	
Mrs. Comeri	Rome	a 1878 r 1881?	
Mrs. Folchi	Rome	a 1878 d 1881	
Mrs. Cardin	Venice	a 1878 r 1879	preacher's wife
Camilla Mattioli (Rev. S. Stazi)	Milan Alexandria Venice Milan	a 1878 married (m) 1881 1884 1885 1886 r 1892	preacher's wife
Mrs. Borelli (Rev. Enrico Borelli)	Venice	a 1879 r 1885?	preacher's wife replaced Cardin
Miss Querci[a]	Rome	a 1881 r 1885?	replaced Conversi
Miss Benincasa (Rev. G. Benincasa)	Rome	a 1881 r 1885?	preacher's wife replaced Folchi
Miss Monta	Turin	a 1881 r 1892	
Miss Nota	Bologna	a 1881	withdrew after three months
Mrs. Palmieri	Perugia Pisa Forli	a 1881? 1885 1886 r 1887?	
Mrs. Cavelleris [Cavalleris] (Rev. E. Cavalleris)		a 1882 r 1885?	preacher's wife
Mrs. Stasio (Rev. Edoardo Stasio)	Perugia	a 1882 1885 r 1887?	preacher's wife
Mrs. Conte[i] (Rev. Gaetano Conte)	Venosa Naples	a 1882 1885 r 1887?	preacher's wife teacher
Mrs. Tollis	Venice Bari	a 1883 1884 r 1886?	preacher's wife Marchioness
Mrs. Cruciani [Cruceani (Rev. Federico Cruciani)	Modena	a 1883 1884 r 1887?	preacher's wife Swiss woman
Mrs. Polsinelli (Rev. Domenico Polsinelli)	Naples Bologna	a 1883 1886 r 1887?	preacher's wife
Mrs. Lopa	Bologna	a 1883 r 1887?	ten years a colporteur

(*Continued*)

Name	Post	Events	Status
Mrs. Marini		a 1883 r 1885?	teacher
Mrs. Campani [Campari]	Milan	a 1884 r 1892	
Mrs. Mando [Mondo]	Rome	a 1884 1892 still active	
Mrs. Taglialatela (Rev. Pietro Taglialatela)	Foggia	a 1885 r 1887?	preacher's wife
Mrs. Mondi	Rome	a 1885 r 1887?	
Miss Biondi [Beondi]	Pisa	a 1886 1892 still active	
Mrs. Fabroni	Florence	a 1886 r 1887?	
Miss Nitti	Venosa	a 1886 r 1887?	
Miss Gay	Tarento	a 1886 r 1887?	
Miss Passesini	Forli	a 1890 1892 still active	

Notes

1 On the work of Bible Women in Christian mission, see Ruth A. Tucker, "The Role of Bible Women in World Evangelism," *Missiology* 13, 2 (April 1985): 133–146, from which the generic portrait of the Bible Woman here has been drawn. See also R. Pierce Beaver, *American Protestant Women in World Mission* (Grand Rapids: Wm. B. Eerdmans, 1969) and Helen B. Montgomery, *Western Women in Eastern Lands: An Outline of Fifty Years of Women's Work in Foreign Missions* (New York: Macmillan, 1910) both of which highlight the work of Bible Women in their historical accounts. None of these resources identify the role of Bible Women in the European context. For a booklet describing these ministries in the Balkans, see Christina Cekov, *Bible Women in the Balkans* (Strumica: United Methodist Church of Macedonia, 2011).

2 Annie [Mrs. J. T.] Gracey, *Eminent Missionary Women* (New York: Eaton & Mains, 1898), 17.

3 Beaver, *American Protestant Women*, 119.

4 For one of the first publications on this topic, see Mrs. S. Moore Sites, "Bible Women in Foochow," *Heathen Woman's Friend* 4, 5 (November 1872): 359–360. She provides the following description of the beginning of this work in China: "The introduction of 'deaconesses,' or Bible women, was a novel feature of missionary work to our native church in China; and it will still require some length of time to get the idea fully before our people. In beginning this work, we have not only to instruct these women more clearly in their knowledge of Christian doctrines, but often to teach them to *read*, beginning with the catechism, the gospels, and the hymns, as translated in their own 'Chinese characters' " (359). The origin of the Bible Women in Europe remains a topic for further research. While a number of studies documents their origins and work in Asia, nothing comparable interprets their work in Europe.

5 Dana L. Robert, *American Women in Mission: A Social History of Their Thought and Practice* (Macon: Mercer University Press, 1997), 169.

6 Frances Hiebert, "Missionary Women as Models in the Cross-Cultural Context," *Missiology* 10, 4 (October 1982): 459.

7 Tucker, "Bible Women," 135.

8 Ibid.

9 Emily F. B. Vernon married Leroy M. Vernon after his first wife, Fannie Elliot Vernon (1840–1869) had died. The Vernons served for 17 years in the Italian mission, helping to establish the MEC in Rome. They had eight children, three of whom died as infants in Rome. Little information remains concerning Emily Vernon's personal life; not even her birth date is known (F. T. Kennedy, "Mrs. Emily F. B. Vernon," in *The Minutes of the Forty-second Annual Session of the Northern New York Conference, MEC*, April 15–20, 1914, 126).

10 Wade Crawford Barclay and J. Tremayne Copplestone, *History of Methodist Missions*, 4 vols. (New York: Board of Missions, 1949–1973), 3: 1047.

11 Tucker, "Bible Women," 134.

12 Ibid.

13 This rationale also provided the impetus for the MEC mission to Bulgaria. Barclay and Copplestone cite the *Journal of the General Conference*, 1856 (p. 260) with a general instruction of the corresponding secretary for the missionaries: "Its chief object is to awaken in the Bulgarian Church, which is of the Greek rite, a desire of the evangelical religion, and lead her people to seek for the same. It will be necessary for you to use all kindness and skill in approaching the people privately and publicly; and you should be well acquainted with the doctrines and customs of the Greek Church, as well as of our own Church, not for the purpose of assailing them in controversy, but, as the occasion offers, to show that they are not agreeable to Scripture" (Barclay and Copplestone, *History of Methodist Missions*, 3: 1018).

14 "Firman [decree] of His Imperial Majesty Sultan Abdul Medjid, granted in favor of his Protestant Subjects," original discovered at a demolition of a Methodist chapel in Strumica, Macedonia. Imprint and explanation by Heinrich Bolleter, "Protestanten-Erlass im Osmanischen Reich im Jahre 1850/51," *EmK Geschichte* 28/1 (2007), 18–26. Cf. Patrick Ph. Streiff, *Der Methodismus in Europa im 19. Und 20. Jahrhundert* (Stuttgart: EmKGM 50, 2003), 58.

15 Streiff, *Der Methodismus in Europa*, 58.

16 Frederick William Flocken (1831–1893), born in Odessa, Russia, but with German roots, emigrated to the United States in 1849, joined the New York Conference in 1853, and was appointed for Bulgaria in 1858. He served at different places, returned 1871 to the United States and went back in 1873 to supervise the Bulgarian mission until 1878. See Barclay and Copplestone, *History of Methodist Missions*, 3: 1019n.

17 Frances J. Baker, *The Story of the Woman's Foreign Missionary Society of the Methodist Episcopal Church 1869–1895* (Cincinnati: Curts & Jennings/New York: Eaton & Mains, 1898), 348, citing the records of the WFMS that documented "supporting one or two Bible women and two or three girls in the school of the American Board in Samokof."

18 Ibid.

19 The *Heathen Woman's Friend*, a news periodical published monthly from the outset of the WFMS, served as the primary voice piece of the Society, providing information on their work and inspirational stories to promote the mission. See Patricia R. Hill, "Heathen Women's Friends: The Role of Methodist Episcopal Women in the Women's Foreign Mission Movement, 1869–1915," *Methodist History* 19, 3 (April 1981): 146–154.

20 Barclay and Copplestone, *History of Methodist Missions*, 3: 1019.

21 "From Bulgaria," *Heathen Woman's Friend* 6, 8 (February 1875): 798.

22 "Our Bulgarian Bible-Woman," *Heathen Woman's Friend* 7, 4 (October 1875): 82. The details concerning her life which follows below in the narrative are drawn from this portrait. Cf. Cekov, *Bible Women in the Balkans*, 16.

23 "Bulgaria," *Heathen Woman's Friend* 9, 1 (July 1877): 21.

24 Barclay and Copplestone, *History of Methodist Missions*, 3: 1026.

25 Ellen Stone (1846–1927) worked for ten years on the editorial staff of *The Congregationalist Magazine*, decided to become a missionary in 1878, and was sent by the ABCFM to Samakov to teach at a school for girls. She inaugurated training classes for Bible Women. In 1901 she was kidnapped with Katarina Cilka, a pregnant wife of a native missionary, and held ransom for six months by Macedonian freedom fighters. In 1902 she returned to the USA (see Cekov, *Bible Women in the Balkans*, 10–14). In various sources, there are different spellings of these place names: Samokof or Samokov, Tulča or Tultscha.

26 Cekov, *Bible Women in the Balkans*, 7.

27 Frei examines this agreement carefully according to later tensions about the responsibility in Sofia (see Ueli Frei, *Der Methodimus in Bulgarien, 1857–1989/90* (Frankfurt am Main: Medienwerk der evangelisch-methodistischen Kirche 2012), 77–80, 125–127).

28 Cekov, *Bible Women in the Balkans*, 9.

29 *Twelfth Annual Report of the WFMS* (1881), 50.

30 Ibid., 53.

31 DeWitt C. Challis (1845–1939), studied at the University of Michigan, became a member of the Detroit Conference, committed to mission work in Bulgaria in 1875, and was responsible for building the school in Lovetch (*Minutes of the Eigthy-fourth and final Session of the former Detroit Annual Conference, Michigan* (June 21–23, 1939) (Detroit: The Conference, 1940), 144).

32 It is important to note that in Bulgaria, as well as in Italy, the first stage of the WFMS mission strategy was to establish schools for girls and to teach women (Bible Women) with the hope that this would transform traditional Christian life.

33 This "Mrs Callis" is Dewitt C. Challis's second wife, Irene L. Shepherd, whom Challis married after his first wife, a physician, whose name we could not uncover, died from smallpox shortly after the birth of their first child in Bulgaria in 1877.

34 *Thirteenth Annual Report of the WFMS* (1882), 41.

35 Baker, *The Story of the WFMS*, 351.

36 Ibid.

37 *Sixteenth Annual Report of the WFMS* (1885), 49. Both women continued to work for some time at the primary Methodist school at Loftcha. As other schools were developed, native women typically filled positions of leadership in these new institutions. Mikala Motchora, for example, directed the educational activities at Orchania in later years (see *Nineteenth Annual Report of the WFMS* (1888), 49).

38 *Eighteenth Annual Report of the WFMS* (1887), 53.

39 *Nineteenth Annual Report of the WFMS* (1888), 49.

40 Baker, *The Story of the WFMS*, 351. There is added: "Most of the students expected in after years to refund the amount expended on their education."

41 *Twentieth Annual Report of the WFMS* (1889), 51.

42 Paul Benjamin Mojzes, "A History of the Congregational and Methodist Churches in Bulgaria and Yugoslavia," PhD dissertation, Boston University, 1965.

43 Ibid., 163.

44 Ibid., 164

45 Leroy M. Vernon, DD, LLD (1838–1896) graduated from Iowa Wesley University and became a member of the Arkansas Conference in 1862. He served as a pastor in St. Louis, Missouri and was later appointed Presiding Elder of the Springfield District, Southwest Missouri. In 1871 Vernon was appointed missionary and superintendent of the MEC in Italy. Together with his second wife, Emily Vernon, he "laid wisely the foundation of our Italy mission," working in Rome and the surrounding area for 17 years. In 1888 Vernon resigned and served as pastor of the First MEC in Syracuse, New York, where he was subsequently elected Dean of the College of Fine Arts at Syracuse University in 1893. He died in 1896 as the consequence of an accident. Vernon served both as member of the General Conference several times and as a member of the first Ecumenical Methodist Conference in 1881. In 1881 he also received the silver medal from the Italian government "for service rendered in the taking of religious census of the country" (E. C. Bruce, "Leroy M. Vernon," in *Minutes of the Twenty-Fifth Session, Northern New York Conference, MEC* (Watertown, April 14–19, 1897), 63–5).

46 *Eighth Annual Report of the* WFMS (1877), 33.

47 Ibid.

48 Ibid., 34.

49 *Eleventh Annual Report of the* WFMS (1880), 33.

50 *Thirteenth Annual Report of the* WFMS (1882), 42.

51 When Vernon began his work in Italy in 1873, he "followed a policy of using Italian evangelists, pastors, and teachers who had been converted, rather than delaying rapid evangelism until workers could be trained into a thorough understanding of Methodist religious experience, aims, and policies. This had been the practice of the Waldensian and Wesleyan groups which in their beginnings had availed themselves of native converts" (Barclay and Copplestone, *History of Methodist Missions*, 3:1044). The policy with regard to the Bible Women paralleled this basic approach.

52 Ibid., 43.

53 Emily Vernon had actually broached this issue as early as 1879, writing to the WFMS: "It would be wise to send out some capable young woman whose exclusive business might be to direct the Society's work and greatly enhance its efficiency. She could be a great power for good" (*Eleventh Annual Report of the* WFMS (1880), 44).

54 *Fourteenth Annual Report of the* WFMS (1883), 41.

55 *Sixteenth Annual Report of the* WFMS (1885), 51.

56 *Seventeenth Annual Report of the* WFMS (1886), 51.

57 See Barclay and Copplestone, *History of Methodist Missions*, 3:1050–1057. Tension arose, in particular, between Dr. Vernon and William Burt who had been appointed as a missionary to Italy in 1886. Later elected an MEC bishop in 1904, Burt represented a vehement counter-cultural approach to mission in Roman Catholic areas.

58 William Burt (1852–1936), born in England, emigrated with his family to the USA, studied at Wesleyan University in Middletown, Connecticut and at Drew Theological School in Madison, New Jersey. He served at churches in Brooklyn before being transferred to the Italy Annual Conference in 1886. In 1888, he became superintendent of the Italy Mission. Among other things he helped to establish the Methodist Building, the Boy's College, a Theological School, Publishing House, and Young Ladies College in Rome. In 1904 Burt was elected a Bishop of the MEC and appointed resident Bishop of Europe. He organized the France Mission Conference, the Austria-Hungary Mission Conference, the Russian Mission Conference, and the Denmark and Finland Annual Conferences. In

1910 he organized all the Methodist work in Europe into the European Central Annual Conference. His episcopal areas included Europe (1904–1912) and the Buffalo, New York area (1912–1924). Burt received several honorary doctorates. He was also knighted by King Victor Emmanuel II of Italy.

59 *Twenty-first Annual Report of the WFMS* (1890), 50.

60 *Twenty-third Annual Report of the WFMS* (1892), 81.

61 Phoebe Palmer (1807–1874), was an evangelist and writer. She promoted the doctrine of Christian perfection and became one of the founders of the Holiness movement at the end of the nineteenth century – a movement that spread from the USA to the UK and at least the European Continent.

62 On the influence of the nineteenth century holiness movement on Methodist women's mission, see Robert, "Holiness Piety for Missions," in *American Women in Mission*, 144–148.

63 *Twenty-fourth Annual Report of the WFMS* (1893), 75.

64 Tucker, "Bible Women," 134.

Sources

Annual Report of the Woman's Foreign Missionary Society. New York: Woman's Foreign Missionary Society of the Methodist Episcopal Church.
  – *Eighth* (1877).
  – *Eleventh* (1880).
  – *Twelfth* (1881).
  – *Thirteenth* (1882).
  – *Fourteenth* (1883).
  – *Sixteenth* (1885).
  – *Seventeenth* (1886).
  – *Eighteenth* (1887).
  – *Nineteenth* (1888).
  – *Twentieth* (1889).
  – *Twenty-first* (1890).
  – *Twenty-third* (1892).
  – *Twenty-fourth* (1893).
Baker, Frances J. *The Story of the Woman's Foreign Missionary Society of the Methodist Episcopal Church 1869–1895*. Cincinnati: Curts & Jennings/New York: Eaton & Mains, 1898.
Barclay, Wade Crawford, and J. Tremayne Copplestone. *History of Methodist Missions*. 4 volumes. New York: Board of Missions, 1949–1973.
Beaver, R. Pierce. *American Protestant Women in World Mission*. Grand Rapids: Wm. B. Eerdmans, 1969.
Bolleter, Heinrich. "Protestanten-Erlass im Osmanischen Reich im Jahre 1850/51." *EmK Geschichte* 28, 1 (2007): 18–26.
Bruce, E. C. "Leroy M. Vernon." In Minutes of the Twenty-Fifth Session, Northern New York Conference, MEC. Watertown, April 14–19, 1897, 63–65.
"Bulgaria." *Heathen Woman's Friend* 9, 1 (July 1877): 21.
Cekov, Christina. *Bible Women in the Balkans*. Strumica: United Methodist Church of Macedonia, 2011.
Frei, Ueli. *Der Methodimus in Bulgarien, 1857–1989/90*. Frankfurt am Main: Medienwerk der evangelisch-methodistischen Kirche, 2012.
"From Bulgaria." *Heathen Woman's Friend* 6, 8 (February 1875): 798.

Gracey, Annie [Mrs. J. T.] *Eminent Missionary Women*. New York: Eaton & Mains, 1898.

Hiebert, Frances. "Missionary Women as Models in the Cross-Cultural Context." *Missiology* 10, 4 (October 1982): 455–460.

Hill, Patricia R. "Heathen Women's Friends: The Role of Methodist Episcopal Women in the Women's Foreign Mission Movement, 1869–1915." *Methodist History* 19, 3 (April 1981): 146–154.

Kennedy, F. T. "Mrs. Emily F. B. Vernon." In The Minutes of the Forty-second Annual Session of the Northern New York Conference, MEC, April 15–20, 1914, 126.

Minutes of the Eigthy-fourth and final Session of the former Detroit Annual Conference, Michigan, Detroit: The Conference, 1940, June 21–23, 1939.

Mojzes, Paul Benjamin Mojzes. "A History of the Congregational and Methodist Churches in Bulgaria and Yugoslavia." PhD dissertation, Boston University, 1965.

Montgomery, Helen B. *Western Women in Eastern Lands: An Outline of Fifty Years of Women's Work in Foreign Missions*. New York: Macmillan, 1910.

"Our Bulgarian Bible-Woman." *Heathen Woman's Friend* 7, 4 (October 1875): 82.

Robert, Dana L. Robert. *American Women in Mission: A Social History of Their Thought and Practice*. Macon: Mercer University Press, 1997.

Sites, Mrs. S. Moore. "Bible Women in Foochow." *Heathen Woman's Friend* 4, 5 (November 1872): 359–360.

Streiff, Patrick Ph. *Der Methodismus in Europa im 19. Und 20. Jahrhundert*. Stuttgart: EmKGM 50, 2003. English translation: Methodism in Europe: 19th and 20th Century. Tallinn: Baltic Methodist Theological Seminary, 2003.

Tucker, Ruth A. "The Role of Bible Women in World Evangelism." *Missiology* 13, 2 (April 1985): 133–146.

2 The pioneering deaconess movement in Germany

Mareike Bloedt

Elise Heidner, First German Methodist Deaconess

An examination of the Methodist women pioneers in Europe begs an important question: Why did women again and again dedicate their lives to becoming deaconesses? To be a deaconess means to live a life filled with service and to work for the kingdom of God as God's instrument. This work entails struggling against the misery endured by others and to live a life involving continuous social service. The work of the Deaconess Societies in Germany started at the beginning of the nineteenth century and offered a great opportunity for unmarried women, at that time, to receive a high quality education.[1] As a deaconess, a single woman became equal in status to a married woman and, additionally, attained financial security. The development of this official appointment for Protestant women within religious life afforded single women the opportunity to gain a higher social status in society.[2]

The social situation in nineteenth century Germany

The nineteenth century in Germany was turbulent because "the time between the French Revolution in 1789 and the European Revolution in 1848 was a period of political unrest. Intellectual and political powers, which in the pre-revolutionary time period were still hidden below the surface, now gained historical shape."[3] It was inevitable that the church would become embroiled in the struggles between intellectual and political powers in nineteenth century Europe. The industrial revolution further exacerbated the political and social problems of this period. The theologian and sociologist Günter Brakelmann states:

> A new class of dependent industrial workers was created, selling their manpower to the owners of production equipment in return for a fixed wage. Because of the capitalistic economic system the business community gained high profits, but on the side of the employees extreme poverty increased.[4]

Dedicated Christian leaders developed diaconal and missionary work in response to the extreme poverty that was pervasive in the society.[5] During the second half of the century mass poverty and societal grievances as a consequence of the industrial revolution only intensified.

At the same time the church had to face the challenge of the Enlightenment, reacting necessarily against many of its ideas and attitudes. This clash of worldviews paved the way for a Christian revival movement that swept throughout Germany, in particular. This revival was organized, according to Fischer, "as a self-contained, private initiative apart from the national Churches, often using the legal structure of an unincorporated association. The essential momentum for the different kinds of work of the inner mission and diaconate arises from this movement."[6] Despite the fact that there were already many attempts, on the part of men and women, to ameliorate the problems of poverty and distress prior to the nineteenth century, "Theodor Fliedner (1800–1864) was the first to break new ground for a comprehensive, interregional, and church-based work for women and especially for single women."[7] He modernized the work of deaconesses (at Kaiserswerth in 1863) and by doing so he changed the face of the medical care system from a male-oriented profession to one in which women played a major role. These new professional nurses became the force which was needed to tackle the catastrophic conditions of hospitals during these times.

Three deaconess centers in Germany

Three Methodist Deaconess Centers became the hub of this pioneering work in Germany. First, the Methodist Episcopal Church (MEC) founded the *Bethanienverein, Diakonissenverein für allgemeine Krankenpflege* (Bethany Society, Deaconess Society for Medical Care and Nursing) in 1874 in Frankfurt am Main. In 1886 the Evangelical Association (EA) established a similar center, the *Bethesdaverein für allgemeine Krankenpflege* (Bethesda Society for Medical Care and Nursing) in Elberfeld. Just three years later, in 1889, the Wesleyan Methodist Church (WMC) founded the *Martha-Maria-Verein für allgemeine Krankenpflege* (Martha Maria Society for Medical Care and Nursing) in Nuremberg. So three different branches of Methodism in Germany began this work, essentially, simultaneously. In each of these developments individuals had the idea of starting a Deaconess Society and campaigned for this entrepreneurial work. Once these societies were founded, women handed their lives over to God and entered into a full-time ministry for the church. At that time this was the only way a woman could obtain a full-time position in the church as they were not allowed to become preachers. Despite the fact that women stood at the forefront of this movement, men quickly claimed leadership of these new German institutions, served as directors of the Deaconess Societies, and the women found themselves outside the corridors of power and control.

Bethanienverein (MEC)

Leaders within the MEC in Germany had considered the establishment of a Deaconess Society along the lines of those in other denominations as early as 1864.[8] Two reasons, in particular, prompted this idea. First, Methodists believed that the proclamation of the gospel required accompanying acts of love. And second, some women wanted to make themselves available to the service of the church as a consequence of their conversions. They felt that involvement in such a society attached to the MEC would enable them to fulfill their calling without having to leave their own denomination. But both the Church and the Methodist mission department were not ready to found their own Deaconess Society at that time. Consequently, individuals attempted to start their own diaconate within their congregations.

Heinrich Mann was one of the first to try to recruit nurses committed to this kind of caregiving in Calw in 1868.[9] Pforzheim and Karlsruhe assisted in these recruiting activities. Rev. Ludwig Nippert also tried to begin a deaconess program in his congregation in Frankfurt am Main.[10] Another ordained pastor, Carl Weiß, was the last to try to start a congregational diaconate in the early 1870s.[11] Having launched this effort in Bremen, it disintegrated following his appointment to a different church. In 1873 the members of the Annual Conference of Germany-Switzerland decided to take the first steps towards founding a Deaconess Society.[12] They developed a roadmap for the foundation of a new institution at the following conference in 1874. Their plan, however, was rejected by the Conference in Schaffhausen after a long debate, the majority of conference members having been convinced that this issue should no longer be a concern of the annual conference.

Four preachers, however, could not accept this decision. "Soon after the vote," according to the records, "the preachers Carl Weiß, Heinrich Mann, Friedrich Eilers and Jürgen Wischhusen left the conference room and went into a neighboring room."[13] Here they briefly discussed their plan, shook hands and, looking to God, founded an independent Deaconess Society on their own which they named *Bethanienverein*. They decided to locate the mother house in Frankfurt am Main because Friedrich Eilers – one of the founding fathers – was transferred as a preacher to this city in 1875.[14] The work of pioneer women formally commenced the following year:

> [In 1876] the first deaconess made herself available to the society. She moved into a room attached to the apartment of the preachers' family (Großer Kornmarkt 4). . . . Fortunately some of the city's doctors supported the society as they believed that they would be able to receive great support and help from the deaconesses for their patients in the future.[15]

The number of deaconesses rose continually in the following years, and they were able to rent an additional apartment for these women in the same house. In this apartment, one of the rooms served as a hospital room in which the first operation for a life-threatening condition was successfully performed. "But the deaconesses," according to the centennial history, "mainly continued to work in the area of private care."[16] In 1878 one deaconess was sent from Frankfurt am Main to Hamburg to nurse a child suffering from diphtheria. But the child had already died by the time Sister Louise Schmidt arrived. She stayed nonetheless to care for the mother of the deceased child and to support her.[17] Dr. Prausnitz, the doctor who had attended to the child, urged Sister Schmidt not to return to Frankfurt because of the need he had for her there. As a consequence, in December 1878 the first private care unit began its work formally in Hamburg. Over the years the so-called Bethanien deaconesses extended their work from Frankfurt and Hamburg to Berlin, St. Gallen, Zurich, Neuenhain (Taunus), Lausanne, Strasbourg, Vienna, Budapest, Rotterdam, Norway, and to the USA.[18]

Bethesdaverein (EA)

The great poverty and misery that was widespread at the end of the nineteenth century led the EA to consider what it could do to alleviate sickness and to help those who could not afford hospitalization or professional treatment by doctors or nurses.[19] One of the memoranda associated with the founding of this Deaconess Society made this connection clear:

> The whole procedure in the former Bethesda hospital teaches us, that well-ordered healthcare without distinction based on the status or standing of a person or their religious beliefs is necessary and that the human help and the divine help have to go hand in hand with each other. The Lord needs people that feel the pull of love to assist, help, visit and console his sick, poor, abandoned, prisoners, widows and orphans.[20]

Faithful women within the Association were anxious to get involved in social welfare work and felt the need to interface this service activity with their evangelistic and missionary ethos. The idea to provide training for deaconesses arose from this impetus.[21] Leaders within the EA discussed this idea at a meeting of the preachers in Heidenheim in 1880.

"Mister Kächele, the director of the theological seminary in Reutlingen, hit the ground running," claims Hans Mistele. "Furthermore there were some benefactors of charitable Christian projects that agreed to spend money on the building of the hospital that was planned to be established in Reutlingen."[22] Given the fact that deaconess institutions of other denominations had already begun work in the region, they decided to drop the project for the time being. In parallel fashion to the MEC, three preachers of the EA, however, decided to take up the initiative and founded a Society for deaconesses in 1884. Jakob Knapp, Jakob Klenert, and Carl Bader[23] discussed the issue at a public meeting of the preachers in Großalmerode and authorized a committee to prepare a draft statute. Two years later, on August 12, 1886, the board of administration founded the *Bethesdaverein für allgemeine Krankenpflege zu Elberfeld*.[24] Jakob Knapp became the Director of the Society and established the headquarters in Elberfeld because he was already stationed there as the superintendent.[25]

Historians of the Society claimed that "it was a start into unknown territory. They barely had the funds, nor did they own appropriate buildings or had the experience. Nevertheless these men risked it anyway, trusting in God's help."[26] But from these modest beginnings, a wonderful work emerged. Sister Marie Kreuder from Rheydt was the first deaconess secured by the Society.[27] She had been trained in the *Bethanienverein*, but with the understanding that she would be part of the EA efforts once they were launched. She arrived in Elberfeld on July 3, 1886.[28] Growth of this movement necessitated the construction of a mother house, which also served as a hospital and opened on August 14, 1890.[29]

In subsequent years, from this base on Distelbecker Strasse in Elberfeld, the *Bethesdaverein* expanded with branch offices in Berlin (1887), Hamburg (1888), Strasbourg (1889; independent after 1892), and Dresden (1891).[30] Likewise, the ranks of the deaconesses swelled, with 184 in service by 1900.[31] The Bethesda deaconesses sought to emulate the Hebrew meaning of their name – to become a "house of mercy" – noted, above all else, for loving service and healing.

Martha-Maria-Verein (WMC)

By 1889 the time had come for the British Wesleyan Methodists to establish a Deaconess Center of their own. But the foundation of this Society had a different journey than those of its sister Methodist denominations. While the MEC and the EA had groups of preachers who devoted themselves to the task of creating those centers, in Nuremberg, for the Wesleyans, everything revolved around two young women and a man who had to face a multitude of challenges.

The WMC sent Rev. Jakob Ekert to Nuremberg in 1884.[32] On arriving it was impressed upon him that "the care of the soul" must also entail "the care of the body" – and he decided, therefore, to get involved in social welfare as well as traditional pastoral work. Around the same time, the idea of founding a deaconess center reawakened in the mind of a young woman in his church, Elise Heidner.[33] She, in fact, asked him to train her as a deaconess. Despite the fact that he did not agree to this at this time, the idea simply would not let him go. One year later he shared this idea with the synod of the Wesleyan Methodists. While supporting his and Heidner's idea in theory, no one was ready to advance the initiative. Ekert quickly realized that he would need to initiate the foundation of a Deaconess Center.[34]

At this point, another young woman, Luise Schneider, entered the unfolding saga.[35] Ekert had first learned of her interest in this work in 1887 when she had been shunned by her church in Heilbronn for her entrepreneurial ideas. It was not until December 1888, however, before providence brought their paths together. At a meeting in Lorch towards the end of the year, Ekert, his brother, Wilhelm, and Schneider laid the plans for future collaboration:

> They determined the principles and discussed the education of the sisters and talked about other things. As a result of this meeting, Sister Luise went to Nuremberg on the February 4, 1889. Alongside her, Novice Elise Heidner was enrolled. She had been preparing herself in the field of nursing in Nuremberg since 1888 and had been sent to get further training in Berlin at the "Königliche Charité" in the spring of 1889.[36]

The beginning of their journey proved to be extremely difficult. Sister Hei-dner remained in Berlin until September as she was continuing her education there, and during this period Sister Schneider had little work to do. Under the circumstances, Heidner went to Munich upon completion of her stud-ies, hoping to be more successful in finding work there. Given the fact that the deaconesses and their work were not officially recognized by the state she was frustrated in these efforts.[37] The police actually prohibited her from doing her work. Back in Nuremberg, the city officials were adapting their constitution at the general meeting and their modifications which declared the legitimacy of deaconess work were enacted in September 1889.[38]

On September 16, 1889, therefore, the Wesleyan Methodist Society was officially licensed as the *Martha-Maria-Verein für allgemeine Krankenpflege in Nürnberg*.[39] All these approvals came in a timely way as a major influ-enza epidemic at the end of 1889 brought the two women an abundance of patients. On May 19, 1895, the WMC released Ekert from his pasto-ral responsibilities so he could become the first Director of the Deaconess Center.[40] As in the case of the other Methodist Centers, the *Martha-Maria-Verein* had extended its work by that time from Nuremberg to Munich (1889), Vienna (1890), Magdeburg (1892), and Halle.

Some of this growth can be attributed to the philanthropic interventions of the Baroness of Langenau who helped the *Martha-Maria-Verein* a great deal with regard to many areas of its further development.[41] She partially financed the acquisition of new buildings for the Society in Nuremberg and later in Magdeburg.[42] It was her efforts that led to the establishment of a Deaconess Center in Vienna.

These three Centers, then, became the hub of Methodist deaconess work in Germany. The primary task of these foundations was to educate women for the servant ministry into which they felt called. But becoming a deacon-ess did not only entail the acquisition of a quality education, it also led to the elevation of these single women. It provided them an opportunity to be treated equally with their married counterparts, and what they wore actu-ally reflected this new-found status.[43] The deaconess cap or bonnet and the originally floor-length dress of the deaconess distinguished these women as people of stature and honor. They also established a professional "distance" when dealing with doctors, male nurses, and male patients and afforded them the ability to perform their duties without being questioned. Publica-tions made these connections clear:

> The apparel of a deaconess is not of unimportance. Even though it is not essential, because one can have an attitude of serving without the cap and the gown . . . but the apparel was supposed to reflect, which social status the woman represents. It prevents the sisters from the moods of fashion. It protects the sisters, especially at night. It lets everyone know, that a deaconess is standing in front of them and such prevents her from unnecessary questions, temptations, and small talk. It is an apparel of

honor because it is the clothing of charity of which everyone knows the value of, even if they don't own it.[44]

Apart from a higher social status, the cap and gown also helped others recognize the deaconesses immediately. Every Deaconess Society had its own apparel and so it happened that an "insider" was able to distinguish the different deaconesses and their societies. Bishop Ernst Sommer, a noted leader of the MEC, described the feelings of pride and delight elicited by simply seeing a uniformed deaconess:

> Whenever I see the typical bonnet on one of our deaconess's head at a train station somewhere, a great joy floods my heart; I know I am not alone. There is help close by. And so I always greet the bonnet. Some sisters have said to me: "I'm surprised you know me," and I unfortunately haven't always been honest in saying: "I'm sorry, but I don't know you, I was just greeting the bonnet.[45]

But apart from the recognition effect, Sommer observed, more importantly:

> Whereas other caps hold together their folds without contiguity, the bonnet holds together the folds of the cap of our deaconesses. As such it symbolizes our view of diaconal ministry [among these women]. Deaconesses and church – one unity, a God-given, mutual give-and-take.[46]

The servant character of the deaconess

The elevated status enjoyed by these pioneer women did not cloud their judgment in terms of their primary vocation. A clear sense of calling informed the work of the deaconess.

Bishop Nuelsen described the deaconess as a servant; she is a servant by decree of God.[47] The extraordinary thing about this occupation is not, according to Nuelsen, the service to the sick and the poor, but the motivation of the women related to this kind of service. Those who advocated this work felt that it was important for these women to embody, testify, and preach the good news in everything they did and in what they avoided. Nuelsen was convinced that the work of a deaconess far exceeded that of a normal occupation, or even the work of a qualified nurse. He felt that a clear calling was essential and believed that God called women to this special service. Moreover, this vocation demanded the virtue of obedience in relation to the call of God. An early guidebook for deaconesses prepared by Philipp Lutz provides a typical description of the deaconess's servant ministry:

> If someone believes of being able to be a deaconess and simultaneously being able to act like a lady or a mademoiselle, she is going to be disappointed and can neither herself be content as a deaconess, nor make

others happy. . . . A servant has to be willing and able to subordinate herself, to learn and to give up her own will and opinion in order to be able to obey.[48]

Director of the *Bethanienverein* in Hamburg (1889–1892), Lutz identified three distinct characteristics of the deaconess: First, a deaconess is a servant of Christ. Second, she is a servant to the poor and the sick. Third, she is a servant to her own deaconess sisters.[49]

The office of deaconess has its origins in the New Testament. The word "deaconess" is derived from the Greek verb *diakonein* (to serve). "The word is solely to be found in the gospels," observe Voigt and Gänzle, "and within it, mostly in the words and parables of Jesus."[50] The basic meaning of *diakonein* is "to attend to the table" (see Matt 22:13). It encompasses service in someone else's favor. It stands in contrast to the Greek word *douleuein* which means the service in dependency to someone, for example the work of a slave. This meaning is mirrored in the book *Lebensordnung für Diakonissen* (Order of Life for Deaconesses), where we read: "Diaconal ministry as a work for Christ means living and responding in and to the love of Christ with and for the people."[51] Jesus himself provides the primary model for the deaconess because he was also called "to serve and not to be served" (Mark 10:45). Since the deaconess lives and works for and with the people, it is right to define her vocation as a service of love. The deaconesses "not only care for the sick body," claims Voigt and Gänzle, "but also stand witness to the love of Christ and convey safety, comfort, and healing."[52]

Areas of diaconal service

The commemorative publication, *50 Jahre Diakonissenarbeit* (50 Years of Deaconess Work) identifies several areas of service in which deaconesses were active.[53] Three are of particular significance. "Private care" entailed caring for sick individuals in their own homes. This type of care was so successful that the deaconesses started to found institutions built upon the principles of this field work and thereby created a new arena dubbed "institutional care." Deaconesses also functioned as social workers, often describing this work as "district nursing." As was the case with many women outside the structures of the deaconess movement, they also engaged in foreign mission.

Private and institutional care

"The private care (or relief of the poor) was the first and most important field, as well as the seed for the expansion in the fields of work of Methodist deaconesses," claim Voigt and Gänzle. "The societies in the Methodist churches did not start with, as with Fliedner, the founding of hospitals, but with the founding of so-called private-care-stations."[54] Since hospitals were frequently unavailable, deaconesses visited both poor and rich people in need of care at their homes in order to offer them this service. Records demonstrate that "the deaconesses were able to reach thousands of families over the course of half a century" through these efforts.[55] The sisters offered direct care to those who were sick but also provided childcare and household services in situations where the mother was incapacitated.[56]

The work of the deaconesses often led to the expansion of institutional care and the development of the first clinics and hospitals in some areas of the country. According to the commemorative magazine, *50 Jahre Diakonissenarbeit*, in the year 1885 the *Bethanienverien* was able to open their first hospital in Frankfurt am Main after the deaconesses gained the trust of the doctors, authorities, and the public.[57] Inevitably, assistance provided to patients who were part of the lower classes opened larger channels of social service to them as well. Whereas most sisters received their nurse's training at institutions such as the *Königliche Charité* in Berlin, one of the oldest hospitals in the German capital founded by the Prussian King in the early eighteenth century, later they trained at their own institutions, which also became noted for the high standard of their education.[58]

District nurses

Deaconesses also served as district nurses. "When we talk about district nurses today," observe Voigt and Gänzle, "we often mean deaconesses who are active in their church district. In the beginning though, these deaconesses were often working in their civil communities, so today we would probably refer to this more as welfare work."[59] The role of district nurse demonstrates how comprehensive the work of the deaconesses could be. It was a holistic profession that naturally pulled these women into a wide spectrum of service to others. The first district nurse was Elise Heidner of the *Martha-Maria-Verein* in Nuremberg. She began her service on June 15, 1900 on the old Bahrendorf manor. The memorandum of the 40th anniversary of the *Martha-Maria-Verein* describes her work: "Primarily she was supposed to serve the day laborers, not only in physical, but also in moral and religious concerns."[60] The personal report of Sister Sabine Eichenmüller affords one of the most vivid descriptions of the work entailed in his district nursing:

> The care-taking in the community is very diverse. You don't only have to care for one patient, but you have to care for the whole family, especially if the patient is the housewife. You have to take care of the sick and the healthy; of the food, the laundry, the garments, and the most important one, making sure that the house is clean. If it's cold you must look after heating, and often also the cattle. In most cases you don't have to do this work all alone, but a district nurse, especially in rural areas, has to take care of these things. In the communities a district nurse is a "Jack of all trades." If she can do this, she wins the people over. . . . Being a district nurse is, if it's being done with a correct

understanding and in the love of Christ, a blessed work. . . . A district nurse can and should be part of all the good work in her community; for instance the society of young women, in the distribution of the paper, etc. If she is doing her job right, she can enjoy a lot of love. . . . That she also has to encounter uncomfortable situations and difficulties goes without saying.[61]

Hans Mistele's reflections on the district nurses reveal a similar level of diversity,

visiting service to members and friends, the journal- and calendar-mission, having the leadership over or being part of the women's group, preparing and carrying out the bazaar; helping with Sunday school, the female scouting group, youth group and in the catechistic instruction, including the sacristan duty.[62]

Foreign mission

Deaconesses were not only needed in Germany, but were also sent into foreign mission (or the so-called "pagan mission" at that time), starting in 1896. Sometimes these deaconesses were sent only after a request from these areas had been received; sometimes the sisters themselves received a calling from God into certain places.[63] Elise Heidner was the first deaconess sent into foreign mission. In 1896 the missionary Karl Ulrich sent a letter to Jakob Ekert and requested that he send out a *Krankenschwester* (hospital nurse) to *Deutsch-Togo* (modern Togo). Ekert dispatched Heidner almost immediately.[64] "Sister Elise Heidner," reports the *Martha-Maria-Verein* memorandum, "who had wanted to go into foreign mission since she was a young girl, was now designated to go to Togo. She was lying in bed after a night shift, and when the answer came and Sister Luise delivered her the message, she jumped out of bed with joy."[65]

In the following century more deaconesses were sent into foreign mission. The mission projects with which they were affiliated exerted a great influence, even though they only represented a small percentage of the work of the Deaconess Societies.[66] In the period covered in this chapter, Emilie Wiesmüller and Anna Class of the *Martha-Mary-Verein* were sent to Bismarck Archipelago (east of Papua New Guinea) in 1913.[67] The commitment that the deaconesses displayed beyond their own national borders demonstrates just how connected the diaconate and mission work were. Hans Mistele got to the heart of this when he said that "the work of the deaconesses and mission have the same root; they are grounded in the gospel of Jesus Christ. Mission promotes missionary deaconesses and the missionary deaconesses promote mission as the compassionate service of love."[68]

A life full of serving – a personal statement

"A life full of serving" means to live a life for and with God. It means to do everything for the glory of God and I believe that is exactly what the Methodist deaconess movement in Germany tried to do and why they began their diaconate in the first place. Strong characters, women and men, initiated the founding of Methodist Deaconess Centers. All these people were convinced that they were following and living God's will. Despite the lack of funds or the lack of sisters, they always trusted in God and this trust in God was rewarded in the end by the success of their work. In my research related to the founding of the *Martha-Mary-Verein*, in particular, I was reminded of the importance of trusting God. For the two deaconesses, Elise Heidner and Luise Schneider, in their social context it was difficult to recruit nurses and to be respected for their work as deaconesses. Despite these initially difficult conditions, the Society quickly expanded its work after having been officially registered. In a short space of time all the Societies founded multiple branches – so many that Jakob Ekert became the first full-time employee and director of the *Martha-Mary-Verein* work.

Today I get the impression that some people in both church and society look on the profession of being a deaconess with condescension. It seems that deaconesses are women who just do not fit into the postmodern, individualistic world anymore, especially on account of their ordered lives and dedication to their community. I find it pitiful and unjustified that our society and some people in the church choose to belittle deaconesses and their work. The deaconesses played a large part in the development of a more just society and particularly in the development of the Methodist Church. They did everything they did for God and spent their lives in service for the church and for the poor and sick. In my opinion they deserve honor and gratitude and not a dismissive attitude.

Without the deaconess's work, the Deaconess Centers in the UMC in Germany would not exist – and who knows if there would be Methodists in Germany at all? More importantly, perhaps, the deaconesses provided the impetus for many changes in society, especially in regard to the role of women. I, as a modern woman, can hardly imagine what it must have been like to have been prohibited an education or been forbidden to become a pastor or to be subordinated to men, without having any rights. In my opinion the ministry of deaconesses was a first step for the emancipation of women both in the church and society. And the work of the deaconesses, as we have seen, was not restricted to Germany. Women were courageous and willing to spread their work throughout the whole world. Developments and connections with the USA are of particular interest because of the strong emphasis placed on education there (see the following chapter in this volume).

Deaconesses trusted in God and lived "a life full of serving." Those pioneers can serve as role models and mentors for us today.

Notes

1   Scholars have just recently begun more extensive study of the deaconess movement in Germany, and the Methodist tradition, in particular. For a comprehensive history of the German deaconess movement, see Ruth Felgentreff, *Das Diakoniewerk Kaiserswerth 1836–1998: Von der Diakonissenanstalt zum Diakoniewerk – ein Überblick* (Düsseldorf-Kaiserswerth: Heimat- und Bürgerverein Kaiserswerth, 1998); Silke Köser, *Denn eine Diakonisse darf kein Alltagsmensch sein. Kollektive Identitäten Kaiserswerther Diakonissenm, 1836–1914* (Leipzig: Evangelische Verlagsanstalt, 2014); and Jochen-Christoph Kaiser, "Diakonie. I. Kirchengeschichtlich," in *Religion in Geschichte und Gegenwart: Handwörterbuch für Theologie und Religionswissenschaft*, Volume 2, 4th ed., edited by Hans Dieter Betz (Tübingen, 1999), 792–4. On the Methodist work, see Marc Nördinger and Thomas Bauer, *Der Schwestern Werk: Die Geschichte des Bethanien-Krankenhauses in Frankfurt am Main von, 1908–2008* (Frankfurt am Main: Frankfurter Diakonie-Kliniken, 2008); Paul Nollenberger, Jakob Ekert, *Eine Pioniergestalt der Diakonie* (Stuttgart: Christliches Verlagshaus, 1988); Ulrike Voigt, *Haus der Barmherzigkeit: 100 Jahre Bethesda Krankenhaus in Stuttgart, 1912–2012* (Stuttgart: Agaplesion Bethesda Krankenhaus Stuttgart GmbH, 2012); and Ulrike Voigt and Sigrid Gänzle, "Ein Weg, auf dem man sein Leben wirklich einsetzen kann für die Sache Gottes – Diakonissen in der Evangelisch-methodistischen Kirche," in *Mit Weisheit, Witz und Widerstand: Die Geschichte(n) von Frauen in der Evangelisch-methodistischen Kirche* (Stuttgart: Medienwerk der Evangelisch-methodistischen Kirche, 2003). The author wishes to express appreciation to Sarah Bach and Claire Hamer for their assistance in the preparation of this chapter.
2   Voigt and Gänzle, "Diakonissen," 137–138.
3   Günter Brakelmann, *Kirche und Sozialismus im 19. Jahrhundert: Die Analyse des Sozialismus und Kommunismus bei Johann Hinrich Wichern und bei Rudolf Todt* (Witten: Gütersloh, 1966), 7.
4   Ibid., 8.
5   Kaiser, "Diakonie," 792.
6   Helmut Fischer, *Schnellkurs Christentum*, 3rd ed. (Köln: DuMont-Literatur-und-Kunst-Verl, 2005), 154–155.
7   Voigt and Gänzle, "Diakonissen," 139.
8   August Rücker, ed., *Im Dienst der Liebe und Barmherzigkeit, 1874–1949: Fünfundsiebzig Jahre Diakonissendienst des Bethanien-Vereins* (Bremen: Anker Verlag, 1949), 11.
9   Philipp Heinrich Friedrich Mann (1844–1920), Methodist preacher and Dean of the Theological Seminary of the MEC. He assumed the leadership of the Methodist Deaconess Society in Frankfurt am Main in 1905. See Karl Heinz Voigt, "Philipp Heinrich Friedrich Mann," in *Biographisch-bibliographisches Kirchenlexikon*, Volume 5, edited by Friedrich Wilhelm Bautz (Herzberg: Traugott Bautz, 1993), 682–684.
10 Ludwig Nippert (1825–1894) was recruited by the MEC as a traveling preacher 1846 and sent to Germany in 1850. See Karl Heinz Voigt, "Ludwig Nippert," in *Biographisch-bibliographisches Kirchenlexikon*, 6: 948–951.
11 Ludwig Daniel Carl Weiß (1841–1883), Methodist preacher and founder of the "mother house" for the deaconesses of the *Bethanienverein* and editor of a variety of different journals of the MEC. See Karl Heinz Voigt, "Ludwig Daniel Carl Weiß," in *Biographisch-bibliographisches Kirchenlexikon*, 13: 676–682.
12 Rücker, *Im Dienst der Liebe*, 12.
13 Friedrich Eilers (1839–1923), co-founder and first Director of the *Bethanienverein* from 1882 to 1889. See ibid., 70.

14 *60 Jahre Bethanien-Verein: Diakonissenanstalt Frankfurt am Main, 1874–1934* (Bremen: Bethanien-Verein, 1934), 11.

15 *Diakonie hilft weiter: 100 Jahre Bethanien-Verein* (Wuppertal: Diakoniewerk, 1986), 7.

16 Ibid., 7–8.

17 Rücker, *Im Dienst der Liebe*, 15–16.

18 *Diakonie hilft weiter: 100 Jahre Bethanien-Verein*, 8–10.

19 Hans Mistele, *Bethesda: Geschichte eines Diakoniewerkes* (Wuppertal: Diakoniewerk Bethesda e. V., 1974), 22.

20 *Denkschrift zur 25 jährigen Jubelfeier der Diakonissenanstalt Bethesda zu Elberfeld, 1886–1911* (Elberfeld: np, 1911), 4.

21 Mistele, *Bethesda*, 22.

22 Ibid., 23.

23 Jakob Knapp (d. 1913) was Director of the *Bethesdaverein* from 1886 to 1896; see Mistele, *Bethesda*, 112. Jakob Christoph Klenert (1859–1933) was a pioneer preacher of the EA. He studied at the seminary of the EA in Reutlingen 1880–1882; see Karl Heinz Voigt, "Jakob Christoph Klenert," in *Biographisch-bibliographisches Kirchenlexikon*, 4: 35. Carl Bader (1860–1918) served as Director of the *Diakonissenanstalt Bethesda zu Elberfeld* from 1914 to 1918.

24 Despite a formal change of name in 1893 from *Bethesdaverein* to *Diakonissenanstalt Bethesda zu Elberfeld* (Deaconess Center Bethesda in Elberfeld), this Deaconess Center, obviously, retained its heart-connection with the Pool of Bethesda in Jerusalem and the healing narratives related to Jesus there (see John 5). Historical documents demonstrate how important this name was to those who were involved in this work. See *Denkschrift zur 25 jährigen Jubelfeier*, 3; cf. Voigt, *Haus der Barmherzigkeit*, 21

25 Mistele, *Bethesda*, 23–4.

26 *Diakonie hilft weiter: 100 Jahre Bethanien-Verein*, 19.

27 Marie Kreuder was senior nursing officer in the Bethesda Hospital in Berlin 1887–1889. See Mistele, *Bethesda*, 117.

28 *Diakonissen-Anstalt Bethesda zu Elberfeld: Denkschrift zum 40. Jahresfest – 1886–1926* (Düsseldorf: Lindner-Verlag, Lindner & Braun 1926), 17.

29 Voigt, *Haus der Barmherzigkeit*, 21.

30 Mistele, *Bethesda*, 21.

31 Ibid., 25.

32 Friedrich Wilhelm Ekert (1849–1904), preacher of the Wesleyan Methodists from 1874 has been called "the gentle" co-founder of the *Martha-Mary-Verein* in Nuremberg.

33 Elise Heidner (1865–1935) was one of the most significant pioneer deaconesses – a woman of many firsts, not only in the *Martha-Maria-Verein*, but among all these early women. See Paul Nollenberger, *Chronik 1889–1989: 100 Jahre Diakoniewerk Martha-Maria* (Frankfurt: Frankfurter Diakonie-Kliniken, 2008), 5.

34 Nollenberger, *Ekert*, 42–3.

35 Luise Schneider (1864–1950), co-founder of the *Martha-Mary-Verein* in Nuremberg. See Nollenberger, *Chronik*, 5.

36 See Nollenberger, *Ekert*, 151; cf. *Denkschrift zur 25 jährigen Jubelfeier*, 8.

37 Nollenberger, *Chronik*, 5–6.

38 *Zehn Jahre des Martha-Maria-Vereins für allgemeine Krankenpflege* (Nürnberg: Martha-Maria-Vereins, 1899), 8.

39 In the 10th annual report of the Society the following suggestions for the name of the new institution are recorded: " 'Sisters with willingness to serve,' 'Mary Martha Society,' 'Deaconess Center – Star of Hope,' and 'Deaconess Society Anchor of Hope' " (*Zehn Jahre des Martha-Maria-Vereins*, 6). The leadership chose the Martha Mary designation because of the connections, again, with the

biblical Bethany narratives and the connections of this community with the healing activity of Jesus (see Luke 10: 38–42).

40 Nollenberger, *Chronik*, 5–9.

41 Baroness Amelie of Langenau (1833–1902) sought a new orientation for her life after the death of her husband Ferdinand Freiherr of Langenau (1817–1881) and worked for almost a decade with the deaconesses of the evangelical *Gallneukirchener Verein* whom she supported with her wealth to the end of her life. During her stays in England she got to know the Methodists and participated in their services in Vienna. Despite her social status she supported the Methodist Church, which had found little acceptance and support for its social welfare activities. See Karl Heinz Voigt, "Baronin Amelie von Langenau," *Biographisch-bibliographisches Kirchenlexikon*, 4: 1107–9 and chapter 8 in this volume by Michael Wetzel.

42 Nollenberger, *Chronik*, 7–8.

43 Voigt and Gänzle, "Diakonissen," 137.

44 *Martha-Maria-Verein für allgemeine Krankenpflege e.V. Nürnberg: Denkschrift zum 40 jährigen Bestehen des Vereins, 1889–1929* (Düsseldorf: Selbstverlag des Vereins, 1929), 11–12.

45 Christian Jahreiss, ed., *Schwestern erzählen: Ein Buch von irdischer Not und helfender Liebe* (München: Anker Verlag, 1948), 12–13. Johann Wilhelm Ernst Sommer (1881–1952), Methodist missionary, professor, and bishop from 1946 to 1952, was a strong proponent of connecting his personal faith with social action in ministry. See Karl Heinz Voigt, "Johann Wilhelm Ernst Sommer," *Biographisch-bibliographisches Kirchenlexikon*, 10: 778–785.

46 Ibid., 13.

47 John Louis Nuelsen (1867–1946), American-born bishop of the MEC who studied at Drew Theological Seminary and later in Berlin and Halle (1893–1894). After election to the episcopacy in 1908 he was assigned the supervision of the MEC in Europe. See Karl Heinz Voigt, "John Louis Nuelsen," *Biographisch-bibliographisches Kirchenlexikon*, 6: 1049–1052.

48 Philipp Lutz, *Wegweiser zum Diakonissen-Beruf* (Bremen: n.p., 1890), 6. Philipp Lutz (1845–1930) was Director of the *Bethanienverein* in Hamburg from 1889 until 1892 and board member until 1911 when the separation of northern Germany took place. See Rücker, *Im Dienst der Liebe*, 22, 70, 78–79.

49 Ibid., 6, 9, 11.

50 Voigt and Gänzle, "Diakonissen," 136. The authors provide an extended discussion of these terms.

51 *Lebensordnung für Diakonisse* (Hamburg/Wuppertal/Nürnberg: np), 11.

52 Voigt and Gänzle, "Diakonissen," 144.

53 *50 Jahre Diakonissenarbeit 1874–1924 in Verbindung mit der bischöfl. Methodistenkirche in Deutschland und der Schweiz* (Bremen: np, 1924), 7–11.

54 Voigt and Gänzle, "Diakonissen," 142.

55 *50 Jahre Diakonissenarbeit*, 7.

56 Voigt and Gänzle, "Diakonissen," 143.

57 *50 Jahre Diakonissenarbeit*, 7–8.

58 *Denkschrift zum 40 jährigen Bestehen des Vereins*, 15. With the increased number of clinics founded by the Deaconess Societies and other bases of institutional care, private care declined into the twentieth century when this field of service was discontinued (see Voigt and Gänzle, "Diakonissen," 143).

59 Voigt and Gänzle, "Diakonissen," 144.

60 *40 Jahre Martha-Maria-Verein*, 25. Her success, however, soon led to jealousy and suspicion, and she was forced to leave because the superintendent did not want "foreign planting" in his district.

61 Ibid., 27.

62 Mistele, *Bethesda*, 79. Hans Mistele (1909–1976), was Director of the Diakoniewerk Bethesda from 1955 until 1966 and in Wuppertal from 1966 until 1974. See Mistele, *Bethesda*, 112. Based on the appointment listings, the Methodist Church in Germany only had one district nurse left in the year 2002. See Voigt and Gänzle, "Diakonissen," 147.

63 Voigt and Gänzle, "Diakonissen," 147–150.

64 *40 Jahre Martha-Maria-Verein*, 36.

65 Ibid.

66 Voigt and Gänzle, "Diakonissen," 150.

67 Emilie Wiesmüller was 30 years old when she finished her education and was originated from Ulm. Anna Class was 29 years old when she was sent into foreign mission and was originally from Waiblingen. See *40 Jahre Martha-Maria-Verein*, 37.

68 Mistele, *Bethesda*, 80.

Sources

50 Jahre Diakonissenarbeit 1874–1924 in Verbindung mit der Bischöfl. Methodistenkirche in Deutschland und der Schweiz. Bremen: np, 1924.

60 Jahre Bethanien-Verein: Diakonissenanstalt Frankfurt am Main, 1874–1934. Bremen: Bethanien-Verein, 1934.

Bautz, Friedrich Wilhelm, ed. *Biographisch-bibliographisches Kirchenlexikon.* Multi-volumes. Herzberg: Traugott Bautz, 1970.

Brakelmann, Günter. *Kirche und Sozialismus im 19. Jahrhundert: Die Analyse des Sozialismus und Kommunismus bei Johann Hinrich Wichern und bei Rudolf Todt.* Witten/Gütersloh: Luther-Verlag, 1966.

Denkschrift zur 25 jährigen Jubelfeier der Diakonissenanstalt Bethesda zu Elberfeld, 1886–1911. Elberfeld: np, 1911.

Diakonie hilft weiter: 100 Jahre Bethanien-Verein. Wuppertal: Diakoniewerk, 1986.

Diakonissen-Anstalt Bethesda zu Elberfeld: Denkschrift zum 40. Jahresfest – 1886–1926. Düsseldorf: Lindner-Verlag, Lindner & Braun, 1926.

Felgentreff, Ruth. *Das Diakoniewerk Kaiserswerth 1836–1998: Von der Diakonissenanstalt zum Diakoniewerk – ein Überblick.* Düsseldorf-Kaiserswerth: Heimat- und Bürgerverein Kaiserswerth, 1998.

Fischer, Helmut. *Schnellkurs Christentum.* 3rd edition. Köln: DuMont-Literatur- und-Kunst-Verl, 2005.

Jahreiss, Christian, ed. *Schwestern erzählen: Ein Buch von irdischer Not und helfender Liebe.* München: Anker Verlag, 1948.

Kaiser, Jochen-Christoph. "Diakonie. I. Kirchengeschichtlich." In *Religion in Geschichte und Gegenwart: Handwörterbuch für Theologie und Religionswissenschaft.* 4th edition. 2 Volume. Edited by Hans Dieter Betz, pp. 792–794. Tübingen: Mohr Siebeck, 1999.

Köser, Silke. *Denn eine Diakonisse darf kein Alltagsmensch sein. Kollektive Identitäten Kaiserswerther Diakonissenm, 1836–1914.* Leipzig: Evangelische Verlagsanstalt, 2014.

Lebensordnung für Diakonisse. Hamburg/Wuppertal/Nürnberg: np.

Lutz, Philipp. *Wegweiser zum Diakonissen-Beruf.* Bremen: np, 1890.

Martha-Maria-Verein für allgemeine Krankenpflege e.V. Nürnberg: Denkschrift zum 40 jährigen Bestehen des Vereins, 1889–1929. Düsseldorf: Selbstverlag des Vereins, 1929.

Mistele, Hans. *Bethesda: Geschichte eines Diakoniewerkes.* Wuppertal: Diakoniewerk Bethesda e. V., 1974.

Nördinger, Marc, and Thomas Bauer. *Der Schwestern Werk: Die Geschichte des Bethanien-Krankenhauses in Frankfurt am Main von, 1908–2008.* Frankfurt am Main: Frankfurter Diakonie-Kliniken, 2008.

Nollenberger, Paul. *Chronik 1889–1989: 100 Jahre Diakoniewerk Martha-Maria.* Frankfurt am Main: Frankfurter Diakonie-Kliniken, 2008.

Nollenberger, Paul. *Jakob Ekert: Eine Pioniergestalt der Diakonie.* Stuttgart: Christliches Verlagshaus, 1988.

Rücker, August et al, ed. *Im Dienst der Liebe und Barmherzigkeit, 1874–1949: Fünfundsiebzig Jahre Diakonissendienst des Bethanien-Vereins.* Bremen: Anker Verlag, 1949.

Voigt, Ulrike. *Haus der Barmherzigkeit: 100 Jahre Bethesda Krankenhaus in Stuttgart, 1912–2012.* Stuttgart: Agaplesion Bethesda Krankenhaus Stuttgart GmbH, 2012.

Voigt, Ulrike, and Sigrid Gänzle. *"Ein Weg, auf dem man sein Leben Wirklich Einsetzen kann für die Sache Gottes – Diakonissen in der Evangelisch-Methodistischen Kirche."* In *Mit Weisheit, Witz und Widerstand: Die Geschichte(n) von Frauen in der Evangelisch-methodistischen Kirche.* Stuttgart: Medienwerk der Evangelisch-methodistischen Kirche, 2003.

Zehn Jahre des Martha-Maria-Vereins für allgemeine Krankenpflege. Nürnberg: Martha-Maria-Vereins, 1899.

3 The European roots of
the American Methodist
deaconess movement

Margit Herfarth

Methodist National Training School, Toronto, 1899–1900, Deaconess Graduates

In 1888 the General Conference of the Methodist Episcopal Church (MEC) formally recognized a new office: the deaconess. Women who held this office were called to "minister to the poor, visit the sick, pray with the dying, care for the orphan, seek the wandering, comfort the sorrowing, save the sinning, and, relinquishing wholly all other pursuits, devote themselves in a general way to such forms of Christian labor as may be suited to their abilities."[1] At this particular time deaconesses were already at work in most Protestant churches in the USA. Between 1880 and 1930 almost 200 deaconess-led institutions were established in multiple denominations, such as the Methodists, Lutherans, Episcopalians, and Evangelical Synod.[2] The story of the American deaconess movement is a story of a transatlantic exchange of ideas closely connected to the process of European immigration.

The ancient deaconess office was based upon a biblical precedent, fully developed by the fourth century and then for many centuries more or less forgotten. Its revival took place in the little town of Kaiserswerth in Germany. During the first decades of the nineteenth century the young Lutheran pastor Theodor Fliedner and his wife Friederike devised new ways to address the social problems of the time. Appalled by the suffering of the sick, the poor, and the outcasts of society, Fliedner found inspiration in the work of Christian social reformers he met in the Netherlands and in England. He eventually established a new female profession based on the ancient female diaconate. Starting in 1836 Theodor and Friederike Fliedner invited young unmarried women to live in the "Deaconess Motherhouse," offering room, board, and – most important of all – a thorough training in nursing or teaching in exchange for their work.

Befitting the social customs of the time, this newly designed religious profession provided women with the only alternative to either marriage or the dreaded position as the wholly dependent, financially and socially insecure "spinster."[3] While the deaconesses thus gained a respected position, the lifelong security of a sisterhood, the chance to answer a religious vocation and to find satisfaction through professional training and work, they nevertheless paid a price. The Deaconess Motherhouse, not unlike their families of origin, was a patriarchal organization, demanding full compliance to strict regulations and fostering the "deaconess ideal" of obedience, meekness, humility, and subordination. The character of the new profession and status thus proved to be ambivalent. On the one hand, it expanded women's sphere; on the other hand, anything resembling the goals of feminism and women's liberation were strongly discouraged.[4]

The Kaiserswerth Deaconess Motherhouse became a model for deaconess work not only in Germany, but all over the world. Theodor Fliedner himself transplanted the deaconess idea to the USA. In 1849, answering an urgent request of the German-American pastor William Passavant, he sent four Kaiserswerth deaconesses to Pittsburgh, Pennsylvania, giving rise to an immensely diverse American deaconess movement. This movement was shaped by the economic and social changes of the late nineteenth century and the emergence of professional nursing and social work. In some denominations, it was an expression of German-American culture and was inextricably linked to the history of German immigration. In all churches, however, the Kaiserswerth model and the characteristic identity markers of the deaconess office – non-salaried work, distinctive deaconess garb, unmarried status, communal living, consecration, and professional training – were adapted to American society and culture.[5]

The deaconess movement in the Methodist Episcopal Church

In the Methodist context the deaconess movement started in two different groups: the Woman's Home Missionary Society (WHMS) and the Chicago Training School for Home, City, and Foreign Missions (CTS). The deaconess work resulting from those organizations was shaped and intensely influenced, in both cases, by its respective female leaders: Jane Bancroft Robinson and Lucy Rider Meyer.

Jane Bancroft Robinson (1847–1932), professor of French language and literature at Northwestern University in Evanston, Illinois, traveled extensively to study the European deaconess movement.[6] In addition to Kaiserswerth she visited several other Motherhouses in Germany, France, Scotland, and England, including Methodist institutions. Upon her return to the USA she not only published the classic, "Deaconesses in Europe and Their Lessons for America" (1889), but also established deaconess work under the auspices of the Woman's Home Missionary Society which subsequently founded deaconess homes, schools, and hospitals.[7] A long-time vice-president of the WHMS, Robinson became president in 1908, serving in that position until 1913 while fulfilling the role of field secretary of the Deaconess Bureau as well. She later became the general superintendent of deaconess work.

Lucy Rider Meyer (1849–1922) graduated from Oberlin College in 1872 with a degree in literary studies, studied science at the Boston School of Technology, and later completed a medical degree at the Women's Medical College of Chicago.[8] After a stint as professor of chemistry at McKendree College in Lebanon, Illinois, Rider Meyer became Field Secretary for the Illinois State Sunday School Association. Her experiences in that capacity convinced her of the urgent need for better training of women wishing to contribute meaningfully to church-related work. In 1885, when she met and married Josiah Shelley Meyer,[9] the couple opened the CTS.[10] The school offered a broad curriculum of Bible studies, theology, church history, music, economics, sociology, and basic medical training. The afternoons were spent with practical work, both visiting in the immigrant neighborhoods of Chicago and teaching in the so-called "Industrial Schools," mostly started by the students themselves, where children and adults afflicted by poverty could take classes in practical skills like sewing and cooking.[11]

Over the years the CTS prepared deaconesses, nurses, Sunday school teachers, parish workers, and missionaries in the widest sense of the word for their work in different fields. Rider Meyer resigned as principal of the

CTS and died in 1922. In the following years, the CTS faced difficulties in recruiting students and in raising the necessary funds for the institution. In 1934, the school merged with the Garrett Biblical Institute in Evanston, Illinois, now Garrett-Evangelical Theological Seminary. Three faculty members, one secretary and 21 students from the CTS subsequently went to the Garrett campus in Evanston.[12]

Different ideas about the structural organization of deaconess work and competition for candidates and funds resulted in a bitter conflict which could not be resolved.[13] This conflict was aggravated by differing narratives about the origin and development of the deaconess movement in the Methodist context: Should Lucy Rider Meyer be considered the originator and pioneer of the movement or should that honor be given to the band of women working for the WHMS?[14] Despite the conflict there were personal and professional connections between the two groups within the movement. Both the deaconesses who trained in Chicago with Lucy Rider Meyer and those who trained in one of the training schools of the WHMS studied along the lines of the same curriculum devised by Rider Meyer.[15] Some deaconesses who had graduated from the CTS staffed institutions founded and administered by the WHMS.[16]

The official recognition of the deaconess office in 1888 eventually led to its revival throughout Methodism, within the MEC's German-speaking Annual Conferences, the Church of the United Brethren in Christ (UB), the Evangelical Association (EA), the United Evangelical Church (UEC), the Methodist Episcopal Church, South (MECS), and the Methodist Protestant Church (MPC).[17] Not intending to judge one of these as more influential or worthwhile than the others, I have limited the focus of this essay on the deaconess work resulting from the CTS. These "Chicago deaconesses" were by far the most prolific in terms of public relations. They wrote and published articles, newsletters, pamphlets, books, stories, and novels promoting the deaconess cause. An examination of all these sources offers some answers to questions about the developments and experiences that shaped the women pioneers in Continental European Methodism. Even though the modern female diaconate originated in Europe, it is reasonable to assume that the American sisters influenced their European sisters as well. The American deaconesses of the nineteenth century, not only among the Methodists, but also in other denominations, were pioneer women in more than one respect. In the remainder of this chapter I examine the Chicago deaconesses in order to identify those traits that may have inspired the women pioneers in Europe.

The beginning of work in the Chicago Training School

At the end of the second school year at CTS, in the summer of 1887, the growing student body as well as the witnessed need for professional service by Christian women in the crowded, poverty-stricken tenements of the slums of Chicago had proved Lucy Rider Meyer and her husband right. A training school was definitely needed. When the three-month long summer break approached, ten of the 15 graduates of that year expressed the wish to stay on to continue the social work they had started as part of the curriculum. Why not use the empty schoolrooms to house those young women during the summer months? The combination of diaconal work and the communal living of women were identified, rather offhandedly, with the adjective "deaconess," when Rider Meyer wrote about this pragmatic summer plan in the CTS periodical *The Message and Deaconess Advocate* in June 1887:

> The opportunities for work in a large city are often better in summer than in winter. This fact, together with the desire we have that our building which would otherwise be nearly vacant for months, may be used for the advance of the Kingdom, has determined us upon opening a Deaconess Home during the summer months.[18]

During that first summer, eight young women accomplished 2,751 visits in the crowded tenements of Chicago, took care of the sick and dying, and taught children in Sunday schools. While they did not call themselves deaconesses yet, they started to call the house "Deaconess Home," albeit "with bated breath."[19] They were strengthened by living together and nourishing their spirituality through their community, which the following excerpt from Rider Meyer's account of that summer of 1878 clearly shows:

> Our family seems very small. We all sit at one very long table. Somebody sent us a crate of berries the other day. It is remarkable what appetites we all have – six loaves of bread every day and eight quarts of milk! . . . The first hour after breakfast is always Bible hour. One of us leads in the responsive Bible reading, and then gives some practical talk on some verse of the lesson. We sing a good deal and pray, and grow strong by communion with God.[20]

At summer's end, donations made it possible to rent an apartment in order to house those women who were willing to continue the "experiment." Fannie Reeves, one of the first deaconesses, later wrote about the inauspicious beginnings of the permanent Deaconess Home:

> One day in October my room-mate and I were called into the office at the Training School, and asked if we were willing to become the nucleus of a Methodist Deaconess Home. And so it happened that one cold evening we began house-keeping on a small scale in the flat on Erie Street. . . . Standing later in our little dining-room we viewed the landscape o'er. A bed lounge, four chairs and a lamp! Could we be happy here? We all knelt in prayer, dedicating ourselves and our Home to the Father above, and then we two were left alone. How large the house

seemed! Four or more large, cold, dark rooms and a large dark hall separated us from the outside world.[21]

Eventually, though, the little community grew, while a "house mother," Isabella Thoburn, "remained with us a whole year, making our home home-like with her motherly presence," as Fannie Reeves remembered.[22] Thoburn (1840–1901), the first missionary appointed by the newly founded Woman's Foreign Missionary Society (WFMS) in 1869, had begun a program of education for Indian women in North India and culminated in the founding of the Lucknow Woman's College (later renamed Isabella Thoburn College).[23] While on furlough in the USA from 1886 until 1896, Thoburn studied at the CTS, became one of the first deaconesses, and was appointed to serve as the first house mother and superintendent of the new Deaconess Home.

The story of the Chicago summer of 1887 and the spontaneous emergence of the Deaconess Home became the often-told narrative of the Chicago deaconesses, marking their identity as strong, resourceful women who were able to create a new reality without resorting to male leadership, tradition, or even secured funds. Deaconess advocates interpreted these humble beginnings in biblical terms as the mustard seed that would grow into a huge tree. Rider Meyer wrote in June 1887:

> We believe this thought of a Headquarters for lady missionaries and an organization of their work, may be a seed with a life-germ in it which shall grow. It is very small, but so was the mustard seed. We will plant it, and wait for the showers of Heaven and the shining of the sun.[24]

Where did the mustard seed come from? It is safe to assume that Rider Meyer knew of the German revival of the deaconess office as well as of the American groups already in place at that particular time. The Methodist pastor J. C. Jackson had even called the CTS and its close community of teachers and students an "American Kaiserswerth" when he wrote about the school in the Methodist periodical *Northwestern Christian Advocate*.[25] However, Rider Meyer, at least in the early years of the Chicago deaconess movement, refused to acknowledge her indebtedness to the European roots of the movement, claiming her ignorance of any forerunners at the time of the initiation of the Chicago deaconess work. In her essay "The mother in the church," published in the *Methodist Review* in 1901, she claimed:

> Not till months afterward did the founders of the work in America learn that the effort in the United States was closely akin to the work of the Lutheran deaconesses across the water and that there was in existence in that country a little nucleus of Methodist deaconesses.[26]

This ignorance is hard to believe considering not only that the above-mentioned article by J. C. Jackson drew a parallel between the Chicago work and that of the Kaiserswerth Motherhouse, but also that the professor for theology, Charles Bradley,[27] who gave the commencement speech in the summer of 1887, talked at length about Kaiserswerth:

> Many of us have read much and with intense interest of the movement instituted by pastor Fliedner of Kaiserswerth. It began in a little summer-house in his garden, into which he took some poor discharged prisoners, for whom his wife tenderly cared. That work has developed into a great charitable organization extending all over Europe. There are similar well-organized sisterhoods in our own Methodist church in Germany whose members, dressed in their uniform, are doing untold good. Our German brethren have found them invaluable – why may not we?[28]

Why would Lucy Rider Meyer distance her endeavor from the venerable albeit nascent tradition of the modern female diaconate? The following paragraph, taken from her above-mentioned article "The Mother in the Church" almost has the ring of a declaration of independence about it:

> But the deaconess movement in American Methodism is strikingly spontaneous. It is not a growth from the German root. Its workers bear the same name as those in Germany, and do in some respects a similar work, but it originated independently and on a far broader and more evangelistic basis.[29]

The last sentence gives a hint to her motives: while the Kaiserswerth deaconesses chiefly, albeit not exclusively, worked as nurses, Rider Meyer's school curriculum prepared women for a broader line of work. The future deaconesses worked as missionaries overseas, as preachers, journalists, pastor's assistants, social workers, to name just a few occupations. By distancing herself from the German model, Rider Meyer claimed the freedom to "invent" a new and different kind of deaconess whose characteristics differed noticeably from the Kaiserswerth prototype, as will be shown below.

While Theodor Fliedner was revered and constantly held up as the epitome of the deaconess cause, such a "Fliedner-cult" was never practiced among the English-speaking Methodist deaconesses. Rider Meyer and her colleagues and students were willing to acknowledge the beneficial effects of Fliedner's work but never willing to "adore" Kaiserswerth. Kaiserswerth could be described as "wonderful work for God and humanity being carried on by these thousands of trained and devoted women, to whom with their honored founder belongs the imperishable glory of resurrecting the ancient order of deaconesses, and giving to the world the modern trained nurse."[30] But the Chicago deaconesses neither felt the need to ask any existing deaconess homes for help or advice nor to closely study the German prototype.

The more established and successful the Chicago deaconess movement became, however, the more explicitly Rider Meyer inscribed her work into the history of the general deaconess movement. In 1897 she described her visit to Kaiserswerth during her tour of Europe the year before. She concluded the article with the expressed hope for a growth of the American deaconess institutions similar to that of Kaiserswerth.[31] Deaconess Isabelle Horton, student and most important coworker of Rider Meyer, even claimed that Fliedner's "mantle fell upon the shoulders of those (i.e. Lucy and Josiah Meyer) who could nourish a native plant to vigorous growth and accomplish the work for which Fliedner longed and prayed."[32]

The Chicago deaconesses claimed their independence, not only from Kaiserswerth, but also from the Methodist church's official channels of recognition. The church, in fact, never contributed financially to the deaconess homes and showed a certain ambivalence towards the deaconess endeavors during the first decades.[33] Perhaps in light of these attitudes and actions, Rider Meyer and her coworkers stressed the timing of the office's emergence: it existed before the church's recognition of it, i.e., it was instituted by the women themselves and not by the church, as Rider Meyer was want to make clear:

> We have, indeed, received official sanction . . . and we receive it gratefully, believing our power is many times greater thus allied directly with the thoroughly organized and divinely appointed church of God. But that does not change its character. It existed both in thought and in definite form, before any ecclesiastical action.[34]

Even stronger words are used by Rider Meyer in her essay "The Mother in the Church," published in the *Methodist Review* and as such intended to be read not only by deaconesses and their supporters, but also by the Methodist public in general:

> The most striking feature of deaconess work in American Methodism is its spontaneity. Though greatly aided and strengthened by the recognition of the General Conference, it did not originate with that body. The women themselves had inaugurated the work, had mastered the initial difficulties, and had carried on the work almost a year before General Conference recognition. That recognition was, indeed, almost wholly because of the work.[35]

Nevertheless, the recognition of the office removed some of the obstacles the deaconesses had had to deal with before and saved them from having to constantly explain their role and to refute the reproachful notion that they were nothing but "impostors and self-seekers."[36] The relationship between the church and the deaconesses, though, was – at least for the period covered in this chapter – never an easy one, due to conflicting visions. Deaconess Isabelle Horton voiced a perception shared by many, albeit not by all deaconesses, in a speech at the First National Conference of the Social Workers of Methodism in St. Louis, Missouri, in 1909:

> From the beginning it was evident that there was a slight divergence, if not in spirit, in ideals, between the deaconess and the Church. The deaconess would seek out the lost sheep; the Church would have her rebuild the walls of Zion. As soon as the deaconess had demonstrated her ability to do anything worthwhile there was the tendency to annex her to the church as a sort of assistant pastor, church visitor – what you will – a servant of the church whose success should be measured by the number of new children brought into the depleted ranks of the Sunday school or the vacant pews filled at the church service.[37]

Chicago versus Kaiserswerth: the adaptation of the Kaiserswerth identity markers

Not all branches of the American Methodist deaconess movement claimed its independence from the German roots of the modern female diaconate. German-speaking Methodists, for example, faithfully replicated the Kaiserswerth model. Deaconess Louise Golder (1857–1929)[38] and her brother, the pastor Christian Golder (1849–1922),[39] both first-generation German immigrants, founded the German Methodist Deaconess Home in Cincinnati, focusing – like their counterparts in Germany – on nursing as the primary deaconess occupation.[40] When German Methodism in the USA was compelled to "Americanize" during Word War One, however, the distinct German Methodist deaconess work merged with that of the English-speaking branch of Methodism and thus disappeared.[41]

The type of deaconess life and work that grew from the CTS, however, proved to be decidedly different from the German prototype. Even though Lucy Rider Meyer's feigned ignorance of Kaiserswerth does not seem plausible, the locus of information about the European deaconess work might be one of the reasons for the liberty of interpretation taken by the Chicago deaconesses. While Jane Bancroft, as well as the German-Lutheran and German Methodist pastors and deaconesses learned about the Kaiserswerth model first-hand, either from the newly immigrated Germans, or by study trips to Germany or German literature, Lucy Rider Meyer received her knowledge from English-language sources, for example from Florence Nightingale's short book on Kaiserswerth.[42]

Nightingale had studied with the Fliedners at Kaiserswerth on two occasions, even staying there for three months in 1851, before beginning her own work in England.[43] Even though Nightingale's book covers many core aspects of Fliedner's institution, some characteristics such as the strict, hierarchical, and patriarchal structure of the Motherhouse are not mentioned. In other English-language books on the European deaconess movement,

Kaiserswerth figures as one among many different institutions.[44] Since these books were mandatory reading for the CTS students, their view on Kaiserswerth consequently differed from that of those deaconesses trained in German-American branches of the American deaconess movement. They neither felt the need nor the compulsion to emulate Kaiserswerth, but freely interpreted the basic elements of the deaconess office, adapting it to the context of the urban situation of their time.

What makes a woman a deaconess? Certain identity markers developed by Theodor Fliedner constituted the earliest definition of the office: a deaconess was a woman living in community with other women, was unmarried in order to donate her whole time and strength to her work, did not receive a salary for her work, and wore a distinctive garb. The specific way in which the Chicago deaconesses shaped those markers, shows the emergence of a new female role model that enabled women to be pioneers in multiple ways. While the Kaiserswerth deaconesses lived under the administration of a (male) pastor and his wife as "daughters" in a patriarchal and hierarchical setting, the Chicago deaconesses never even considered inviting a man to head the deaconess family. A female superintendent, sometimes called house mother, was put in charge of the group. Rules were negotiated and explained – unlike in Kaiserswerth where obedience to rules was tantamount to the deaconess ideal.[45]

The deaconesses were not considered children who were expected to obey their "parents," but adult women who learned to live together not by the order of a male authority. Isabella Thoburn, the first house mother of the Chicago Deaconess Home, explained their shared intent: "But it is the work that mainly imparts the cohesive quality. We have common joys and common cares, and these make common interests. When you have spent the day looking after a social outcast, it is helpful to come into a household of those who believe in your success, and who are doing similar work."[46] By the communal life – a learning process in and of itself – the deaconesses were being prepared to network and foster communities of their own. It is telling that the first three Chicago deaconesses eventually founded their own institutions. The majority of the Chicago-trained deaconesses proved to be well educated, highly mobile, and capable of taking on responsible positions.[47]

The unmarried status of the deaconesses, in Kaiserswerth as in Chicago, needed to be defended against its critics who saw marriage as woman's proper goal in life. The Chicago deaconesses argued that "God wanted some of us to be the mothers of humanity's orphans."[48] Yet, contrary to the Kaiserswerth customs and rules that were designed to keep deaconesses from the temptation to leave the vocation, the Chicago deaconesses seem to have been rather unperturbed in the face of a deaconess's decision to get married. Marriage did not devaluate the years spent as a deaconess – and some deaconesses even celebrated their wedding in the Chicago Deaconess Home's small chapel.[49] The deaconess years could be seen as preparation for all possible ways of life, as the Methodist Bishop John Vincent stressed:

In this way, the life of the Deaconess becomes a school, preparing her for all possible future relations of life, as wife of a minister, as foreign missionary, as wife of a layman, as mother, as possessor of wealth and social prestige. Her life as a Deaconess prepares her for all that is noblest and best.[50]

While both the non-salaried work and the garb as characteristic traits of the Kaiserswerth deaconess were not only motivated by practical reasons but also by religious and educational considerations, both traits were employed rather pragmatically by the Chicago deaconesses. During the first years of the CTS and the Chicago Deaconess Home, neither Lucy Rider Meyer as the superintendent nor the students and deaconesses received any salary because there simply were no funds available.[51] Also, the abdication of a salary could be construed as a conscious stance against the emerging capitalist consumer society which produced the social inequality whose victims the deaconesses encountered in their daily work. Isabelle Horton wrote about the non-salaried deaconess work:

And is there not needed, in this money-mad, materialistic age, such a resetting of the almost forgotten standard of sacrifice and service "for Jesus' sake." When the dollar is often the standard of value, not only in commerce but in character, it may be good to learn again the Christ lesson that not what a man gains but what he gives is the measure of his worth to the world. And just this is the lesson of the office and the work of the deaconess.[52]

The reasons for choosing a distinctive dress for the deaconesses resemble those found in the Kaiserswerth sources, with two important differences. The deaconess garb, as the leaders of both institutions agreed, economized time and money, strengthened the "corporate identity," made her recognizable and safe. But both the educational motive behind the Kaiserswerth garb, chosen by the Fliedners, to remind the wearer of her deaconess duties, as well as the exacted compliance with all the details of the garb, were conspicuously lacking in Chicago. The garb was designed not by Rider Meyer alone, but by the group of the first-generation deaconesses, "and many were the discussions we had over the matter," as Rider Meyer later recalled.[53] Those discussions continued and led eventually to the revocation of the rules concerning both the garb and the non-salaried work.[54]

Deaconesses as pioneer women

By reinventing the modern female diaconate on their own terms, freely making use of the Kaiserswerth tradition but not letting themselves be governed by it, the Chicago deaconesses created a new role model for women in Christian work. While the humble Kaiserswerth deaconess was either working as a nurse (in a hospital or in a parish) or as a teacher, the Chicago deaconesses proclaimed to have virtually no limits on what they could do – a remarkable stance, considering that at this particular time women were still denied laity rights in the MEC.[55] In 1898, Lucy Rider Meyer wrote:

> The deaconess is not the traditional bible reader who creeps softly up shabby back stairs and pats the heads of dirty little children (but never washes them) and reads and prays with poor sick women (but never gives them a bath or sweeps the room). Deaconesses are visitors, but they do more. They are nurses, and kindergartners, and kitchen-gardeners, and housekeepers, and teachers, and evangelists, and gospel singers and pastors' assistants, and editors and physicians, and managers of orphanages, and superintendents of hospitals. They are – anything that a broad Christian woman may be to advance the cause of Christ.[56]

Comparable to the women of the Woman's Christian Temperance Union (WCTU), the WFMS and the WHMS, the deaconesses greatly extended their female sphere. They diplomatically circumvented the patriarchal establishment through their use of a language of domesticity which softened their feminist ambitions. This "soft" or "maternal" feminism paved the way for the more radical and political feminism of the twentieth century.[57] Politically and theologically, the Chicago deaconesses were pioneers of the Social Gospel before it became – at least for a while – widely accepted in the MEC.[58] They participated in the socio-political discussions of their time, taking a stand against the so-called "scientific philanthropy" and its differentiation between the "worthy" and the "unworthy poor." They learned from and cooperated with the American pioneers of the settlement movement, for example, with Jane Addam's Hull House in Chicago.[59] True charity, as deaconess Isabelle Horton put it in her essay "What the Deaconess Says to the Churches," should be an all-embracing love:

> True charity is . . . an all-embracing love that sees in the most debased of mankind a brother – a sister. . . . There is no charity in employing a brother man at starvation wages, and then expecting him to be grateful for a basket of food and a suit of cast off clothing.[60]

Through their work among the mostly immigrant population of the Chicago tenements, the predominantly middle-class deaconesses learned to navigate difficult social and cultural boundaries. Without necessarily crossing the seas, they left home and adjusted to new worlds. Confidently, they agreed that the deaconess office was an opening for women into meaningful Christian work, but also a door leading out of the church, into the world, as deaconess Kate Morrison Cooper explained:

> It was the vision of the overwhelming need of the unchurched masses in our larger towns and cities that brought the Deaconess into the field.

It was the thought of the bitter poverty and need which the churches are not touching by their ordinary lines of service, which leads most women into Deaconess work. . . . The Deaconess Order is often called the "open door" for Christian work for women, but it is a door opening not into the enclosure of the church, but leading from that out into the "highway and hedges," where the cry is heard, "No man careth for my soul."[61]

The Chicago deaconesses were pioneer women: they saw the need for diaconal work, they trained and studied in order to work professionally, they did their own public relations work and fund raising, they ventured into fields unknown to most pastors and lay people, they acted without male leadership, they fostered their independence as well as their spiritual and practical sisterhood, they cooperated with other women's organizations, they did not shy away from responsible positions, and they took a stand in the political and theological debates of their time. With great confidence they could proclaim:

Who are the women that make the best missionaries? Not those who fail in everything else. The successful teacher, or one who would succeed as a teacher – the prosperous dress-maker – in short, the women who have success in them – they are the ones we want for Deaconesses.[62]

Notes

1 David S. Monroe, ed., *Journal of the General Conference of the Methodist Episcopal Church, held in New York, May 1–31* (New York: Phillips & Hunt; Cincinnati: Cranston & Stowe, 1888), 435.
2 Jennifer Legath, *The Phoebe Phenomenon: The Protestant Deaconess Movement in the United States, 1880–1930* (Princeton: Princeton University Press, 2008), 8–27.
3 For a comprehensive history of the German deaconess movement, see Ruth Felgentreff, *Das Diakoniewerk Kaiserswerth, 1836–1998: Von der Diakonissenanstalt zum Diakoniewerk – ein Überblick* (Düsseldorf-Kaiserswerth: Heimat- und Bürgerverein Kaiserswerth, 1998); Silke Köser, *Denn eine Diakonisse darf kein Alltagsmensch sein: Kollektive Identitäten Kaiserswerther Diakonissen, 1836–1914* (Leipzig: Evangelische Verlagsanstalt, 2014; and Jutta Schmidt, *Beruf: Schwester Mutterhausdiakonie im 19. Jahrhundert* (Frankfurt: Campus-Verlag, 1998).
4 Margit Herfarth, *Leben in zwei Welten:Die amerikanische Diakonissenbewegung und ihre deutschen Wurzeln* (Leipzig: Evangelische Verlagsanstalt, 2014), 58–63.
5 See Herfarth, *Leben in zwei Welten*, 65–452.
6 Carolyn DeSwarte Gifford, "Robinson, Jane Marie Bancroft," in *The Westminster Handbook on Women in American Religious History*, edited by Susan H. Lindley and Eleanor J. Stebner (Louisville: Westminster John Knox Press, 2008), 184–5.
7 For the deaconess work of the WHMS, see Ruth Esther Meeker, *Six Decades of Service (1880–1940): The Woman's Home Missionary Society of the Methodist Episcopal Church.* (Cincinnati: The Woman's Home Missionary Society of

78

the Methodist Episcopal Church, 1969), 91–110 and Elizabeth Meredith Lee, *As Among the Methodists: Deaconesses Yesterday, Today and Tomorrow* (New York: Woman's Division of Christian Service Board of Missions, 1963), 35–39.

8 For a biography of Lucy Rider Meyer see Isabelle Horton, *High Adventure: Life of Lucy Rider Meyer* (New York: The Methodist Book Concern, 1928) and Carolyn Henninger Oehler, "Lucy Rider Meyer," in *Women Building Chicago, 1790–1990*, edited by Rima Lunin Schultz and Adele Hast (Bloomington: Indiana University Press, 2001), 587–591.

9 See Mary Agnes Dougherty, "The Meyers: Josiah Shelley and Lucy Jane Rider," *Methodist History* 37 (October 1998): 48–58.

10 William Bernard Norton, *The Founding of the Chicago Training School for City, Home, and Foreign Missions* (Chicago: James Watson & Co., 1912).

11 For the curriculum of the CTS, see Lucy Rider Meyer, *A Wonderful Work or Large Results from Small Beginnings* (Chicago: Deaconess Advocate, 1899).

12 For the history of Garrett Theological Seminary, see Frederick A. Norwood, *From Dawn to Midday at Garrett* (Evanston: Garrett-Evangelical Theological Seminary, 1978).

13 Two competing ideas were voiced: Should the deaconess work be overseen by the general church, according to Rider Meyers "Church Plan" or be housed in the WHMS, according to Bancroft Robinson as the head of their "Deaconess Bureau?"

14 See Priscilla Pope-Levinson, "A 'Thirty Year War' and More: Exposing Complexities in the Methodist Deaconess Movement," *Methodist History* 47, 2 (January 2009): 101–116.

15 See Mary Agnes Dougherty, *My Calling to Fulfill: Deaconesses in the United Methodist Tradition* (New York: Women's Division, General Board of Global Ministries, 1997), 132.

16 Dougherty, *My Calling to Fulfill*, 46.

17 Ibid., 38.

18 Lucy Rider Meyer, "Deaconess Work," *The Message and Deaconess Advocate* 2, 6 (June 15, 1887), 3.

19 Lucy Rider Meyer, *Deaconesses, Biblical, Early Church, European, American. With an Account of the Origin of the Deaconess Movement in the Methodist Episcopal Church of America*, 3rd ed. (Cincinnati: Cranston & Stowe, 1892), 69.

20 Ibid., 71.

21 Quoted in ibid., 72–73.

22 Quoted in ibid., 74.

23 For a biography of Isabella Thoburn, see Earl Kent Brown, "Isabella Thoburn," *Methodist History* 22, 4 (July 1984): 207–220.

24 Rider Meyer, "Deaconess Work," 3.

25 Jackson J. C., "An American Kaiserswerth," reprinted in *The Message and Deaconess Advocate* (March 1, 1887), 3.

26 Lucy Rider Meyer, "The Mother in the Church," *Methodist Review* (September–October 1901), 728.

27 For a short biography of Charles Bradley, Professor for New Testament at Garrett Bible Institute from 1883, see Norwood, *From Dawn to Midday at Garrett*, 57.

28 For a reprint of the full speech, see Charles Bradley, "Commencement Address," *The Message and Deaconess Advocate* (July 1, 1887), 1–2.

29 Rider Meyer, "The Mother in the Church," *Methodist Review* (September–October 1901), 728.

30 Lucy Rider Meyer, "Origin and Organization of the German Lutheran Deaconess Work," *The Message and Deaconess Advocate* (February 1897), 5–6.

31 Lucy Rider Meyer, "A Visit to Kaiserswerth," *The Message and Deaconess Advocate* (January 1897), 3.

32 Isabelle Horton, *The Builders: A Story of Faith and Works* (Chicago: The Deaconess Advocate Co., 1910), 90–2.

33 While the deaconess cause found ardent admiration and support among the Methodist pastors, some of whom contributed articles to the periodicals published by the CTS, the refusal to contribute financially to the deaconess work and training seems to be a reflection of the general church's stance towards the deaconesses. For a list of supportive articles, see Herfarth, *Leben in zwei Welten*, 353, footnote 145.

34 Lucy Rider Meyer, "Deaconesses and the Need," *The Message and Deaconess Advocate* (September 1890), 10.

35 Rider Meyer, "The Mother in the Church," 10.

36 Lucy Rider Meyer, "From Day to Day, May 24th, 1888," *The Message and Deaconess Advocate* (July 16, 1888).

37 Isabelle Horton, "The Deaconess in Social Settlement Work," in *The Socialized Church: Addresses before the First National Conference of the Social Workers of Methodism*, edited by Worth M. Tippy (New York: Eaton & Mains, 1909), 153.

38 See the biography of Louise Golder in Paul Douglass, *The Story of German Methodism* (New York: Methodist Book Concern, 1939), 143.

39 See the biography of Christian Golder by Karl Heinz Voigt in *Biographisch-bibliographisches Kirchenlexikon*, Vol. 18, edited by Friedrich Wilhelm Bautz (Herzberg: Traugott Bautz, 1993), 520–525.

40 See Lee, *As Among the Methodists*, 42–5.

41 See Donald Carl Malone, "German Methodism and the Great War," *Methodist History* 9 (July 1971): 3–21.

42 Florence Nightingale, *The Institution of Kaiserswerth on the Rhine* (London: London Ragged Colonial Training School, 1851).

43 For Nightingale's sojourn at Kaiserswerth, see Anna Sticker, "Florence Nightingale und Kaiserswerth," *Der Brief: Kaiserswerther Diakonie Magazin für Mitarbeiter der Kaiserswerther Diakonie* (2001): 18–29.

44 See the bibliography in Rider Meyer, *Deaconesses*.

45 With regard to the subject of "rules and regulations" in deaconess life, see Herfarth, *Leben in zwei Welten*, 399–400.

46 Isabella Thoburn, "Our Deaconess Home," *The Message and Deaconess Advocate* (December 1890), 10.

47 See Mary Agnes Dougherty, "The Methodist Deaconess 1885–1919: A Study in Religious Feminism" PhD dissertation, University of California at Davis, Davis, CA, 1979, 97–100.

48 See the novel by Elizabeth Holding, *Joy, the Deaconess* (Cincinnati: Cranston & Curtis, 1893), 92.

49 John Vincent, "On Deaconesses," *The Message and Deaconess Advocate* (October 1890), 5.

50 Ibid., 6–7.

51 Rider Meyer, *A Wonderful Work*, 10.

52 Isabelle Horton, "The Burden of the City," in *The American Deaconess Movement in the Early Twentieth Century (Women in American Protestant Religion 1800–1930)*, edited by Carolyn DeSwarte Gifford (New York/ London: Garland, 1987), 132.

53 Rider Meyer, *Deaconesses*, 96–97.

54 See Dougherty, *My Calling to Fulfill*, 29.

55 For a discussion of the peculiar situation during the late nineteenth century in which the female role was simultaneously constrained and extended see

Rosemary Skinner Keller, "Creating a Sphere for Women: The Methodist Episcopal Church, 1869–1906," in *Perspectives on American Methodism. Interpretive Essays*, edited by Russell E. Richey (Nashville: Kingswood Books, 1993),
332.

56 Lucy Rider Meyer, "Relation of the Deaconess to the Church," *The Message and
Deaconess Advocate* (January 1898), 6.

57 See Donna Behnke, "Forgotten Images: Women in American Methodism,"
Explor. A Journal of Theology 5 (1979): 28; Mary Agnes Dougherty, "The
Methodist Deaconess. A Case of Religious Feminism," *Methodist History* 21
(January 1983): 90–98; Rosemary Skinner Keller, "Leadership and Community
Building in Protestant Women's Organizations," in *Encyclopedia of Women
and Religion in North America*, Vol. 2, edited by Rosemary Skinner Keller and
Rosemary Radford Ruether (Bloomington: Indiana University Press, 2006), 852.
Rosemary Skinner Keller, "The Deaconess: 'New Woman' of Late Nineteenth
Century Methodism," *Explor. A Journal of Theology* 5 (1979): 40.

58 See the discussion in Herfarth, *Leben in zwei Welten*, 424–41.

59 Horton, *High Adventure*, 182–183.

60 Isabelle Horton, "What the Deaconess Says to the Churches," *The Message and
Deaconess Advocate* (March 1896), 11.

61 Kate Morrison Cooper, "The Real Deaconess Idea," *The Message and Deaconess Advocate* (August 1903).

62 *The Message and Deaconess Advocate* (December 1, 1888), 4.

Sources

Bautz, Friedrich Wilhelm, ed. *Biographisch-Bibliographisches Kirchenlexikon*.
Multi-volumes. Herzberg: Traugott Bautz, 1970.

Bradley, Charles. "Commencement Address." *The Message and Deaconess Advocate* (July 1, 1887): 1–2.

Brown, Earl Kent. "Isabella Thoburn." *Methodist History* 22, 4 (July 1984):
207–220.

Dougherty, Mary Agnes. "The Methodist Deaconess 1885–1919: A Study in Religious Feminism." PhD dissertation, University of California at Davis, Davis, CA,
1979.

Dougherty, Mary Agnes. "The Meyers: Josiah Shelley and Lucy Jane Rider." *Methodist History* 37 (October 1998): 48–58.

Dougherty, Mary Agnes. *My Calling to Fulfill: Deaconesses in the United Methodist Tradition*. New York: Women's Division, General Board of Global Ministries,
1997.

Douglass, Paul. *The Story of German Methodism*. New York: Methodist Book Concern, 1939.

Felgentreff, Ruth. *Das Diakoniewerk Kaiserswerth 1836–1998: Von der Diakonissenanstalt zum Diakoniewerk – ein Überblick*. Düsseldorf-Kaiserswerth: Heimat-
und Bürgerverein Kaiserswerth, 1998.

Herfarth, Margit. *Leben in zwei Welten: Die amerikanische Diakonissenbewegung
und ihre deutschen Wurzeln*. Leipzig: Evangelische Verlagsanstalt, 2014.

Holding, Elizabeth. *Joy, the Deaconess*. Cincinnati: Cranston & Curtis, 1893.

Horton, Isabelle. *The Builders: A Story of Faith and Works*. Chicago: The Deaconess
Advocate Co., 1910.

Horton, Isabelle. "The Burden of the City." In *The American Deaconess Movement in the Early Twentieth Century (Women in American Protestant Religion 1800–1930).* Edited by Carolyn DeSwarte Gifford. New York/London: Garland, 1987.

Horton, Isabelle "The Deaconess in Social Settlement Work." In *The Socialized Church: Addresses before the First National Conference of the Social Workers of Methodism.* Edited by Worth M. Tippy. New York: Eaton & Mains, 1909.

Horton, Isabelle. *High Adventure: Life of Lucy Rider Meyer.* New York: The Methodist Book Concern, 1928.

Jackson, J. C. "An American Kaiserswerth." *The Message and Deaconess Advocate* (March 1, 1887): 3.

Köser, Silke. *Denn eine Diakonisse darf kein Alltagsmensch sein. Kollektive Identitäten Kaiserswerther Diakonissenm, 1836–1914.* Leipzig: Evangelische Verlagsanstalt, 2014.

Lee, Elizabeth Meredith. *As Among the Methodists: Deaconesses Yesterday, Today and Tomorrow.* New York: Woman's Division of Christian Service Board of Missions, 1963.

Legath, Jennifer. *The Phoebe Phenomenon: The Protestant Deaconess Movement in the United States, 1880–1930.* Princeton: Princeton University Press, 2008.

Lindley, Susan H., and Eleanor J. Stebner, eds. *The Westminster Handbook on Women in American Religious History.* Louisville: Westminster John Knox Press, 2008.

Malone, Donald Carl. "German Methodism and the Great War." *Methodist History* 9 (July 1971): 3–21.

Meeker, Ruth Esther Meeker. *Six Decades of Service (1880–1940): The Woman's Home Missionary Society of the Methodist Episcopal Church.* Cincinnati: The Woman's Home Missionary Society of the Methodist Episcopal Church, 1969.

Monroe, David S., ed. *Journal of the General Conference of the Methodist Episcopal Church, held in New York, May 1–31.* New York: Phillips & Hunt; Cincinnati: Cranston & Stowe, 1888.

Nightingale, Florence. *The Institution of Kaiserswerth on the Rhine.* London: London Ragged Colonial Training School, 1851.

Norton, William Bernard. *The Founding of the Chicago Training School for City, Home, and Foreign Missions.* Chicago: James Watson & Co., 1912.

Norwood, Frederick A. *From Dawn to Midday at Garrett.* Evanston: Garrett-Evangelical Theological Seminary, 1978.

Oehler, Carolyn Henninger. "Lucy Rider Meyer." In *Women Building Chicago, 1790–1990.* Edited by Rima Lunin Schultz, and Adele Hast, pp. 587–91. Bloomington: Indiana University Press, 2001.

Pope-Levinson, Priscilla. "A 'Thirty Year War' and More: Exposing Complexities in the Methodist Deaconess Movement." *Methodist History* 47, 2 (January 2009): 101–16.

Rider Meyer, Lucy. "Deaconess Work." *The Message and Deaconess Advocate* 2, 6 (June 15, 1887): 3.

Rider Meyer, Lucy. *Deaconesses, Biblical, Early Church, European, American. With an Account of the Origin of the Deaconess Movement in the Methodist Episcopal Church of America.* 3rd edition. Cincinnati: Cranston & Stowe, 1892.

Rider Meyer, Lucy. "Deaconesses and the Need." *The Message and Deaconess Advocate* (September 1890): 10.

Rider Meyer, Lucy. "From Day to Day, May 24th, 1888." *The Message and Deaconess Advocate* (July 16, 1888).

Rider Meyer, Lucy. "The Mother in the Church," *Methodist Review* (September–October 1901): 723–728.

Rider Meyer, Lucy. "Origin and Organization of the German Lutheran Deaconess Work." *The Message and Deaconess Advocate* (February 1897): 5–6.

Rider Meyer, Lucy. "A Visit to Kaiserswerth." *The Message and Deaconess Advocate* (January 1897): 3.

Rider Meyer, Lucy. *A Wonderful Work or Large Results from Small Beginnings.* Chicago: Deaconess Advocate, 1899.

Schmidt, Jutta. *Beruf: Schwester Mutterhausdiakonie im 19. Jahrhundert.* Frankfurt am Main: Campus-Verlag, 1998.

Skinner Keller, Rosemary. "Creating a Sphere for Women: The Methodist Episcopal Church, 1869–1906." In *Perspectives on American Methodism. Interpretive Essays.* Edited by Russell E. Richey. Nashville: Kingswood Books, 1993.

Sticker, Anna. "Florence Nightingale und Kaiserswerth." *Der Brief: Kaiserswerther Diakonie Magazin für Mitarbeiter der Kaiserswerther Diakonie* (2001): 18–29.

Thoburn, Isabella. "Our Deaconess Home." *The Message and Deaconess Advocate* (December 1890): 10.

Vincent, John. "On Deaconesses." *The Message and Deaconess Advocate* (October 1890): 5.

4 Methodist women missionaries in Bulgaria and Italy

Paul W. Chilcote and Ulrike Schuler

Kate B. Blackburn, Methodist Missionary to Bulgaria

Bible Women laid the foundation for mission among women and girls in Bulgaria and Italy within the broader context of the work of the Methodist Episcopal Church (MEC), but they were soon joined by Woman's Foreign Missionary Society (WFMS) missionaries from the USA and other countries.[1] These second-wave pioneers – highly educated and deeply pious women – quickly moved into positions of leadership and supervision, consolidating the efforts of their sisters in the faith. As was the case with regard to the stories of the Bible Women, information concerning these WFMS missionaries "had to be teased out, pulled from below, dragged through the cracks," since "their work was little recorded, little regarded, and little known."[2] Obviously, the relationship between the Bible Women and the other women missionaries was critical, but it was also extremely complex. Their experience reveals a typical pattern of growing expatriate control and subsequent domination. As the scales of power shifted in the direction of the missionaries, the Bible Women fell increasingly under their shadow and eventually disappeared. In this chapter we examine the role and influence of the WFMS missionaries and describe their relationship with incumbent missionary wives and indigenous counterparts.

Women missionaries for Bulgaria

During the period between 1884 and 1906, the WFMS deployed six women to Bulgaria (see a full listing of the names and vital information for each of these women at the conclusion of this chapter). Linna Schenck was the first woman appointed to service as a missionary in this context, a decade after the work of the Bible Women had begun in 1874 under the auspices of the MEC. Ella E. Fincham joined her three years later. Only two appointments were made in the 1890s, Kate B. Blackburn in 1892, the year of Schenck's resignation, and Lydia Diem, seconded to the WFMS the following year from the Swiss Methodists. Both of these second-wave pioneers served lengthy tenures in Bulgaria, 34 and 18 years respectively. Dora Davis also dedicated a lengthy period of her life to Bulgaria, serving from 1900 to 1926. The average term of service for these women in this area of Europe was over 18 years.

With the authorization of the MEC mission board, Dewitt Challis opened a school for girls in Loftcha in November 1880 with nine students, a parallel institution to the more famous Samokov school.[3] He and his wife accommodated the school in their own home. As important as they considered this work to be, it was but one facet of their whole ministry, and Dr. Challis expressed the hope in his 1881 report that "some American lady may be sent to take the place."[4] In this simple statement he expressed the primary expectation and projected the pattern related to the WFMS missionaries that would soon follow. The missionaries of the WFMS, in fact, were deployed primarily in educational ministries, both for the establishment and the supervision of schools for girls and for the training of Bible Women. In

1882, the General Executive Committee of the WFMS approved the purchase of the Loftcha Girls' Boarding School, but difficulties with the government delayed its official recognition.

Linna Schenck arrived in November 1884 to serve as principal of the school under the support of the Northwestern Branch of the WFMS. Challis reported that she "entered upon her duties with enthusiasm, giving several hours per day to the study of the language, and other hours to English teaching and general management of the school."[5] Once Schenck was in place, almost all of the reporting back to the WFMS revolved around the new institutions and the progress related to their educational endeavors.[6] The remark of Frances Baker provides something of a window into the attitudes and the strategic vision of the day: "Miss Schenck did not expect to make teachers of all her pupils; some, she hopes, would make good wives and mothers."[7] The American ideology of domesticity still reigned and shaped the mission.

Linna Schenck was born in Fulton, New York, on July 23, 1846, entering mission service at 38 years of age.[8] Raised in the Presbyterian Church, she transferred her allegiance to the MEC as a youth. In late life, after her return to the USA, a friend asked her why she became a missionary. "There were three influences," she wrote in response, "letters from my missionary cousin in the Sandwich Islands, the influence of a dear sister who went to an early reward, and the reading of the *Missionary Herald*."[9] After only six years' service in Bulgaria, she returned to Michigan on a health leave, never to return, dying in Grand Rapids in 1898. One can only conjecture that Fincham had been deployed to assist Schenck in her efforts to consolidate the work of this educational mission, both teaching and providing administrative assistance. As Schenck's health deteriorated it would only have been natural for Fincham to assume more responsibilities related to the school. But no clear evidence remains to document the nature of her contribution; not even the most rudimentary aspects of her life story have been recovered.

Kate Blackburn was appointed in 1892 to replace the ailing Schenck.[10] The report of Blackburn's perilous journey to Loftcha, including days snowbound in Austria, quarantine in Rustchuk, a steamer trip through cold, fog, and floating ice, and a final carriage drive of 50 miles, all made for exceptional reading in the 1893 annual report.[11] She was born near Jacksonville, Illinois, on January 26, 1865. Her English father and American mother trained her in the doctrine and discipline of the MEC, of which she became a member at 11 years of age. The same year she graduated from Illinois Female College in her home town (1883), she became an ardent member of the WFMS. After a lengthy inner struggle, she gave herself to God for mission service, entering the Chicago Training School for Home, City, and Foreign Missions (CTS) under the direct teaching of Lucy Rider Meyer during 1890–1891.[12] Soon after Blackburn's arrival in Bulgaria, Fincham returned home, leaving her with the entire responsibility of the school, the pastoral care of the community (in the absence of the pastor), and the supervision of the other schools as well. She shared this responsibility with Lydia Diem[13] for many years, from the time of Lydia's arrival in 1893 until her untimely death in 1911, not long after her wedding.

This relationship testifies to the fact of close collaboration between American and German-speaking Methodists in the expansion of these mission enterprises. Lydia was born in Kassel, Germany, on July 14, 1871, the daughter of a German Methodist pastor. She had a vivid imagination, shaped no doubt by the beautiful areas in which she was privileged to live along the Rhine River near the Falls of Schaffhausen, by Lake Zürich in Constance, and in Lausanne, St. Gallen, and Basel. She was well trained in instrumental and choral music. Her sister, although not connected with the WFMS, later joined her in her appointment as a French and music teacher at the school in Loftcha.

Another colleague in ministry, Dora Davis, joined the work from the United States in 1900.[14] She was born in Greencastle, Indiana, on January 4, 1868 and died in Tuolumne, California, on June 15, 1951. Her parents blended a Scotch-Irish and English ancestry. She was educated at Kalamazoo College and Albion College, receiving her degree from Albion in 1889. She served at Loftcha as a teacher and finally assistant principal. Blackburn and Davis both retired from mission service in 1926. A tribute to the 34-year ministry of Kate Blackburn in Bulgaria, published at the time of her death, speaks of her courage and perseverance: "Miss Blackburn faced loneliness, political disturbances, riotous uprisings and her own school problems, met each as it came, used all her resources of faith, courage, and consecrated commonsense, and left results with God."[15]

Women missionaries for Italy

The WFMS sent seven women missionaries to Italy in the parallel period between 1885 and 1902, whose work followed the same pattern as their counterparts in Bulgaria (see a full listing of the names and vital information for each of these women at the conclusion of this chapter). Emma Hall was the first missionary of the WFMS to serve in Italy. Having been appointed in 1885, she retired in 1900 after 15 years of service. She spent six years as the only woman missionary until she was joined in 1891 by Martha Ellen Vickery. The longest serving missionary in Italy during this period, Vickery retired after 29 years, in 1920. The only other appointment in the nineteenth century came in 1897, following another six-year hiatus, but Ida May Bowne terminated her service in 1903 with her marriage to Manfred Perry. The Society appointed four new women in the early years of the new century (1900–1902), despite the fact that only one of the women, Emma Hall, had retired from active service during that period. The average tenure for these women was 13 years.

These women who served in Italy under the auspices of the WFMS, like their counterparts in Bulgaria, were highly educated. Their work, however, at least at the beginning, seemed to be more evenly divided between supervising the work of the Bible Women – which was much more extensive in Italy – and developing new educational institutions. Emma Hall was born in Madison County, New York, on November 30, 1849.[16] Her father, a graduate of Wesleyan University, was a strong supporter of the abolitionist movement and inculcated a deep concern for justice in his children. Emma's mother consecrated her to mission service at her baptism. A graduate of Cazenovia Seminary,[17] she entered the first class of Michigan University that admitted women in 1870. She later completed her master's degree in 1875. During a decade of teaching in the USA she experienced recurring dreams about being a missionary, applied to the Northwestern Branch of the WFMS and was accepted. When she arrived in Italy in 1885, work among women had been pioneered for a decade by the large circle of Bible Women.

Her first task was to enlist and train Sunday school teachers for whom she prepared weekly lessons that were published in the Methodist periodical.[18] In October 1888, she established a Home and Orphanage in Rome in which nine or ten girls formed the nucleus of a genuine Christian family.[19] Emily F. B. Vernon, and her husband, Leroy M. Vernon, the first MEC missionary to Italy, served for 17 years in the Italian mission with primary responsibility for the establishment of the MEC in Rome. Emily may have been the most instrumental force behind the development of the first Bible Women in Italy.[20] For years, the Vernons and Hall had requested greater support from the WFMS for the more formal training of Bible Women. In 1889, therefore, the WFMS provided funds for Hall to board candidates for this purpose and to "prepare a course of study in the Bible" as part of their curriculum.

This directive would soon be eclipsed, however, by the reappraisal of the mission during these years. Representative of a new spirit in a new generation of missionaries, William Burt, the newly appointed supervisor of the Italy mission, severely criticized the supervision of the mission, particularly shocked by the prevalence of smoking and drinking among the indigenous clergy.[21] He reappraised the work and inaugurated what might be properly described as a purge. Hall was caught up inevitably in these developments, which not only affected the Bible Women under her supervision, but also entailed educational reforms within the wider connection. As a consequence, she invested more and more of her energy in the developing school system and less and less on the Bible Women. A new vision of "higher education" quickly mitigated what was considered by many to be a non-productive strategy of the past. In 1891 the WFMS sent Martha Ellen Vickery to assist Hall in her work, and she came with her own vision for the future.

Vickery was born in Evansville, Indiana, on November 22, 1866. Her education at DePauw University, from which she graduated in 1887, impressed upon her the importance of higher education, and she entered her work with a strong emphasis on the need of advanced education among women. She was convinced that this would be the key to the success of "evangelical

Christianity" in Italy. She immediately published her impassioned appeal in her first report to the WFMS:

> The power of the Romish Church is in the faith of their women. The crowd of earnest devotees is composed largely of the peasant women and ignorant people. Very rarely do you see a man among the worshipers, or an intelligent looking woman. The government free schools in Rome are very good, and all, even the University, are open to girls. Still, owing to prejudices of co-education – much stronger than ever existed in America – they are sent to the convent schools.[22]

On May 10, 1894, during the Italian Conference session, Bishop John P. Newman dedicated the new school and applauded the work and vision:

> May 10th was "Woman's Day in Rome," crowning the generous efforts of the W.F.M.S. of our church. . . . Near the traditional sight of St. Peter's crucifixion, not far from the tomb of Tasso, between the City Hospital and the Italian Acadamy [sic] of Fine Arts, of which the Pope is president, and within sight of the Vatican, is located this valuable property, with its spacious building and ample grounds, the Girls' School of Methodism, so long under the fostering care of Miss Hall, and now in her absence honored with the supervision of Miss Vickery. There forty Italian girls are educated for the Lord, from whose womanhood shall issue holy influences on their native land.[23]

We have found little evidence concerning the work of Ida May Bowne who arrived in 1897. When Hall returned to the USA in 1900, of the four women sent out to replace her, Alice Llewellyn, the daughter of a prominent Welsh family, born in Mt. Carmel, Pennsylvania on June 7, 1865, became the long-time friend and collaborator with Vickery.[24] They would work together for nearly 20 years in the administration of Crandon Institute in Rome, one of the centers of higher education founded by Vickery. The Italian Protestant paper paid tribute to Llewellyn at the time of her death in 1927.

> The teachers, the pupils of Candon Institute, the families of the pupils, felt for her great deference, admiration, affection, because love begets love. . . . Her heart was a temple erected to the Divine Master; now it is silent, but the angels sing in heaven, and here on earth the faithful are grateful, blessing her for the work that she has accomplished in the name of God and for the uplifting of her neighbors.[25]

These later WFMS missionaries were singularly devoted to the education of girls and women, pouring their hearts and souls into this strategy for mission.

The context, into which these missionaries were thrust, as well as the changing theories of mission during this period, shaped their attitudes about their vocation. In addition to these external factors, however, the internal concerns of the mission and the interrelationships of the women reveal a fascinating dynamic within the missionary community.

Complex contextual dynamics

The women missionaries in Bulgaria and Italy, in these very early stages, faced typical contextual challenges including misunderstanding, resistance, isolation, and even persecution. Expatriate missionaries, limited in number and also poorly prepared to deal with the cultural diversity they would encounter in an alien context, were pushed to their limits. Bulgaria and Italy presented unique challenges. The first Methodist mission efforts coincided with extreme political as well as social and confessional turmoil – in every case interwoven with each other and difficult to understand at that time. As an illustration of this complex tapestry of influences and historic developments, Ueli Frei has demonstrated how the new translation of the Bible in Bulgaria became a symbol of national identity and created a common language for Bulgarians in a time of national rebirth.[26]

These circumstances in and of themselves would have been enough to provide the impetus for mission boards to send missionary couples in the earliest pioneering stage of the work with the intention to support renewal. But the dominant mission theory of the antebellum period also supported this strategy. So, men and their spouses were sent "two by two," as it were, into fairly complex dynamics. Italy had just faced a revolution in 1848/49 with the abolition of the temporal authority of the Pope, restriction of Vatican City State, and union of a highly fractured Italy under the rule of King Victor Emmanuel I. Bulgaria was embroiled in a political process leading to independence from the Ottoman Empire. This struggle for political liberation brought nearly a half millennium of foreign rule to an end but witnessed a quarter century of war during the last quarter of the nineteenth century. Simultaneously, other power blocks began to play a role in the politics of the Balkan Peninsula; regardless, by 1878 a constitutional monarchy was established in Bulgaria.

In both countries, the established Churches, defending their "canonical rights" as state churches – the only churches authorized and permitted to care for the religious life of the country – were deeply involved in all these struggles. In Bulgaria, the Orthodox Church found itself defending national independence at the same time it fought for the right of its own religious domination. In Italy, a Roman Catholic Church that had lost its original power sought to reassert its primacy under Pope Leo XIII. In light of all these social and political complexities, to say nothing of the brokering for power that dominated this era, opposition to the various Protestant missions was bound to occur.

In both contexts the Methodist (Protestant) mission was viewed as a foreign "sect" and unsolicited intruder – not least suspect because of a different

cultural ambiance in a time of national and ethnic resurgence. The statement of Rev. T. Constantine, a minister in Sistov, about the difficulties of
Methodist work in Europe, reflects the suspicion and mistrust in the minds
of many:

> [The] difficulty is the spirit of suspicion that the missionaries are politi-
> cal agents of Great Britain or America whose object is to prepare the
> people of the country by making them Protestants to accept the suprem-
> acy of the Protestant States, when they see their convenience to invade
> this territory which they consider to be the envy of the world, and which
> they poetically describe as being – "Bulgaria land of paradise". . . they
> think that it is patriotism to remain in the Orthodox Church and trea-
> son to become a Protestant. They cannot see why Protestant countries
> should have any care about the spiritual welfare of other nations unless
> they had some ulterior objects in view.[27]

This contextual dynamic made the work of the indigenous Bible Women
all the more critical. Being both inside these issues by virtue of heritage and
birth, but also outside them by virtue of gender, status, and role, gave these
women a unique space to inhabit in the missionary movement. While the
Bible Women had this advantage, with the attendant difficulties nonetheless,
one can only imagine the challenges faced by American women or women
from other Western contexts. The experience of missionary wives in this
inaugural period of mission activity contrasted somewhat dramatically with
the experience of WFMS single women missionaries who, though still pioneers, entered the drama of mission service in the 1880s.

Women prepared for educational ministries

Shaped by the changes in women's education in America, in particular, and
schooled in the nascent training centers for mission service, it was only natural that the attitudes and educational practices of the women sent to serve
in Bulgaria and Italy would mirror the values and vision inculcated by their
mentors. The motivation that led women into this training and service for
these European contexts also exerted its own influence on their lives, attitudes, and practices.

Female seminaries throughout the course of the nineteenth century educated young women especially to teach.[28] Many of the ideas related to
women in mission, as well as the attitudes about the education of women in
the global context, found initial expression in these centers of learning. The
seminaries existed to prepare women for "usefulness," defined primarily
in terms of building the kingdom of God on earth. In this project, women
were being given and took the initiative to assume a role equal to their male
counterparts. It was in these seminaries that women first conceived their
education and that of other women as "a means of world regeneration."

While rooted, in some ways, and emanating from the "cult of domesticity," the provision of a broad liberal education for women also helped them, in an ironic fashion, to transcend an exclusively domestic frame of reference. As Leonard Sweet has concluded: "Seminaries trained women not for public positions of authority but for private positions of influence."[29] The influence of a Kate Blackburn in Bulgaria or an Ellen Vickery in Italy would be profound.

The birth of the WFMS immediately following the American Civil War coincided with another educational innovation related to women, the inauguration of the mission training school.[30] "Intended primarily for lay people, and most of them for women," as Virginia Brereton demonstrated, "these schools emphasized the acquisition of skills and practical experience, particularly in the areas of Bible teaching and missions."[31] These institutions immersed their students in the study of the Bible. Although their programs were of short duration – students typically receiving instruction in these schools for no more than two years – these schools provided an education that was intense, practical, and missional in nature. According to Brereton, "their most important objectives were to promote knowledge of the English Bible, provide a high proportion of practical subjects, and expose their students to varied forms of religious work by sending them outside the schools."[32] The purpose of the study of the Bible in particular, she argued, was to guide the student in her approach to non-Christian religious practitioners and to learn, quite simply, how to teach the Bible. No school had a greater impact on the Methodist women missionaries, according to Dana Robert, among others, than the Chicago Training School under the direction of Lucy Rider Meyer.[33]

The concept of God's call to mission dominated conversations within the newly established network of WFMS branches, the primary purpose of which was the recruitment of young women. "The call" remained the primary motivation for mission service throughout the course of the nineteenth century. According to Dana Robert, the overall bias of those who approved women for missionary service was in the direction of candidates "who could point with certainty to their conversion, calling to missions, and experience of the Holy Ghost."[34] Wendy Deichman has identified their sense of vocation – a critical call that propelled single women into mission – as one of eight "interrelated ministerial characteristics" that were both desired and cultivated at one of the earliest training schools.[35] Among the other motivating factors that drew women into this new sphere were the desires to participate in the cultivation of God's kingdom, to learn ministry by doing it, and to teach others the story of salvation. Add to these the virtues of courage, intelligence, gentleness, and a general capacity to lead, and you have a pretty clear and compelling portrait of the ideal woman missionary. According to Lydia Hoyle, on the basis of her examination of the correspondence of women seeking mission appointments, "a desire for usefulness, a sense of calling, and a concern for the souls of the heathen were the primary motivating factors mentioned by the missionary candidates."[36] Kate Blackburn and Ellen Vickery closely resembled this portrait.

Kate Blackburn and Ellen Vickery – the passing of the baton

During the earliest phase of mission work in Bulgaria and Italy, the educational program fell under the jurisdiction of the early missionary wives, Irene Challis and Emily Vernon, respectively and in particular. From the outset, these women managed this work because they were the ones who had access to women. They met women at the market place, visited them in their homes, and connected as mothers. Bible Women, having been trained at mission schools of the American Board of Commissioners of Foreign Mission (ABCFM) initially, and then later in those under the auspices of the MEC and WFMS, supported the work of the missionaries' wives, particularly in the arena of evangelism. An intimacy of fellowship and mutual support characterized their working relationship. Increasingly, the Bible Women found themselves on the "front line" of mission, as it were, while the missionaries provided the necessary support systems behind the scenes. The missionary wives provided and regulated education; the Bible Women engaged directly in evangelization. So when the single women missionaries of the WFMS arrived on the scene in the 1880s, they found it necessary to navigate two primary and fairly well-established networks of women – missionary wives and Bible Women.

The arrival of the WFMS missionaries, however, coincided with fairly monumental changes in mission theory and practice, and they had been prepared through their own education to conceive their ministry with a different trajectory in mind from that of their incumbent counterparts. Even if the dialectical elements of the missional vision were never intended as bifurcations, and changes of emphasis only, these changes profoundly affected the missions in both Bulgaria and Italy. The "second-wave" women came with the goals of transforming the world rather than converting individuals to the Christian faith, of liberating women from the constraints of an oppressive culture/religion rather than elevating the souls of the heathen, and of consolidating the work of newly established institutions rather than relying on the power of personal connection and appeal. While an over simplification, nevertheless, the shift from evangelism to education, from conversation to institution, from Christian witness to transformer of culture became increasingly apparent in these women. How would the new generation of female missionaries relate to the missionary wives and the Bible Women, or would they even really need to? Kate Blackburn and Ellen Vickery provide something of a window through which to peer with regard to these unfolding relationships in the mission field.

Both Blackburn and Vickery were highly educated women, as we have seen. Having received her initial training at a well-known female seminary in her home town, Blackburn entered the newly established CTS in 1890 and became the immediate protégé of the founder, Lucy Rider Meyer. Upon completion of her studies there, the WFMS appointed her to the Bulgarian mission, where she served for 34 years. Her reports reflect the passion for education that her mentor had planted in her heart. Ellen Vickery's service in Italy was essentially concomitant. Having arrived at her station in 1891, she retired 29 years later, the longest serving missionary in Italy during this period. In 1867 Indiana Asbury University admitted its first female students, in part due to the heavy losses of young men from Indiana in the Civil War, but also on account of the leadership of Methodists in women's education. By the time Vickery graduated 20 years later, her alma mater had transitioned to DePauw University, one of the great flagship institutions of the MEC. The curriculum stressed the importance of higher education in the global Christian crusade and strongly encouraged its students to consider Christian vocations in ministry and mission. It was only natural for her to enter her work under the WFMS in 1891 with a strong emphasis on the need of advanced education among women.[37] She was convinced that this would be the key to the success of genuine Christianity in Italy and that women educated in their schools would transform their world.

When Blackburn and Vickery arrived in their respective missions, the new policies that had been put in place by those superintending the Methodist work – men like William Burt, for example – had already led to the marginalization of indigenous Bible Women. After 1890, Bible Women essentially disappear from the records and reports of the WFMS in Bulgaria. In Italy, Burt's "purge" provides dramatic evidence of their decline. Only six Bible Women were still active in 1889, three in 1891, one year after Vickery arrived, and only two in 1895. The actions of those in leadership ended their era and their influence by the turn of the century. So there was little interaction between these two long-tenured second-wave missionaries and those who had done so much to lay the foundation for Methodist mission in both these contexts. Likewise, their relationship with the missionaries' wives was really characterized by nothing more than their reaching for the baton extended by their retiring colleagues. Irene Challis returned to the USA with her husband in 1888, after about 12 years' service in Bulgaria. As far as we can tell from the records, she never met Kate Blackburn. Emily Vernon and her husband left Italy in disgust, having dedicated their lives to a three-self vision of the church that was being undermined by his successor, William Burt. Having built a strong foundation for the church upon the indefatigable labor of indigenous Bible Women, whom Vernon held in high esteem, both she and her husband's hopes were dashed by the policies of the new regime. They resigned under duress and with not a little heartache. By the time Vickery arrived in 1891, the new policies were firmly entrenched, and there is no evidence that she opposed them in any way.

A thorough examination of the attitudes about ministry espoused by Blackburn and Vickery lies outside the parameters of this study. Much more research needs to be conducted to determine with any level of certainty how their attitudes or theory of mission was shaped by the many years they lived and worked in these difficult contexts. We can hope that the sentiments of Barbara Welter might just be true:

> The ethnocentric attitude and national and religious absolutism of these men and women cannot be denied. In almost every case, however, if they remained in the field any length of time, there was identification with and sympathy for some aspects of the host culture. Missionaries were far more sensitive to the societies in which they worked than is generally believed.[38]

"The lady missionary," claimed Elaine Magalis in a similar vein, "wanted to change the world, but found the relation could only be reciprocal; the world changed her."[39] Having discovered a rich legacy in the stories of Bulgarian and Italian Bible Women, of missionaries' wives, and of the "second-wave" single women missionaries of the WFMS, we are left with as many questions as answers, and know that there is much more to these stories than these initial explorations have revealed. With regard to this last group, we can say without any question that these were extremely intelligent women, deeply committed to Christ, who were also captive in many ways to the currents of culture that shaped their age. Can we say anything different about ourselves? So our admiration, respect, and esteem for these women is mingled with a sense of critical awareness only made possible by our vantage point. What is abundantly clear to us is that these are women well worth knowing – well worth knowing much better.[40]

Women's Foreign Missionary Society of the Methodist Episcopal Church Missionaries in Bulgaria 1884–1937

Name	Events	Sources
Linna Schenck	appointed (a) 1884 Resigned (R) 1892 died (d) 1898	UM Archives #60 ID 2021
Ella E. Fincham	a 1887 R 189?	
Kate B. Blackburn	a 1892 retired (r) 1926 d 1936	UM Archives #21 ID 424
Lydia Diem	a 1893 married (m) 1911 (Wenzel) d 1911	UM Archives #31 ID 788
Dora Davis	a 1900 R 1926	UM Archives #30 ID 772
Edith Burt	a 1906 R 1913	daughter of missionaries

Name	Events	Sources
Edith Perry	Sailed (S) 1923	
	m (Morgan)	
Fern E. Perry	S 1923	UM Archives #56 ID 1834
	d 1926	
Mellony F. Turner	S 1925	UM Archives #69 ID 2311;
		ms Turner Collection
Margaret R. Gongwer	S 1926	
	r 1935	
Beredene Kill	S 1928	
	r 1935	
Etta Mary Gifford	S 1931	
	r 1937	
Esther Carhart	S 1937	UM Archives #26 ID 573

Women's Foreign Missionary Society of the Methodist Episcopal Church Missionaries in Italy 1885–1935

Name	Events	Sources
Emma M. Hall	appointed (a) 1885	UM Archives #38 ID 1067
	Resigned (R) 1900	
M. Ellen Vickery	a 1891	UM Archives #69 ID 2340
	R 1920	
	died (d) 1936	
Ida May Bowne	a 1897	
	married (m) 1903	
	(Manfred Perry)	
Laurea E. Beazell	a 1900	
	m 1906 (Andreas)	
Evaline A. Odgers	a 1900	UM Archives #54 ID 1763
	R 1908	
Alice A. Llewellyn	a 1901	UM Archives #49 ID 1508
	retired (r) 1919	
	d 1927	
Edith T. Swift	a 1902	UM Archives #66 ID 2228
	R 1914	
Artele B. Ruese	a 1918	UM Archives #60 ID 1987
Alice E. Brooks	Sailed (S) 1919	contract worker
	m 1919 (Updegraff)	
	d (in the field)	
Ellen Louie Stoy	S 1919	
	r 1923	
Mildred Foster	S 1922	
	R 1935	
Lena Ware	S 1922	
	r 1931	
Ellen H. Dearmont	S 1928	
	R 1929	

Notes

1 With regard to the work of missionaries in Bulgaria and Italy, more recent studies supersede the earlier classic work, Wade Crawford Barclay and J. Tremayne Copplestone, *History of Methodist Missions*, 4 vols. (New York: Board of Missions, 1949–1973). Of particular interest in this regard is the remarkable inventory of the history of Methodism in the different European countries, Patrick Ph. Streiff, *Der Methodismus in Europa im 19. und 20. Jahrhundert* (Stuttgart: EmKGM 50, 2003). English edition, *Methodism in Europe: 19th and 20th Century* (Tallinn: Baltic Methodist Theological Seminary, 2003). See also, Ulrike Schuler, *Die Evangelische Gemeinschaft: Missionarische Aufbrüche in gesellschaftspolitischen Umbrüchen* (Stuttgart: EmK Studien 1, 1998), Peter Stephens, *Methodism in Europe* (Peterborough: Methodist Publishing House, 1998), and Patrick Ph. Streiff, ed., *Der europäische Methodismus um die Wende vom 19. zum 20. Jahrhundert* (Stuttgart: EmKGM 52, 2005). An older study that is still of great significance is D. John Nuelsen, Theophil Mann, and J. J. Sommer, eds., *Kurzgefasste Geschichte des Methodismus* (Bremen: Verlagshaus der Methodistenkirche GmbH,1929).

2 Using here the language of Jocelyn Murray in "British Women in Mission in the Nineteenth Century: A Survey of the Literature," *Mission Studies* 11, 2 (1994): 254.

3 Barclay and Copplestone, *History of Methodist Missions*, 3: 1028. DeWitt C. Challis (1845–1939), studied at the University of Michigan, became a member of the Detroit Conference, committed to mission work in Bulgaria in 1875 (*Minutes of the Eighty-fourth and final Session of the former Detroit Annual Conference, Michigan*, June 21–23, 1939, Detroit: The Conference, 144). His second wife, Irene L. Shepherd, could only devote limited service to this endeavor due to her many responsibilities.

4 *Twelfth Annual Report of the WFMS* (1881), 53.

5 *Sixteenth Annual Report of the WFMS* (1885), 49.

6 By 1889 the WFMS supported schools in Loftcha, Rustchuk, Sistof, Orchania, and Hotanza, all under the supervision of Schenck, with the support of Ella Fincham.

7 Frances J. Baker, *The Story of the Woman's Foreign Missionary Society of the Methodist Episcopal Church 1869–1895* (Cincinnati: Curts & Jennings/New York: Eaton & Mains, 1898), 351.

8 Methodist Archives, Drew University, Missionary Records, #60 ID 2021, from which all biographical information is drawn.

9 The *Missionary Herald* was the magazine voice piece of the American Board of Commissioners of Foreign Mission, established in 1821.

10 Methodist Archives, Drew University, Missionary Records, #21 ID 424, from which all biographical information is drawn.

11 *Twenty-second Annual Report of the WFMS* (1893), 73.

12 On the work of this institution and its founder, see Virginia Lieson Brereton, "Preparing Women for the Lord's Work: The Story of Three Methodist Training Schools, 1880–1940," in Hilah F. Thomas and Rosemary Skinner Keller, eds., *Women in new worlds: historical perspectives on the Wesleyan tradition*, vol. 1 (Nashville: Abingdon Press, 1981), 178–199. For Meyer's biography, see Isabelle Horton, *High Adventure: Life of Lucy Rider Meyer* (New York: Methodist Book Concern, 1928).

13 Methodist Archives, Drew University, Missionary Records, #31 ID 788, from which all biographical information is drawn.

14 Methodist Archives, Drew University, Missionary Records, #30 ID 772, from which all biographical information is drawn.

15 Zena U. Baker, "Kate B. Blackburn: A Tribute," *Woman's Missionary Friend* (February 1934): 64.
16 Methodist Archives, Drew University, Missionary Records, #38 ID 1067, from which all biographical information is drawn.
17 In 1825, the MEC established this pre-collegiate school in Cazenovia, New York, from which it took its name. It had close links with the mission work of the church. In 1839, the seminary initiated a three-year course of study, particularly designed for the education of women. The seminary also developed a course of study for missionaries. See J. R. Greene, *Generations of Excellence: An Illustrated History of Cazenovia Seminary and Cazenovia College* (Syracuse: Syracuse Litho, 2000).
18 Barclay and Copplestone, *History of Methodist Missions*, 3: 1048–1049.
19 This school was later named after Mrs. E. P. Crandon. Ibid., 1049.
20 F. T. Kennedy, "Mrs. Emily F. B. Vernon," in *Minutes of the Forty-second Annual Session of the Northern New York Conference, MEC*, April 15–20, 1914 (New York: NNYC, 1915), 126.
21 William Burt (1852–1936), born in England, emigrated with his family to the USA, studied at Wesleyan University in Middletown, Connecticut and at Drew Theological School in Madison, New Jersey. He served at churches in Brooklyn before being transferred to the Italy Annual Conference in 1886. In 1888, he became superintendent of the Italy Mission. In 1904 Burt was elected a Bishop of the Methodist Episcopal Church and appointed resident Bishop of Europe.
22 *Twenty-third Annual Report of the WFMS* (1892), 81.
23 *Twenty-sixth Annual Report of the WFMS* (1895), 64–65.
24 We have only been able to collect the most rudimentary information concerning Laurea E. Beazell, Evaline A. Odgers, and Edith T. Swift. Information for Llewellyn has been drawn from Methodist Archives, Drew University, Missionary Records, #49 ID 1508.
25 "A Tribute," L'Evangeliste (December 28, 1927).
26 See Ueli Frei, *Der Methodimus in Bulgarien, 1857–1989/90* (Frankfurt am Main: Medienwerk der Evangelisch-methodistischen Kirche, 2012), 68. Along these same lines, Mojzes cites a publication of Charles F. Morse, a missionary in Bulgaria of the ABCFM: "They had been bought not to read it [the Bible] but to own it as a sign of loyalty and patriotism, and as a magic thing whereby to drive away bad spirits and assure God's goodwill" (Paul Benjamin Mojzes, "A History of the Congregational and Methodist Churches in Bulgaria and Yugoslavia," PhD dissertation, Boston University, 1965, 59).
27 Minutes of the Second European Methodist Episcopal Church Congress, held in Zürich, Switzerland, from September 17th to 21st 1903 (Zürich: Christliche Vereinsbuchhandlung, 1903), 51.
28 See Leonard I. Sweet, "The Female Seminary Movement and Woman's Mission in Antebellum America," *Church History* 54, 1 (March 1985): 41–55. Dana L. Robert thoroughly documents the establishment of female seminaries in the 1840s under the leadership of Mary Lyon and her five-fold vision of women's education in the areas of basic Christian principles, benevolence, intellectual achievement, good habits of living ("physical culture"), and "social and domestic character" (*American Women in Mission: A Social History of Their Thought and Practice* (Macon: Mercer University Press, 1997), 96).
29 Sweet, "The Female Seminary," 53.
30 This is not the place to rehearse the well-known history of this development. The rise of the training schools is well-documented elsewhere. In particular, see Brereton, "Preparing Women," 178–199; Wendy J. Deichman Edwards, "Domesticity with a Difference: Woman's Sphere, Women's Leadership, and the Founding

of the Baptist Missionary Training School," *American Baptist Quarterly* 9, 3 (Spring 1990): 141–157; and Robert, *American Women in Mission.*

31 Brereton, "Preparing Women," 178.

32 Ibid., 188.

33 See Robert, *American Women in Mission*, 153.

34 Dana L. Robert, "Holiness and the Missionary Vision of the Woman's Foreign Missionary Society of the Methodist Episcopal Church, 1869–1894," *Methodist History* 39, 1 (October 2000): 22.

35 Deichman, "Domesticity with a Difference," 151. Within the Methodist tradition, these women had to be single. If they married, they lost their appointment under the WFMS. If they married a minister, they became the "wife of a missionary" under the supervision of the mission board if their husband was under the appointment of the board.

36 Lydia H. Hoyle, "Nineteenth-Century Single Women and Motivation for Mission," *International Bulletin of Missionary Research* 20, 2 (April 1996): 61.

37 See her report, for example, in *Twenty-third Annual Report of the WFMS* (1892), 81.

38 Barbara Welter, "She Hath Done What She Could: Protestant Women's Missionary Careers in Nineteenth Century America," *American Quarterly* 30, 5 (Winter 1978): 624.

39 Elaine Magalis, Conduct Becoming to a Woman: Bolted Doors and Burgeoning Missions (New York: Women's Division, Board of Global Ministries, The United Methodist Church, 1973), 75.

40 Among the many unfinished tasks associated with this research, the several topics we have identified include the role of the deaconess movement in all these developments, the actual day-to-day nature of the missionaries' activities, the issue of self-reflection and personal transformation around the concerns of mission theory and practice, the tension between various Christian traditions in the context of mission, the "women's sphere" or "domesticity" paradigms as helpful heuristic models to interpret developments in mission related to the female missionary, and the ongoing work of women missionaries in Europe into the twentieth century.

Sources

Annual Report of the Woman's Foreign Missionary Society. New York: Woman's Foreign Missionary Society of the Methodist Episcopal Church.

– *Twelfth* (1881).

– *Sixteenth* (1885).

– *Twenty-first* (1890).

– *Twenty-second* (1891).

– *Twenty-third* (1892).

– *Twenty-sixth* (1895).

Baker, Frances J. *The Story of the Woman's Foreign Missionary Society of the Methodist Episcopal Church 1869–1895.* Cincinnati: Curts & Jennings/New York: Eaton & Mains, 1898.

Baker, Zena U. "Kate B. Blackburn: A Tribute." Woman's Missionary Friend (February 1934): 64.

Barclay, Wade Crawford, and J. Tremayne Copplestone. *History of Methodist Missions.* 4 volumes. New York: Board of Missions, 1949–1973.

Brereton, Virginia Lieson. "Preparing Women for the Lord's Work: The Story of Three Methodist Training Schools, 1880–1940." In *Women in New Worlds: Historical Perspectives on the Wesleyan Tradition*, 1 Volume. Edited by Hilah F. Thomas, and Rosemary Skinner Keller, pp. 178–199. Nashville: Abingdon Press, 1981.

Deichman Edwards, Wendy J. "Domesticity with a Difference: Woman's Sphere, Women's Leadership, and the Founding of the Baptist Missionary Training School." *American Baptist Quarterly* 9, 3 (Spring 1990): 141–157.

Frei, Ueli. *Der Methodimus in Bulgarien, 1857–1989/90*. Frankfurt am Main: Medienwerk der evangelisch-methodistischen Kirche, 2012.

Greene, J. R. *Generations of Excellence: An Illustrated History of Cazenovia Seminary and Cazenovia College*. Syracuse: Syracuse Litho, 2000.

Horton, Isabelle. *High Adventure: Life of Lucy Rider Meyer*. New York: The Methodist Book Concern, 1928.

Hoyle, Lydia H. "Nineteenth-Century Single Women and Motivation for Mission" *International Bulletin of Missionary Research* 20, 2 (April 1996): 58–64.

Kennedy, F. T. "Mrs. Emily F. B. Vernon." In Minutes of the Forty-second Annual Session of the Northern New York Conference, MEC, New York: NNYC 1915, April 15–20, 1914.

Magalis, Elaine. *Conduct Becoming to a Woman: Bolted Doors and Burgeoning Missions*. New York: Women's Division, Board of Global Ministries, The United Methodist Church, 1973.

Minutes of the Eigthy-fourth and final Session of the former Detroit Annual Conference, Michigan, Detroit: The Conference, 1940, June 21–23, 1939.

Minutes of the Second European Methodist Episcopal Church Congress, held in Zürich, Switzerland, from September 17th to 21st 1903. Zürich: Christliche Vereinsbuchhandlung, 1903.

Methodist Archives. Drew University. Missionary Records.

Mojzes, Paul Benjamin Mojzes. "A History of the Congregational and Methodist Churches in Bulgaria and Yugoslavia." PhD dissertation, Boston University, 1965.

Murray, Jocelyn. "British Women in Mission in the Nineteenth Century: A Survey of the Literature," *Mission Studies* 11, 2 (1994): 254–258.

Nuelsen, D. John, Theophil Mann, and J. J. Sommer, eds. *Kurzgefasste Geschichte des Methodismus*. Bremen: Verlagshaus der Methodistenkirche GmbH,1929.

Robert, Dana L. *Robert. American Women in Mission: A Social History of Their Thought and Practice*. Macon: Mercer University Press, 1997.

Robert, Dana L. "Holiness and the Missionary Vision of the Woman's Foreign Missionary Society of the Methodist Episcopal Church, 1869–1894." *Methodist History* 39, 1 (October 2000): 15–27.

Schuler, Ulrike. *Die Evangelische Gemeinschaft: Missionarische Aufbrüche in gesellschaftspolitischen Umbrüchen*. Stuttgart: EmK Studien 1, 1998.

Stephens, Peter. *Methodism in Europe*. Peterborough: Methodist Publishing House, 1998.

Streiff, Patrick Ph., ed. *Der europäische Methodismus um die Wende vom 19. zum 20. Jahrhundert*. Stuttgart: EmKGM 52, 2005.

Streiff, Patrick Ph. *Der Methodismus in Europa im 19. Und 20. Jahrhundert*. Stuttgart: EmKGM 50, 2003. English translation: Methodism in Europe: 19th and 20th Century. Tallinn: Baltic Methodist Theological Seminary, 2003.

Sweet, Leonard I. "The Female Seminary Movement and Woman's Mission in Ante-bellum America." *Church History* 54, 1 (March 1985): 41–55.

"A Tribute." *L'Evangeliste* (December 28, 1927).

Welter, Barbara. "She Hath Done What She Could: Protestant Women's Missionary Careers in Nineteenth Century America." *American Quarterly* 30, 5 (Winter 1978): 624–638.

5 Methodist women's mission societies in Germany and Switzerland

Ulrike Schuler

Methodist Deaconesses at *Bethanienverein* in Frankfurt am Main

Although Methodist mission work began later than elsewhere on the continent, Methodism in Germany emerged as the strongest form of the movement in Europe. Many of the subsequent mission efforts to eastern or southern European countries (Austria, Hungary, Russia, Switzerland, and Yugoslavia) came under the auspices of German Methodism. The work of various Anglo-American mission agencies involving Germany are well documented.[1] Methodist mission boards all initiated this work in the middle of the nineteenth century: the Wesleyan Methodist Church (WMC) from Great Britain in 1830,[2] the Methodist Episcopal Church (MEC) in 1849, the Evangelical Association (EA) in 1850,[3] and the Church of the United Brethren in Christ (UB) in 1869. The work of German MEC preachers expanded into Switzerland in 1856, with the EA following soon thereafter in 1866. Both these branches, in particular, developed their missions aggressively in both countries, developed comity agreements so as not to impede one another, and evolved their growing organizations into conferences, in their own right, as quickly as possible.[4]

Methodist women in Germany and Switzerland

The little that is known about women in this story must be ferreted out of discrete histories, minutes, and records written mainly by men. The historiography with regard to this matter did not change until the twentieth century when women were permitted to become delegates to annual conferences and prepared their own reports, affording more information than traditional statistical data entailed. Irene Kraft-Buchmüller was one of the first to examine the publications of the church related to the beginnings of the MEC in Germany with a particular view of the women. She also discussed women's activities in relation to the possibilities afforded them by the *Discipline* of the church. She concluded that there were actually more choices available to women at that time (e.g., serving as class leaders and lay preachers) than the contextual situation permitted them in Germany and Switzerland, although these were sometimes prohibited by male ministers.[5]

On the national level in Germany the women's movement of the second half of the nineteenth century demanded many women's rights, including the right to vote and to provide leadership on a more equal footing with men. Unfortunately, this trend tended to affect the situation of the women churches more negatively than positively given the conservative ethos of the Methodist mission. Kraft-Buchmüller argues that these changes actually impeded the expansion of Methodist women's roles. Their demand for education was welcomed and their fight against prostitution and alcohol supported, as long as they did not press their claim for equality with men.

Despite the fact that this battle was not won until the twentieth century, Methodist women of the late nineteenth century did much more than serve as dutiful housewives. As a consequence of the industrial revolution – in full swing by the middle of the nineteenth century – Methodist women also worked in factories, as maid-servants, governesses, and teachers.[6] There was a surplus of women in society, especially after World War One, and women had to fill vacancies left by absent men in all parts of social as well as church life. On the one hand, while women were forced by church leaders to work for the church – caring for fiscal as well as social matters – on the other hand men reminded them constantly not to overstep their bounds and to remember their "creature-like determination" and their plain work, like sewing and knitting.

Official MEC mission work in Germany began in Bremen in 1849. Soon thereafter missionaries established *Missions-Nähvereine* (mission sewing societies). These were popular meeting points for women and became widespread in Methodist churches. These mission-oriented small groups for women were also known as "sister societies," "bee societies," "women and virgin societies," and "Tabatha societies" (according to Acts 9:36–41). In 1856 the work commenced in Zürich, Switzerland, and Methodist missionaries established a parallel *Nähverein* (sewing society) there in 1861. Women met for prayer, edification, and care of the community. In addition, as the name infers, they produced handcrafts that were sold or sent to the USA to support the work of mission.[7] These funds also supported local congregations and were particularly earmarked for the education of preachers. It is not too much to say that sewing and knitting sustained the budgets of the earliest Methodist seminaries in Germany – the MEC *Missionshaus* (mission house), established in Bremen in 1858, and the EA *Predigerseminar* (preacher's seminary) in Reutlingen in 1877.[8] Conference minutes and articles demonstrate how the financial support of the women's organizations were crucial to the maintenance of these crucial institutions.

The Annual Conference of the MEC decided to establish *Schwesternvereine* (sister societies) for the exclusive purpose of generating revenue for the *Martins-Missions-Anstalt*.[9] Pastor Lüring assumed supervision of these societies in 1878 as "corresponding secretary."[10] Evidence of the importance of these women's societies can also be inferred from the action of the Annual Conference to create a committee especially designed to oversee their work. In 1879 Lüring referred to about 25 sister societies within the bounds of the conference. The church periodical (*Der Evangelist*) opened a special column, entitled *Plauderstübchen* (little room for chitchat), where Lüring reported the activities of these mission groups.[11] In 1880 conference required that Lüring produce an article for the promotion of the sister and sewing societies at least twice a year in the church periodical.[12] In 1881 he described their enormous contribution of 7,386 Marks as "a pretty penny." At that time there were – according to the minutes of the Annual Conference – 155 societies with a membership of 1,962.[13] So-called virgin and children societies were soon founded to teach girls how to sew and knit so they also could become active in women's societies.

German and Swiss branches of the WFMS

In 1886 two women of the Woman's Foreign Missionary Society (WFMS) visited the Annual Conference held in Zürich to promote the work of the Society.[14] The members of the conference – exclusively male at that time – agreed to support the WFMS and appointed Philippine Achard-Jacoby to organize a German and Anna Spörri to organize a Swiss branch.[15] Later, both women became the first secretaries of this emerging work.

Philippine Henriette Achard-Jacoby was born on June 17, 1841 in Cincinnati, Ohio, the oldest daughter of the Methodist preacher Ludwig Sigismund Jacoby (1813–1874) and Joanna Margaretha Theresia Amalia Jacoby, née Nuelsen (1814–1889). Ludwig Jacoby was the first official missionary of the MEC to Germany, raised by Jewish parents, but baptized in a Lutheran church at the age of 23. In 1838 he emigrated to the USA, studied medicine, and settled in the USA as a physician in Cincinnati, Ohio. In 1839, he was converted to Methodism by the German-American evangelist William Nast (1807–1899), who founded the German Methodist Church in the USA.

In 1841 Jacoby felt compelled to do mission work and Nast sent him to St. Louis, Missouri, to engage in mission work among the large number of German immigrants who had settled there. In 1849 the family was sent at Jacoby's own request to Bremen, in Germany, where Philippine received a classical education in German schools. She studied for a time in a private school in Württemberg where she lived with relatives of William Nast. At 21 years of age she returned to the USA and attended the Wesleyan Academy in Wilbraham, Massachusetts.[16] Providence brought her there into contact with a native of Wilbraham, Harriet Warren, the two becoming fast friends.[17]

After completion of the four-year course of study she was invited to a position as teacher. In the meantime, however, Philippine received an offer of marriage from C. A. Clement Achard (1833–1902), a widowed Methodist minister with two children in Germany. Feeling called into this relationship, she returned to Bremen in 1864, married Achard, and entered into an itinerant ministry with him that carried them successively to Berlin, Zürich, Basel, and St. Gallen, where the growing family suffered great hardships, particularly the death of their 13-year-old son. After a brief appointment to Stuttgart, Achard served as docent and director of the *Martins-Missions-Anstalt* in Frankfurt am Main from 1886 to 1889. Philippine, as his wife, became the "house mother" of the seminary, as was the case with all wives of seminary directors.

A mother of 11 children, in 1886 Philippine was commissioned as the first secretary of the WFMS in Germany. She accompanied her husband to New York in 1888, where her husband served as a delegate at the General Conference. This trip also provided the opportunity for Philippine to visit her mother, her father having died in 1874. As a consequence, perhaps, of these important connections, the Achard family decided to move with some of their children to the USA in 1889. Clement served pastoral appointments among German congregations in Quincy, Pretoria, and St. Louis prior to retirement in 1900. Just arrived back in the USA, Harriet Warren persuaded Philippine to assume editorial responsibilities for *Frauen-Missions-Freund*, the German counterpart to the *Heathen Woman's Friend* that Harriet edited.[18] In 1895 she became the secretary of the German WFMS. The work was scattered over a wide expanse of territory – in 12 German Conferences, nine of which were located in the USA, two in Germany, and one in Switzerland.

When she relinquished her leadership of the German WFMS, she left behind a large number of letters, tracts, and reports yet to be fully examined. Philippine died on October 5, 1902 at 61 years of age, following a surgery that proved to be lethal.[19] Throughout the course of her life Philippine supported Methodist mission ardently and functioned as a liaison linking German-speaking Methodist in Europe with those in the USA. Her correspondence was enormous, and *Der Evangelist* published a number of her letters every now and then.[20]

A circular letter, prepared just after she was appointed by the Conference to organize the WFMS in Germany, and probably sent initially to Methodist preacher's wives in Germany and Switzerland, reveals her prudence and self-confidence:

Dear sisters!

Because our men – unbeknownst to us – founded a branch of the Women's Foreign Missionary Society [in Europe] – and since this made our sisters in America elated, we must continue the work that has begun. Although we – the subscribers – have large families to manage, we have decided to take on the responsibility of this work with God's help. We want to beg you for your support in this associated work; first that you solicit subscribers by advertising the periodical *Heiden-Frauen-Freund*. We think if each sewing society or sister society could establish a subscription for one copy, this would be a good beginning.

Secondly, we request that you choose members for the society. Because our sisters are wrapped up in duties, we thought to limit the monthly subscription to five pennies. We would assume that whoever pays this is a member of the society. Indeed, higher rates are not excluded.

Maybe you think we already have so many obligations and cannot assume much more. Look! First, we thought the same, but after considering it carefully we came to the conclusion that the Lord will send us the necessary help for the work entrusted to our care, if it only will be done with appropriate wholeheartedness and looking to Him. It's our intention to lend a hand with regard to the work that our sisters in America began. Let us think about the privilege that we as Christian women have as an advantage over heathen women, so that the love of Christ will soak into us to give our might to contribute to the rescue work of the mission. We again beg you not to ignore this, but to do what you can do.

All funds should be sent to Mrs. Preacher, M. Mann in Kaiserslautern, Pfalz.[21] Likewise, let her know how many copies of *Heiden-Frauen-Freund* you want to request. Other matters such as reports about the foundation of the societies, the membership and activities of any particular society or section of the society should be directed to the following address: Mrs. Preacher, Ph. Achard in Frankfurt am Main. In the hope soon to be pleased by your news, we finish with sisterly greetings. Philippine Achard-Jacoby and Magdalene Mann.[22]

Philippine's hopes were realized almost immediately. Twenty societies emerged in Germany before January 1887. Philippine wrote: "The smallest has 5; the biggest 30 members. I think, up to now we have about 120 members and 50 to 60 subscribers of the *Heiden-Frauen-Freund*."[23]

When Philippine left Germany with her family in 1889, Magdalene Mann succeeded her as director of the WFMS. Her successor, Philippine Rieker, assumed those responsibilities in 1897. All of these women were preacher's wives. But Achard stayed connected to the work. She just undertook the editing of the *Frauen-Missions-Freund* and from 1895 on she officially accomplished the supervision of the German-speaking societies.

Anna Spörri was born in Zürich on August 15, 1857, daughter of a baker, Jakob Benzler, and his wife Anna, née Schober. After she finished secondary school, Anna expanded her facility with languages, so as to be able to translate French publications and to speak fluent English with visitors. She also taught languages. When she was 21 she married Jakob Gottlieb Spörri, a Methodist pastor in Bern. "For 34 years," claims the author of her obituary, "with loving appreciation, she shared with him the worries and the joys of his vocation."[24] Their ministry carried the couple to Niederuzwil, Winterthur, Bern, Zürich, St. Gallen, penultimately to Bern for a third time, and then to Zürich for a second and final time. Because of their energy-sapping labors, they received a one-year sabbatical (1909–1910), thereafter caring for the congregation in Horgan for another two years. Jakob Spörri retired from ministry and died soon thereafter. The couple had two sons – both of whom poured their energies into the Methodist cause as well: Samuel served as a pastor; Theophil completed doctoral studies and later served as docent at the *Martins-Missions-Anstalt* in Frankfurt am Main.[25]

Anna was still a young woman when she took on the responsibility of the WFMS for Switzerland in 1886 and then worked for 33 years as its corresponding secretary. At the Conference of 1888, the corresponding secretary of the annual conference, Johannes Schneebeli, reported about the work of the women in Switzerland. No less than 14 little societies had been formed with 565 members and an income of 343 Franken.[26] Two years later the sum had tripled, registering 569 donors and a yearly average of 2,500 Franks.[27] Throughout the course of these years Anna also provided leadership for a children's missionary society and a class meeting. She took care of young deaconesses when her husband served as director of the Bethany Deaconess Center in Zürich, and after her husband's death she still worked as "deaconess mother" for about 30 years, teaching as well at the nursing school.[28] She carried on a sizeable correspondence, especially concerned to comfort people in distress. A gifted author and poet, Anna was also a well-trained singer who even enjoyed composing songs. "Her poems," it has been said, "were the testimonies of person who trusted God and sang with a happy heart."[29] She died on July 25, 1942.

The development of the WFMS in Germany and Switzerland progressed rapidly. It was soon the third largest branch in a church the membership of which approximated 14,000 active members. On the one hand, the conferences needed the women's financial support; but on the other hand, men within the German and Swiss MEC looked at the WFMS with suspicion. Having launched in the USA as an institution autonomous of the MEC, in the European context, men maintained a firmer grasp with regard to institutional control. Women who affiliated with the WFMS in Germany and Switzerland debated these issues. Philippine Achard, for example, had offered a choice: women could remain in their original society and support the new one or create a new women's society. In both instances, however, the women's groups remained under the control of the annual conference. With regard to Germany, Kraft-Buchmüller concluded that the WFMS reached a zenith during the time of the Weimar Republic, where between 1925 and 1932 the number of deaconesses and women societies doubled.[30]

Methodist women missionaries from Germany and Switzerland

Much of the work of the WFMS in Switzerland and Germany was local, despite the name. Members of the Society, for example, often functioned as Godparents for orphans or Bible Women, engaged in acts of compassion, and promoted the work of local mission.[31] But women also applied to become foreign missionaries. On the basis of agreements struck between American and European counterparts, missionaries from Europe had to be educated in and then sent from the USA to their sphere of mission. Given the fact that women from Switzerland and Germany could not be sent directly from their home Conference into the mission fields of the MEC, this meant that they had to function somewhat independently of the European Conference and the WFMS in Germany or Switzerland. Kraft-Buchmüller discovered that secretaries only maintained records for those women who were daughters of German or Swiss preachers; church periodicals only reported tersely when missionaries entered service. It is even difficult to determine, therefore, who went to the USA or Great Britain to enter mission service or found another missionary society with which to affiliate. Concerning some of these pioneers, however, some detail has been recovered to sketch out the following portraits.

Lydia Diem, a preacher's daughter, was the first female Swiss Methodist missionary, sent eventually by the WFMS from the USA for mission service.[32] She was born in Kassel in Germany and served from 1893 to 1906 as a teacher at the Methodist girl's school in Loftcha, Bulgaria.[33] After Lydia married H. P. Wetzel, they traveled together as a missionary couple to the Bismarck-Archipel where she died in 1911.[34] Her Sister Amélie Diem worked with her at the girl's school in Loftcha from 1894 to 1896 until her marriage to Gottfried Alder, Methodist pastor in Switzerland.[35] She later served as the Secretary of the WFMS in Switzerland.[36]

Debora Gebhardt, daughter of a famous song writer and evangelist in the holiness movement, is featured in *Der Evangelist*.[37] She went to Chicago to prepare for mission service but failed because of difficulties there.[38] Only a cryptic reference remains, maintaining that she had not been "humble" enough.[39]

Sarah Sommer, daughter of the German pastor, Johann Jakob Sommer (1850–1925), went as a physician on behalf of the WMC from England to India in 1906.[40] Kraft-Buchmüller identifies other women, but there is very little information about them that has been unearthed.[41] *Martha Lebeus* traveled in the 1880s to America; there she became a deaconess and later a missionary. In 1897 she was the first MEC missionary to serve in Sing-lu, China.[42] *Martha Nicolaisen*, originally a deaconess of the Bethany Center, was sent around 1889 as a missionary to China as well. *Emma Betow* entered mission service in 1904.

Paula Seidlmann was the first woman with close connections to Germany and Austria to receive financial support from Europe for her mission service. She came from Vienna where she was a member of the MEC and was educated as a teacher. She went to Berea College in Kentucky for her mission preparation.[43] She was also sent by the American WFMS to China, but the *Jugendbund* (youth association) in Europe paid for her travel expenses and salary for one year.[44] Just prior to World War One, around 1913 or 1914, Paula visited congregations in Germany, reporting on her experiences and missionary endeavors.[45] She encouraged the women to create a distinct German branch with the right to send missionaries autonomously. This was discussed in the Annual Conference, which concluded that this request was "untimely."[46]

In the 1890s there had already been discussions about the conditions that would need to be met to send women missionaries directly from Germany and Switzerland. By that time, more and more women were beginning to surface who had felt the call to mission service. Some were discouraged by the need to spend time in Methodist educational institutions in the USA. Most of them did not have the financial resources to participate in such a protocol. In 1902 Martha Lebeus recommended that German women prepare for mission service in cooperation with the seminary and the Bethany Society in Frankfurt am Main.[47] In 1908 the board of the *Martins-Missions-Anstalt* responded positively to this request to "receive two guest students who would receive their training in the institution."[48] The South German Annual Conference concurred with the perspective that German daughters ought to be educated in the context of their own church and recommend support. Hanna Scharpff and Anna Rauch were the first women to study at the MEC seminary in the academic year 1908–1909. They lived outside the community of male seminarians, but participated in all the classes that were prescribed for them "as suitable." The Seminary Director, Gustav Junker, reported that both women "were held in high esteem by virtue of their humility, attentiveness, and diligence. Their presence had no detrimental effect on the class."[49] While Anna Rauch's name disappeared from the minutes and denominational periodicals, Hanna Scharpff became the first female missionary educated and sent forth by the German branch of the WMFS.

Hanna Scharpff was born on April 4, 1877 in Lausanne, Switzerland and died July 15, 1964 in Pasadena, California.[50] As the daughter of a Methodist minister, Adolf Scharpff (1845–1933) and his wife Christine, née Kilgus (1841–1915), she learned early how to navigate the transitions to several different German and Swiss preaching places to which her father was appointed. She completed studies at a higher girl's school and a women's work school in Ludwigsburg, Germany. In later years she revealed that Sunday school and mission reports read by her mother aroused her interest in the possibility of a missional vocation. Around the time of her confirmation in 1881, she received a personal call for mission, working initially as an educator near Lausanne for four years. In 1902 she returned to her family who then lived in Nuremberg where she became a Sunday school teacher and conducted the virgin society. Hearing that the German Methodist Episcopal Church might be able to send missionaries abroad under their own auspices, she applied but had to wait a long time for the church's decision on this matter. The secretaries of the WFMS in the USA and the representatives of the seminary in Frankfurt am Main discussed where it would be best to train the women missionaries, but they came to no resolutions with regard to the nature of their collaboration.

In this protracted interim period, Hanna served as private tutor and governess in Italy for a year and six months and supported the development of a church development in Lyon, France, where she was employed as a parish worker. It was in France that she received word that the WFMS had approved her application for mission service. At the conclusion of her studies at the *Martins-Missions-Anstalt* in Frankfurt am Main in 1909, and not having received a decision about her place of service, she undertook a course in nursing at the Bethany hospital and a course related to infant care at a hospital of the Red Cross in Karlsruhe.

During this period, the WMFS secretaries in Germany and the US continued correspondence in the hopes of arriving at some resolution of their impasse. After serving a year as a visiting nurse at the Peter Böhler Congregation, a Wesleyan congregation in London – also to improve her English – she met Luise Rothweiler, Phillippine Achard's successor as secretary for the German-speaking branches of the WFMS in the USA. Rothweiler was on a visiting tour of Europe in 1910. Once back in the USA she championed Hanna's cause. Almost immediately she received a telegram from the USA deputizing her to a missionary post in Korea.[51] In Heilbronn, Germany, on January 6, 1911 the church leaders commissioned Hanna as a missionary from Germany to Korea in the presence of the bishop for Europe, William Burt. In Korea, Hanna worked as a teacher at a school for girls, later as a traveling evangelist, as a catechist, and as a preacher for women. Indigenous Bible Women accompanied her on her various journeys throughout Korea.

In 1914 she accompanied an employee for a surgery via Siberia to Berlin. When war broke out it was impossible to get back to Korea. So Hanna used the time to study two and a half years at the Chicago Evangelistic Institute and one more year at Baldwin Wallace College in Berea, Ohio, where she received a Bachelor of Divinity degree. During this period, she also became a naturalized US citizen. Back in Korea in 1920 she was responsible for Bible courses and women's evangelism. The WFMS established a branch in Korea which began to send women to China and funded a mission school in India. In 1932 Hanna was one of the first women consecrated for the mission service through the Korean branch.[52] Two years later she visited congregations in Germany and Switzerland to report about her mission service. Fortunately, Hanna's extensive correspondence was regularly published in church periodicals, but remains a source not yet fully exploited.[53] During World War Two Hanna had to leave Korea because of her US citizenship, dying at age 87 in Pasadena, California.[54]

Women in Switzerland also tried to find their way to participate in mission. In 1921, the first women, the Swiss secretary of the WMFS, Amélie Alder-Diem, presented the report of the WFMS directly to the Swiss annual conference. Her address is recorded in the conference minutes. Amélie courageously addressed the bishop and the conference members, confirming an increase in the women's financial contribution to missions and reminding them about the way in which the WFMS sustained the seminary in Frankfurt am Main. She expressed her surprise that the young men in church,

> in youth societies or trombone choirs are less generous, not encouraged to give, and had not made it their task to contribute according to their capability for the education of their brothers in the ministry. The women societies would then be free to attend to their closest and natural duties: caring for the old and infirm, nursing the poor, and supporting women in mission. The women's mission is working shoulder to shoulder with the common mission society and it is to our credit, indeed, that we give it attention. . . . I cannot see that our daughters have to go five to seven years through a process of Americanizing before they can be sent. During the last year we didn't have less than seven daughters . . . who asked me, if and how they could become appointed a missionary of

our society. I had to give answers that were not sufficient and satisfying in any way. . . . I was about to send those who are making inquiries to the Canadian or Paris Mission. You must concede that this cannot stay like this. Otherwise a secretary for Switzerland would be nothing but a redundant decoration.[55]

Women were very dissatisfied about the fact that the WFMS in the USA presented challenges to the European mission candidates and did not consider the educational system in Europe. People in Switzerland also wanted to have closer connections to missionaries, Bible Women, and godchildren.[56] Amélie lamented the fact that "the path to Africa, China, India – and even France, Italy, and Bulgaria is channeled through America."[57]

A year later Amélie again broached this matter with the Swiss Annual Conference, demonstrating the complications and the need for greater knowledge, leadership, and imagination:

> We celebrate the fact that we, as a conference, have our own missionary in the mission field: Lydia Urech, daughter of the Preacher Urech in Nuremberg. . . . The fact that we have our own missionary does not place any additional burden on our congregations. Lydia Urech, working under British supervision, was assigned to an English-speaking conference in the United States. This conference also pays the costs for the return trip. It is convenient that the English government pays a special sum for her salary and so we have only to take care for $250.00, the money that is taken from the amount that our cashier, Mrs. Dr. Rodemeyer, receives from the congregations. . . . Also this year a number of daughters volunteered for mission service. Most of them have only a primary school education and it was hard to make them understand that they have a lengthy journey, at best, that lays ahead and that they can expect many challenges. . . . It was suggested to us that the candidates should [prepare for their mission service] at the seminary in Frankfurt am Main. The thought is good, that they live outside the seminary, pay their school fees, study diligently, and take their exams. . . . Dear bishop, I pray that this idea captures your interest and that you implement it through concrete action.[58]

There is no evidence that any women from Switzerland enrolled as students in the seminary in Frankfurt am Main.[59] Regardless, between 1911 and 1930, eight young women from Switzerland entered mission service through the WFMS in the USA and were sent to China, India, Japan, and Singapore.[60] Missionaries from Europe were not only supported in overseas missions, but were also deployed to Hungary, Yugoslavia, Macedonia, and Bulgaria.[61]

Lydia Urech was born September 30, 1881 in Backnang, Germany, daughter of a Methodist pastor. She received her education in Stuttgart. In a Methodist congregation in Heilbronn, Germany she engaged in Christian education for young girls. She felt the call to mission early in life and was supported ultimately by Dr. Emil Lüring to serve for 30 years on different mission stations of what was then the Malaysian Peninsula: Singapore, Pengang, Kuala-Lumpur, and Ipoh.[62] Only scattered information about her survives or has been discovered. Her father was stationed at a congregation in London at some point. This explains why she first was sent from England to Malaysia, at that time a British colony. In the Conference Minutes of 1922 we find this cryptic statement: "We note that Lydia Urech in Southeast Asia can be considered our missionary."[63] Increasingly the Swiss women's societies took responsibility for her, especially after the Swiss WFMS branch became self-reliant in 1930. Lydia spent her final years in Zürich, but no obituary for her seems to be extant.

During the 1920s the Swiss and German branches of the WFMS were fully restructured. The 60th anniversary of the founding of the WFMS, celebrated in 1929, may have provided a strong impetus for change. The WFMS invited the global secretaries for a celebration in the USA where they also learned more about the international departments of the WFMS. Simultaneously, the leadership of the mission societies in each country of the Central Conference were reorganized their work. Discussion concerning these changes ensued at the Second Central Conference of the *Mitteleuropäischen Sprengel* (Middle-European Diocese), held in September 1930. One of the main questions had to do with the role of the WFMS in these new structures.[64] Mission leaders in Switzerland organized the *Frauengesellschaft für innere und äußere Mission der Bischöflichen Methodistenkirche in der Schweiz* (Women's Society for the Local and Foreign Mission of the Methodist Episcopal Church in Switzerland) and clarified its relationship to the Swiss Methodist Mission Society through its bylaws. Luella S. Nuelsen-Stroeter, wife of Bishop John Louis Nuelsen, the first bishop of the MEC who was stationed in Europe, became president of the new Swiss organization.[65] In the report of the commission for women's mission and sister societies at the annual conference in Switzerland in 1931, the new board of the Society was introduced: "The wife of Bishop Dr. J. L. Nuelsen as president, Mrs. Preacher Dr. Rodemeyer as secretary, Mrs. M. Peter and Mrs. L. Fankhauser as committee members."[66]

A reorganization of the WFMS also took place in Germany in connection with the foundation of the German Methodist Mission Society, but along different lines.[67] The Germans developed no overarching women's organization as the Swiss had in 1930. In their annual reporting they made no distinction between the German and the American WFMS. In 1939 references appear for the first time with regard to the *Frauengesellschaft für Auswärtige Mission der BMK in Deutschland* (Women's Society for Foreign Mission of the MEC in Germany), but only the officers of the organization are listed. Both the new German and Swiss organizations remained strongly connected to the WFMS in the USA through the international department of the WFMS, but they functioned as independent and fully autonomous bodies which were responsible for the educational and financial support of their own missionaries. Both WFMS organizations also became part of the church's Mission Society, represented in the executive with two delegates for each conference. In other words, they had become departments of the Mission Society in their respective countries. In 1939 the World Federation of Methodist Women was founded as a consequence of church union in the USA, connecting women's organizations in 27 countries.[68] Louise Achard, at that time secretary of the German-speaking branch in the USA and also responsible for Germany and Switzerland, signed the contract.

Pioneering women in the Evangelical Association

Evidence for the work of women within the EA in Germany and Switzerland is more difficult to uncover, but parallels the mission efforts of the MEC. In 1838 the EA founded its own mission agency in North America and established what could be described as a women's auxiliary in Philadelphia the following year for the express purpose of supporting of the church's Missionary Society financially.[69] It was not until 1884 that women organized themselves into a proper missionary society. In 1892 Mrs. E. M. Spreng was elected as president.[70] She immediately made efforts to connect with women in Europe.[71]

Almost all of the local branches of the societies were organized and led by preacher's wives. In contrast to the MEC, the EA maintained a more "conservative attitude" toward the roles of women in both church and society. But the EA did deploy women to missionary service. One woman in particular during the period under study, Elisabeth Schempp, devoted her life to foreign mission.

Elisabeth Schempp was born in Eisenach, Germany, on August 3, 1884. She was the third of ten children of Dr. Johannes Schempp and Fredericke, née Bauer.[72] Her father, a parish pastor, later became director of the *Predigerseminar* (preacher's seminary) of the EA in Reutlingen, Germany. According to her obituary:

> Elisabeth studied in Germany and by the age of twenty-four had developed skills in teaching and handicraft. She had also studied music and was an accomplished artist at the piano and pipe organ. She was profoundly influenced in her academic years by the German version of the Student Volunteer Movement and sensed a call to become a teacher in the overseas missions of the Church. In 1908, she was appointed by the Evangelical Board of Mission to go to China.[73]

Elisabeth spent a year in the USA in language study and orientation to the life of a missionary in Cleveland, Ohio.[74] In 1909, she went to China where she taught Bible, language, and handiwork for women for ten years.

When she was in China she became acquainted with fellow missionary of the EA, a young pastor from the USA, the Reverent Carl B. Wahl.[75] They were married on July 29, 1919. The couple went to Tungjen in Kweichow, a province in the interior of China. While her husband was the headmaster of a school, Elisabeth helped with school projects and women's work. The couple had four children. Problems arose because of uprisings in China and frequent harassment from bands of bandits. In 1934 the family was forced to flee to the refuge of a larger city because a revolutionary movement had become so violent. As they traveled by boat on the Yellow River, Pastor Wahl became ill. He passed away on December 3, 1934 at the age of 48. Elisabeth returned to the USA and organized the education of her two eldest children. Then she went back to China with her two younger children and resumed her work as a missionary teacher. As the threat of Japanese invasion of China deepened, her family members, who were at a boarding school for missionary children nearby Hong Kong, were finally evacuated to the USA in 1943. In later life Elisabeth settled with her children to Park Ridge, Illinois and died at the age of 93 in 1977.

A final discovery and remark

The creation of the Women's World Day of Prayer by a European Methodist woman must be mentioned as a significant ecumenical landmark. Luise Scholz first introduced this practice to Switzerland and Germany in 1927 and Methodist congregations continued to celebrate this event until 1943. After the war, in 1949, through Scholz's enormous efforts, the World Day of Prayer became a central event in the ongoing life of the ecumenical movement.

Luise Scholz (née Junker) was born May 22, 1890 in Bremen. Her father was a Methodist pastor, Paul Gustav Junker, at that time superintendent, later docent and director at the *Martins-Mission-Anstalt*, and her mother Hortense, née Achard. She grew up in Frankfurt am Main. After World War One she assumed the responsibility for the household of the *Martins-Missions-Anstalt*. Two of her brothers were killed in the war and soon after both parents died. In 1922 she married Pastor Ernst Scholz (1894–1972), who studied at the seminary. After several pastoral appointments, Luise became more fully engaged in the Methodist Women's Society, being elected chair of the WFMS of the MEC in Austria. She maintained close connections with Philippine Achard. Through her vigorous advocacy of the mission work of Hanna Scharpff in Korea and Elsa Schwab in Sumatra and Japan as well as Korean Bible Women, it is not too much to say that she fell in love with the world mission. When she and her husband relocated to Berlin, she assumed leadership of the WFMS of the North-East German Annual Conference. In 1936 she co-founded the *Ökumenischen Frauendienst in Berlin* (Ecumenical Women's Service in Berlin) in connection with the *Ökumenischen Dienst* (ecumenical service) where National and Free churches worked together. She was most active in the interdenominational Women's World Day of Prayer movement that she began in Germany in 1927.

This examination of Methodist women pioneers in Germany and Switzerland reveals much about the origins of women's mission and the consolidation of their efforts in the MEC and the EA, providing a broader understanding of the church in these areas of Europe. We can see how the activities of women were much more in the center of the church, especially in its ongoing social ministry and, most particularly, in the financial support of the church's mission. The women discussed here crossed both international and denominational boundaries in their effort to foster an understanding of mission as the Christian response to needs, no matter when they arose. One can also see in their narratives what a crucial role the deaconess movement and the deaconesses of the Bethany and Bethesda Deaconess Centers played in their efforts to respond faithfully to the call placed upon them by God.[76]

Notes

1 See John D. Nuelson, Theophil Mann, and J. J. Sommer, eds., *Kurzgefasste Geschichte des Methodismus* (Bremen: Verlagshaus der Methodistenkirche GmbH, 1929); Karl Steckel and C. Ernst Sommer, eds., Geschichte der Evangelisch-methodistischen Kirche. Weg, Wesen und Auftrag des Methodismus unter besonderer *Berücksichtigung der deutschsprachigen Länder Europas* (Stuttgart: Christliches Verlagshaus, 1982); and Michael Weyer, *150 Jahre Evangelisch-methodistische Kirche. Geschichte des Methodismus in den deutschsprachigen Ländern* (Kehl am Rhein: Sadifa Medis, 2000).

2 See Friedemann Burkhardt, *Christoph Gottlob Müller und die Anfänge des Methodismus in Deutschland, Arbeiten zur Geschichte des Pietismus, Bd. 43* (Göttingen: Vandenhoeck & Ruprecht, 2003).

3 Schuler, *Die Evangelische Gemeinschaft: Missionarische Aufbrüche in gesellschaftspolitischen Umbrüchen* (Stuttgart: EmK Studien 1, 1998)

4 This is also true for "awakening movements" and mission societies at that time (from the eighteenth century on (e.g., the Moravians, Hallesche Mission and Christentumsgesellschaft of the Basel mission). For a helpful overview of the connections between Pietism, Methodism, and other awakening movements in the nineteenth and twentieth century, see Ulrich Gäbler, ed., *Geschichte des Pietismus*, 4 vols. (Göttingen: Vandenhoeck & Ruprecht, 2000–2004), esp. vols. 2 and 3.

5 Irene Kraft-Buchmüller, *Die Frauen in der Anfangszeit der bischöflichen Methodistenkirche in Deutschland. Eine Untersuchung der eigenkirchlichen Schriften von 1850 bis 1914. Beiträge zur Geschichte der Evangelisch-methodistischen Kirche*, Bd. 41 Stuttgart: Christliches Verlagshaus, 1992. All English translations of this text are by Ulrike Schuler.

6 Ibid., 21, 46–47. It is important to note that, in an article in *Der Evangelist*, women workers were portrayed as immoral. Christian women and girls were admonished to take no job that forced them to "leave their natural sphere." They described fabric workers as "starry-eyed" and particularly stereotyped maid-servants as promiscuous.

7 Ibid., 25, fn 273, quoting a formal word of thanks in 1856 from the USA for donations from women, found in *Der Evangelist*.

8 The MEC moved the Missionshaus to Frankfurt am Main, renamed Martins-Missions-Anstalt, after an American donator, the clothier John T. Martin of St. Louis. Eventually, all these institutions merged to establish the Theologische Seminar Reutlingen (Theological Seminary in Reutlingen), where it remains today as the Reutlingen School of Theology (state-acknowledged in 2005).

9 Kraft-Buchmüller, *Die Frauen*, 25.

10 H. L. Emil Lüring (1863–1937) studied theology, philosophy, and oriental languages in Zürich and Strasbourg. He worked first for three years in a congregation in Kiel and then served from 1889 to 1909 as a missionary in Singapore, Borneo, and the Indochina Peninsula. Lüring was able to preach in 25 languages. From 1909 to 1935 he taught at the Methodist seminary in Frankfurt am Main.

11 *Der Evangelist* 30 (1879): 278.

12 Verhandlungen der 25: Sitzung der Jährlichen Konferenz der Bischöflichen Methodistenkirche von Deutschland und der Schweiz, Pforzheim, 22–28 Juli 1880, 43. The English translations of the Confernce records have been translated by Ulrike Schuler throughout.

13 Verhandlungen der 26. Sitzung der Jährlichen Konferenz der Bischöflichen Methodistenkirche von Deutschland und der Schweiz, Winterthur, 14–18 Juli 1881, 45–7. At the Annual Conference of 1886 it was reported that there were 175 sister societies with 2,660 members that collected 10,718 Marks. The Missionshaus was given 2,552 Marks (Verhandlungen der 31: Sitzung der Jährlichen Konferenz der Bischöflichen Methodistenkirche von Deutschland und der Schweiz, Zürich, 24–30 Juni 1886, 52). The church in Switzerland/Germany had at that time 3,033 probationary members, 11,134 full members, 85 circuit preachers, six probationary preachers, 19 preaching helpers, 157 admonishers (Ermahner), 797 children in religion classes, 356 baptisms, 723 preaching places 417 Sunday schools, 1,673 Sunday school teacher, and 22,509 scholars (*Der Evangelist* 37 (1886), 229).

14 Mrs. L. Hagans, board member of the WFMS, and Mrs. B. Ohlinger, a missionary in China (*Der Evangelist* 37 [1886], 245). It was the last conference of Germany and Switzerland combined. The conference split into a Deutschland-Konferenz and a Schweizer Konferenz. The German conference was divided again in 1993 into a North and South German Conference.

15 Verhandlungen der 31, 55.

16 Wilbraham Wesleyan Academy was one of the oldest educational institutions of the MEC. It was established by Methodist clergy of New England in 1818. It was originally located in New Market, New Hampshire, and moved to Wilbraham in 1824. It was intended both for general educational purposes and for young men intending to enter the ordained ministry.

17 Harriet Cornelia Merrick Warren (1843–1893), an American editor. She was a charter member of the WFMS and editor of the *Heathen Woman's Friend* from its beginning and of the German counterpart, *Heiden-Frauen-Freund*, for two years. She is remembered as a major leader of the "Woman's Work for Woman" movement. She married Rev. William Fairfield Warren, the later first president of Boston University, who also taught from 1861 to 1866 at the Missionshaus in Bremen.

18 The *Heathen Woman's Friend* (1869–1896; renamed *Woman's Missionary Friend*, 1896–1940) was a Christian women's monthly publication. Established in May 1869, it was published by the WFMS of the MEC in Boston, Massachusetts. The monthly magazine described conditions in the mission fields of the church, documented the work of the society, and provided assistance to missionaries. The WFMS initiated the publication of a parallel German version was published, *Heiden-Frauen-Freund* in 1885, later *Frauen-Missions-Freund*),

originally for the German women in the USA then also sent to the German-speaking areas in Europe (Germany, Switzerland, Austria).

19 This biography is compiled from different obituaries for Philippine Achard: G. Junker, *Der Evangelist* 53 (1902), 381, 389 and *Frauen-Missions-Freund* 17 (1902), 81–5, in particular. At the time of her death the Annual Report of the WFMS indicates that "there are 205 auxiliary societies in the United States, 107 in Germany and Switzerland. . . . The membership in the United States is 4,557, in Europe 2,303. . . . The amount of money raised is $9,407.49" (Thirty-third Annual Report of the Woman's Foreign Missionary Society (New York: Woman's Foreign Missionary Society of the Methodist Episcopal Church, 1903), 7).

20 *Der Evangelist* 41 (1890), 366.

21 Typically, the wife of a preacher was appropriately addressed as "Mrs. Preacher."

22 *Mit Weisheit, Witz und Widerstand: Die Geschichte(n) von Frauen in der Evangelisch-methodistischen Kirche* (Stuttgart: Medienwerk der Evangelisch-methodistischen Kirche, 2003), 245; *Frauen in der Evangelisch-methodistischen Kirche Schweiz/Frankreich* (Zürich: Self-published, 2000), 17; and *Rundbrief, Frauendienst* 19, 1 (1987): 12. Translation of the letter by Ulrike Schuler. A similar letter addressed to all women was published in *Der Evangelist* 37 (1886): 366.

23 Ibid.

24 Collection of Obituaries, Central Archives of The UMC in Germany, Reutlingen, files: Frauen A–N; Frauen O–Z.

25 Theophil Spörri (1887–1955) studied theology in Basel, Tübingen, Halle, and Münster, receiving his Licentiata in 1924. From 1922 to 1944 he served as docent at the seminary in Frankfurt am Main, and later instructor for students from Switzerland in the mission house of the Basel Mission. His publications influenced generations of Methodists in Germany and Switzerland.

26 *Frauen in der Evangelisch-methodistischen Kirche*, 18.

27 Ibid., 100–133, including many examples of activities of women's societies in the congregations and different districts in Switzerland – also distinguished lists for what the money was appointed to (pp. 100–133).

28 Collection of Obituaries, Central Archives of the UMC in Germany, Reutlingen, file Frauen O–Z.

29 Ibid.

30 Kraft-Buchmüller, *Die Frauen*, 49.

31 *Der Evangelist* 56 (1905), 64.

32 See Chapter 4, in which her ministry is examined as well.

33 *Frauen-Missions-Freund*, May 1929.

34 *Der Evangelist* 62 (1911), 112.

35 Her name appears in two variant forms: Amalie and Amélie.

36 Written record of Hanni Handschin, Switzerland (Central German Archives, Reutlingen/Germany, file "Frauen A–N, Hanna Diem, Lydia Diem"). See also the remarks about her motivational report to the Swiss Annual Conference 1921 below.

37 Ernst (Heinrich) Gebhardt (1832–1899), a Methodist minister of Germany, spent some time in South America, North America, and England, accompanying R. Pearsail Smith as song leader at his evangelistic meetings in the holiness movement. Gebhardt wrote many original hymns and translated over 50 gospel hymns from English into German, most of them Moody and Sankey songs. They appeared in hymnals which were distributed in Europe and America in innumerable volumes.

38 She probably went to the Chicago Training School for Home, City, and Foreign Missions. See Chapter 3 on "The European Roots of the American Methodist Deaconess Movement."

39 Kraft-Buchmüller, *Die Frauen*, 42.

40 *Der Evangelist* 57 (1906), 39.

41 Kraft-Buchmüller, *Die Frauen*, 42f.

42 *Frauen-Missions-Freund* 25 (1910); *Der Evangelist* 53 (1902), 212.

43 Probably this was the Berea College in Kentucky, founded in 1855, and distinctive among post-secondary institutions for providing free education to students and for having been the first college in the Southern United States to be coeducational and racially integrated.

44 *Der Evangelist* 60 (1909), 425 and 65 (1914), 31–32, 256.

45 Verhandlungen der 21: Sitzung der Jährlichen Konferenz der Prediger der Bischöflichen Methodistenkirche in Deutschland, Nürnberg, 10–15 Juni 1914, 82.

46 Kraft-Buchmüller, *Die Frauen*, 42.

47 *Der Evangelist* 59 (1908), 544. Kraft-Buchmüller notes that her name was not mentioned in the report but all what was said fits to Martha Lebeus (*Die Frauen*, 42, fn 494).

48 Citation of the board minutes of June 1908, in Kraft-Buchmüller, *Die Frauen*, 43.

49 The Director's Report for 1909 (Kraft-Buchmüller, *Die Frauen*, 43). Gustav Junker (1884–1919) served as director of the Martins-Missions-Anstalt from 1895–1919.

50 The following biography is based on several articles: "Gehe du auch in den Weinberg, und was recht sein wird, soll dir werden," *Der Missionsbote* 53, 4 (1911), 25; Hanna Scharpf, "Wie Ich Missionarin Wurde," in *Rundbrief, Frauendienst* 20, 1 (1988), 17; and Karl Heinz Voigt, "Hanna Scharpff," in Biographisch-bibliographisches Kirchenlexikon, ed. Friedrich Wilhelm Bautz (Herzberg: Traugott Bautz, 2007), 27: 1188–1193.

51 Methodism mission work began in Korea in 1885. The first missionary was Henry Gerhard Appenzeller (1858–1902), a Swiss who had emigrated to the USA. The Korean mission badly needed a woman as a teacher after the death of Mary F. Scranton, an American pioneer missionary.

52 Ulrike Schuler, ed., Glaubenswege – Bildungswege: 150 Jahre theologische Ausbildung im deutschsprachigen Methodismus Europas (Kempten: Algäu, 2008), 210.

53 See the Collection in the Central Archives of the UMC in Germany, Reutlingen (file: Frauen O–Z).

54 Before the onset of World War One, by 1913, three additional missionaries were sent from Germany – all three deaconesses: Theodora Hanna, a Bethany sister was sent to Oran, Algeria; Emilie Wiesmüller and Anna Class, deaconesses of the Martha-Maria-Society, were sent to the German colony Bismarck-Archipel. The state of the research on these women is such that even basic portraits are impossible.

55 Verhandlungen der 35: Jährlichen Konferenz der Bischöflichen Methodistenkirche der Schweiz, Basel, 16.-20 Juni 1921, 122–123.

56 *Frauen in der Evangelisch-methodistischen Kirche*, 22–24.

57 Ibid., 23.

58 Verhandlungen der 36: Jährlichen Konferenz der Bischöflichen Methodistenkirche der Schweiz, Biel, 8–11 Juni 1922, 222–4. She also describes in great detail the educational steps required of European women training for mission service that were imposed by the WFMS in the USA.

59 In 1922 Lydia Sautter attended the Martins-Missions-Anstalt as a guest student but nothing is known about her time or experience in the seminary. Reports in the *Frauen-Missions-Freund* show that between 1924 and 1928 the question about the education and sending of missionaries was also discussed in other European countries and negotiated with the WFMS in the USA.

60 Report of Hanni Handschin, January 2001, in *Geschichte des Frauendienstes in den Ländern der Zentralkonferenz von Mittel- und Südeuropa. Arbeitsgruppe*

Frauendienst. Anlage 27b (14. Tagung der ZK-MSE 2001, Bülach, Schweiz) – unprinted, unpaginated photocopy.

61 Ibid.

62 Notes in the Collection provide hints about Lydia Urech, Central Archives of the UMC in Germany, Reutlingen, file Frauen O–Z.

63 Ibid., Lydia Urech is mentioned in the report of the commission for women mission and sister societies to the Swiss Annual Conference in 1922. At that time, she is on deputation at home and working in congregations. In that report other Swiss missionaries are named: Miss Frieda Stäubli in China; Miss Klara Kleiner in Bombay; Miss Martha Graf in China – on furlough; and three women who are in preparation for mission: Trudi Schläfli, Marguerite Perrelet, Martha Gertsch (cf. Verhandlungen der 42: Sitzung der Jährlichen Konferenz der Prediger der Bischöflichen Methodistenkirche, Oerlikon, 19–14 Juni 1928, 67–68.

64 Verhandlungen der zweiten Tagung der Zentralkonferenz des Mitteleuropäischen Sprengels der Bischöflichen Methodistenkirche, Berlin-Schöneberg, 23–28 September 1930, 49–50. The Central Conference of Middle Europe included Austria, Bulgaria, Germany, Hungary, Switzerland, and Yugoslavia (1925– 1936). The political changes in Germany later made it necessary for them to form a separate Central Conference for Germany.

65 Luella S. Nuelsen-Stroeter was born on August 25, 1875 and died October 14, 1933. John Louis Nuelsen (1867–1946) was a German-American bishop of the MEC and The Methodist Church, elected in 1908. He was a Methodist pastor, a college and seminary professor and theologian, and an author and editor. In 1912 he was assigned to Europe with residence in Zürich, Switzerland. In 1920 the European work was divided into three Episcopal Areas – Nuelsen remained in the Zürich Area.

66 Verhandlungen der 45: Sitzung der Jährlichen Konferenz der Prediger der Bischöflichen Methodistenkirche, Zürich 1, 16–21 Juni 1931, 428–31; cf. Schuler, "Frauen in der Evangelisch-methodistischen Kirche," 28.

67 See "Bericht des Missionsausschusses," *Verhandlungen* 1930, 101–105. The bylaws of these institutions are also published in this volume.

68 Today titled The World Federation of Methodist and Uniting Church Women.

69 Schuler, *Die Evangelische Gemeinschaft*, 103.

70 Her husband, Samuel P. Spreng (183–1946), was later elected Bishop for Germany.

71 *Frauen in der Evangelisch-methodistischen Kirche*, 44–6.

72 Johannes Schempp Jr. (1880–1955) studied theology in Reutlingen, Tübingen, and Berlin. After serving in congregations he became docent for systematic theology at the seminary of the EA in Reutlingen and succeeded his father there as director of the institution until 1952.

73 Typewritten leaflet with Elisabeth Schempp-Wahl's vita, copy obviously for her funeral (Collection of Obituaries, Central Archives of the UMC in Germany, Reutlingen, file Frauen O–Z). Translated by Ulrike Schuler.

74 Ibid.; this and the following citations.

75 Carl Wahl was the son of German immigrants to the USA. He graduated from North Central College in Naperville, Illinois, before he enrolled in the Evangelical Theological Seminary in Naperville (today part of Garrett Evangelical Theological Seminary in Evanston, Illinois). Upon completion of seminary he was ordained and prepared for China. Carl Wahl went overseas in 1916.

76 Ute Minor and Rosemarie Wenner, "Gemeinsames Engagement – Der Weltgebetstag," in *Mit Weisheit, Witz und Widerstand*, 295–305. Cf. Dorothe Sackmann, "Menschen, die bewegen – Luise Scholz (1890–1972)," *EmK Geschichte* 25, 2 (2004), 10–13.

Sources

Burkhardt, Friedemann. *Christoph Gottlob Müller und die Anfänge des Methodismus in Deutschland. Arbeiten zur Geschichte des Pietismus, Bd. 43.* Göttingen: Vandenhoeck & Ruprecht, 2003.

"Central Archives of The UMC in Germany", Friedrich-Ebert-Straße 31, Reutlingen.

Frauen in der Evangelisch-methodistischen Kirche Schweiz/Frankreich. Zürich: Self-published, 2000.

Gäbler, Ulrich, ed. *Geschichte des Pietismus.* 4 volumes. Göttingen: Vandenhoeck & Ruprecht, 2000–2004.

"Gehe du auch in den Weinberg, und was recht sein wird, soll dir werden." *Der Missionsbote* 53, 4 (1911): 25.

Geschichte des Frauendienstes in den Ländern der Zentralkonferenz von Mittel- und Südeuropa. Arbeitsgruppe Frauendienst. Anlage 27b (14. Tagung der ZK-MSE 2001, Bülach, Schweiz) – unprinted, unpaginated photocopy.

Kraft-Buchmüller, Irene. *Die Frauen in der Anfangszeit der bischöflichen Methodistenkirche in Deutschland: Eine Untersuchung der eigenkirchlichen Schriften von 1850 bis 1914. Beiträge zur Geschichte der Evangelisch-methodistischen Kirche, Bd. 41.* Stuttgart: Christliches Verlagshaus, 1992.

Mit Weisheit, Witz und Widerstand: Die Geschichte(n) von Frauen in der Evangelisch-Methodistischen Kirche. Stuttgart: Medienwerk der Evangelisch-methodistischen Kirche, 2003.

Nuelsen, D. John, Theophil Mann, and J. J. Sommer, eds. *Kurzgefasste Geschichte des Methodismus.* Bremen: Verlagshaus der Methodistenkirche GmbH, 1929.

Periodicals, 1870–1920: Der Evangelist, Frauen-Missions-Freund, Heathen Woman's Friend, Heiden-Frauen-Freund, Woman's Missionary Friend.

Sackmann, Dorothe. "Menschen, die bewegen – Luise Scholz (1890–1972)." *EmK Geschichte* 25, 2 (2004): 10–13.

Scharpf, Hanna. "Wie Ich Missionarin Wurde." *Rundbrief, Frauendienst* 20, 1 (1988): 17.

Schuler, Ulrike. *Die Evangelische Gemeinschaft: Missionarische Aufbrüche in gesellschaftspolitischen Umbrüchen.* Stuttgart: EmK Studien 1, 1998.

Schuler, Ulrike, ed. *Glaubenswege – Bildungswege: 150 Jahre Theologische Ausbildung im Deutschsprachigen Methodismus Europas.* Kempten: Algäu, 2008.

Steckel, Karl, and C. Ernst Sommer (ed.). *Geschichte der Evangelisch-MethodistischenKirche: Weg, Wesen und Auftrag des Methodismus unter Besonderer Berücksichtigung der Deutschsprachigen Länder Europas.* Christliches Verlagshaus: Stuttgart, 1982.

Thirty-third Annual Report of the Woman's Foreign Missionary Society. New York: Woman's Foreign Missionary Society of the Methodist Episcopal Church, 1903.

Verhandlungen der 21: Sitzung der Jährlichen Konferenz der Prediger der Bischöflichen Methodistenkirche in Deutschland. Nürnberg, Juni 10–15, 1914.

Verhandlungen der 25: Sitzung der Jährlichen Konferenz der Bischöflichen Methodistenkirche von Deutschland und der Schweiz. Pforzheim, Juli 22–28, 1880.

Verhandlungen der 26: Sitzung der Jährlichen Konferenz der Bischöflichen Methodistenkirche von Deutschland und der Schweiz. Winterthur, Juli 14–18, 1881.

Verhandlungen der 35: Jährlichen Konferenz der Bischöflichen Methodistenkirche der Schweiz. Basel, Juni 16–20, 1921.

Verhandlungen der 36: Jährlichen Konferenz der Bischöflichen Methodistenkirche der Schweiz. Biel, Juni 8–11, 1922.

Verhandlungen der 42: Sitzung der Jährlichen Konferenz der Prediger der Bischöflichen Methodistenkirche. Oerlikon, Juni 19–14, 1928.

Verhandlungen der 45: Sitzung der Jährlichen Konferenz der Prediger der Bischöflichen Methodistenkirche. Zürich 1, Juni 16–21, 1931.

Verhandlungen der zweiten Tagung der Zentralkonferenz des Mitteleuropäischen Sprengels der Bischöflichen Methodistenkirche. Berlin-Schöneberg, September 23–28, 1930.

Voigt, Karl Heinz. "Hanna Scharpff." In *Biographisch-Bibliographisches Kirchenlexikon*. Edited by Friedrich Wilhelm. Multi-volumes set. Herzberg: Traugott Bautz, 1970.

Weyer, Michael. *150 Jahre Evangelisch-Methodistische Kirche: Geschichte des Methodismus in den Deutschsprachigen Ländern*. Kehl am Rhein: Sadifa Medis, 2000.

6 Methodist women pioneers in Belgium, Czechoslovakia, and Poland

Paul W. Chilcote and Ulrike Schuler

Renee Thonger and Family, Methodist Missionaries to Belgium

Methodist women in Switzerland encouraged women in countries of their Central Conference to send inspirational stories about women to the Women's Society in their conferences. The women then circulated a duplicated collection of papers, *Geschichte des Frauendienstes* (History of the Women's Service) at the Central Conference of Central and Southern Europe in 2001.[1] In the introduction, Hanni Handschin, who at the time was chair of the Women's Society in Europe, wrote that the primary goal of this publication was "to record and cherish the history of our mothers and grandmothers in the church before it is lost [and] to make the contribution of women in our church visible – to know the past and understand the present much better."[2] The contributions, as one might assume, are very diverse. Some authors found it nearly impossible to recover any written material concerning these women. This was particularly true in former Communist countries where Methodists had to work underground. In other areas of Europe, many sources were destroyed during the two World Wars. But this collection has helped to recover some of the history related to Methodist women in several countries.

The 100th anniversary of the birth of the Methodist Mission Society in 1919 provided the impetus for the Methodist Episcopal Church (MEC) and the Methodist Episcopal Church, South (MECS) to negotiate comity agreements with regard to their work in Europe. The Board of Missions met in January 1920 to consider relief efforts in Europe, in particular, and designated Belgium, Czechoslovakia, and Poland as the areas of mission for the MECS. This mission activity revolved primarily around relief efforts to help these nations rebuild following the catastrophic destruction of the war. The role of women in these pioneering efforts remains an untold story. The *Geschichte des Frauendienste* is one of the more recent sources related to the activities of Methodist women, in addition to limited material discovered in missionary histories and records. In all three of these countries, the story of women pioneers remains fragmentary at best, and even the research in this essay only scratches the surface. The statement of O. E. Goddard, Foreign Secretary of the Board of Missions of the MECS, and one of the most respected missioners at that time, whetted our interest about and has inspired us to begin the process of uncovering this story: "In our missions in Belgium, Czechoslovakia, and Poland the women are our largest hope. They are more susceptible to gospel truth and are better leaders than their husbands and sons."[3]

Belgium

In 1816 the WMC established mission work in Brussels to parallel their nascent efforts in France.[4] Around the same time, the MECS developed a connection with Belgium as the consequence of their mission work in the Congo in Africa, which was a Belgian colony. Bishop James Cannon, Jr., in conjunction with his exploratory visits to the Congo mission, broke his journey with a stop in Europe and surveyed the relief needs in Belgium.[5] In 1920 they established two institutions in Uccle, an area in Brussels, an orphanage and a girls' school, named *Les Marronniers*, the only institution of its kind in the country at that time. Most certainly, women formed the core of those who engaged in teaching and social service ministries in these institutions. By 1924 there were approximately 200 girls enrolled in the school.[6] In 1921 the mission board bought a hospital, which stood in close proximity to the girl's school, in a cooperative effort with the Dutch Reformed Church. Soon thereafter they opened a nursing school. From these humble beginnings Methodism spread to Antwerp and Liège, other major cities of the nation, and to Ypres which had been destroyed almost entirely during World War One.

Willam G. Thonger, who formally organized all these efforts from as early as August 1922, served as superintendent of the Methodist mission.[7] He provided the following generic portrait of their endeavors:

> Many interesting details could be given about the methods used to bring the Gospel to the Belgian people with Gospel-tents, intensive open-air work, door to door Bible colportage and religious services in rented ball-rooms, drinking saloons and any other premises which could be secured.[8]

Given the fact that one of Thonger's primary interests revolved around the distribution of Christian literature, it is not surprising that he secured a building in the center of Brussels that served as a headquarters, bookstore, Bible house, and distribution site for the colporteur ministry. By 1930, the Belgian mission had become an Annual Conference. Given the nature of the various ministries in which the church was engaged, one can see how central the role of women would be, and it is not surprising to discover that the MECS deployed quite a number of women into this mission (see this list of missionaries at the close of this chapter).

From the correspondence of Maude Hayes, one of the missionaries sent to Brussels, we ascertain that the MECS deployed the women "in view of constructive relief work" for a minimum of two years.[9] The Hayes file contains letters of application for two other women, Margaret Quayle and Mary L. Tinny, and it would appear that these three women were the first missionaries sent to Belgium by the Woman's Foreign Missionary Society of the MECS (WFMSS). They agreed to a salary of $100 per month and accommodation. The mission board paid their travel expenses to their place of assignment and also allocated them $150 for personal equipment prior to sailing. While it is not possible to determine with certainty, given the fact that Maude received her education at Galloway College (Galloway Women's College in Searcy, Arkansas) and had worked as a teacher of mathematics, it is safe to assume that she would have worked at *Les Marronniers* in Uccle in the educational ministries of the mission. We know Ruth McCain, deployed several years later in 1924, was also identified specifically as a teacher. We can only assume that many of the other women taught at the girl's school as well.

It is clear from the records that if the women did not work in education, they supported the hospital in the areas of nursing and nurse's training.

Appointed to Brussels in 1922, Byrd Boehringer entered mission service with an exceptionally strong resume of training and service. Her primary interest seems to have been in the plan of the mission to develop a school to train indigenous nurses. A graduate of St. Luke's Hospital School for Nurses in St. Louis, Missouri, she had worked as a nursing instructor and supervisor, and spent two years with the American Red Cross in France during the war. She was also fluent in French and noted the great need in the French hospital for French-speaking nurses. She served, therefore, as one of the first training nurses in the hospital in Brussels.

Elizabeth Duncan, apparently caught in the same set of circumstances as Margaret Quayle, was expecting deployment to Poland.[10] But for reasons we are unable to ascertain, she ended up serving in Belgium, despite Quayle's onward journey to Poland.[11] She also came with a full portfolio of potential service. She had taught in both Young Men's Christian Association (YMCA) and Young Women's Christian Association (YWCA) schools before being appointed the YWCA Secretary in Europe, stationed in France for two years. Like her mission colleague, Byrd Boehringer, her fluency in French may have been the impetus for her to stay in Brussels; but she was also fluent in German which would have opened doors for her in Poland. Her primary interests were in relief and social work, motivated by her knowledge of post-war France, Belgium, and Poland, but one could easily see how her talents could have been used in the school, both in teaching and administration. Moreover, she had taught piano, having studied in Vienna in 1913–1914, prior to the war.

The Woman's Missionary Council divided the work in Belgium into Flemish and French Sections.[12] Mrs. W. Thomas, wife of a prominent missionary, served as secretary for the Flemish branch. In the midst of worldwide economic collapse and crisis, the women more than doubled their contributions from the previous year, raising nearly 25,000 Francs for the work of the mission in 1931.[13] Together with Renee Thonger, wife of the director of the mission, these two missionary's wives exerted considerable influence on the Methodist churches. Not only did they visit all the women's societies in the course of the year, they rendered both material and spiritual aid to those in need and assisted their husbands in the evangelistic work of the mission.[14] They organized an annual meeting of the societies on Ascension Day 1931 in Liège, which proved to be a highlight of their year. Unfortunately, as a consequence of the Great Depression, all American missionaries were recalled from Belgium in the coming years, due to the inability of the MECS to fund their work. We can only imagine the deep sorrow among this pioneer class of women missionaries when forced to leave this nascent work.

Czechoslovakia

Vilém Schneeberger wrote the first coherent chapter about Methodism in Czechoslovakia.[15] This area was long a part of the Austro-Hungarian Empire with the territories of Bohemia, Moravia, Slovakia, and Carpathian

Ruthenia until the empire eventually collapsed at the end of World War One and the new state, the Republic of Czechoslovakia, was founded. Schneeberger included absolutely no information about women in his account. His description of early Czech Methodism says nothing about women's activities or their involvement in the growth and spread of Methodism, and particularly, nothing about the suffering they endured. Typically, he focused on male clergy as the primary protagonists and on the decisions of boards or Conference Minutes and statistics with regard to growth or decline. Much remains obscure with regard to women.

Some of the earliest evidence about Methodist evangelism in this arena revolves around a former Czech theater director, Václav Pázdral, a colorful character who converted to Methodism and was educated allegedly at the Wesleyan Methodist *Missionshaus* in Waiblingen, Germany. He appears to have been ordained and was sent, in 1883, as a Methodist minister by an "American mission board" to Bohemia.[16] Pázdral may have also worked at some point in time as an evangelist under the auspices of Wesleyan Methodists. Persecution in a context dominated by the Roman Catholic Church and political upheaval, including the collapse of the Habsburg monarchy and simultaneous dislocation of Catholicism, add deeper levels of complexity to this story.

Czech emigrants, settling in the south of the USA, were affected by the mission work of the MECS, and submitted a request to the mission board not to forget their brothers and sisters in their homeland (Bohemia and Moravia). Most historians consider 1920 to be the official beginning of the Methodist church in Czechoslovakia and, as we shall see, women were there right from these beginnings. Bishop Paul Garber summarized the historical development in Czechoslovakia at that time according to the interweaving of political, national, and religious coherences:

> Because the Hapsburgs had forced Roman Catholicism in religion and autocracy in government upon the Czechoslovak people, it was felt by many in 1918 that release from the autocratic Hapsburg regime should involve freedom from the papacy. In a great "Free from Rome" movement, two million Czechs left the Roman Catholic Church between 1918 and 1926. Such a movement offered a great opportunity for Methodist evangelism.[17]

Robert Sledge reports that the delegation of the MECS guided by Bishop Cannon, including representatives of the Woman's Missionary Council, visited Czechoslovakia and met with the first and newly elected president, Tomáš Garrigue Masary, and the prime minister, Edouard Beneš, to offer "food for numbers of university students who had fled to Prague from Eastern Europe and clothing for Protestant ministers and their families."[18] When the statesmen promptly agreed, the church sent missionaries to the new nation. Schneeberger described some of the difficulties they encountered, particularly the refusal of many to welcome the foreigners in light of re-catholicization efforts, but also described some of the missionary activities. Several weeks of tent missions, later held during the cold season in school buildings, reached people and gave rise to the first congregation in Praha. He also reported the ministers' activities and the support received from abroad that sustained a growing Sunday school program, and choirs – where the only mention of women is made. He does not acknowledge the work of any women in this mission.

An account of Miroslava Procházková in the aforementioned collection of historical essays provides some initial impressions concerning the activities of the women.[19] In addition, Pavel Procházka, a contemporary Methodist who works at the Department of Theology and Christian Education at the Univerzita Mateja Bela v Banskej Bystrici, provided a report about women in Methodism in the Czech and Slovak Republics.[20] Both reports are based on sources like Minutes of Annual Conferences, church periodicals, and a certain "Chronicle of the United Methodist Church" written by Václav Našinec.[21] Concurring with the conclusions of Schneeberger, Procházková believes that the initial attempts to establish Methodism among the Czech peoples failed because "the field was not ripe." She describes the activities of the Czech immigrants in the USA who desired to support people in their homeland, also remembering the Moravian influence on the Wesleys with gratitude. In a letter to the Mission Board, dated February 5, 1919, Josef Dobeš also drew attention to this connection with earliest Methodism.[22] In March 1919 he received a letter from the mission board inquiring as to whether he would be willing to return to his homeland as a missionary. He answered tersely that "he and his wife considered the invitation an answer to their prayers."[23] Upon the return of this Czech MECS minister to his native land, he founded the first Methodist congregation there in November 1920 in Praha Vršovice. Dobeš began his work there with an open-air tent meeting as he had done in Texas.

According to archived records of the MECS Mission Board, three women were appointed that same year to Prague: Emilie Dobešová, Mrs. Bartáková, and Mrs. Neill, all minister's wives with deep connections with Czechoslovakia.[24] Both Mrs. Dobešová, co-founder of Methodism with her husband, and Mrs. Bartáková figure prominently in the unfolding of the Czech mission. We know nothing of Mrs. Neill other than her name. Mrs. Bartáková graduated from Fall's Business College in Nashville, Tennessee, and had worked as an assistant secretary and treasurer at John E. Brown College in Siloam Springs, Arkansas, before entering missionary service. Shortly before the Munich crisis of 1938, when Czechoslovakia was dismembered under the expansion of German hegemony, Mrs. Bartáková and her three children returned to the USA. She remained there during the war years, was reunited with her husband in 1942, and returned to Europe in 1946 where she resumed her mission work alongside her husband in Vienna.[25] She assisted her husband in his pastoral work – teaching in Sunday schools, arranging

fund raising, and engaging in organic evangelistic activities, alongside raising her families.

The women were active in the development of women's missionary societies in their places of assignment and an important part of their work
revolved around the cultivation of indigenous women's leadership for the
church. The first women's missionary society was founded in Praha in 1921,
almost simultaneously with the beginning of the mission work. The following year, the society elected Emilie Dobešová as its chair. The women visited
sick and poor people from house to house and collected money for various
ministries and concerns such as church construction, the preacher's fund,
and a fund for the poor.[26] They were creative in their efforts to raise money.
For example, they prepared evening buffets and always tithed their profits
for the poor. They collected money for church buildings, furnished apartments for single ministers, and raised money for the minister's salary. They
gave money for shoes, clothes, books, and school supplies, and supported
an orphanage in the community. The women's societies, which had grown to
70 members by 1924, held a spiritual meeting every Monday. Two women
are named because of their official positions in the church, but no information is available to provide even biographical sketches for either of them.
Mrs. Vančurová became the secretary of the Sunday school of the church
and M. Bartáková, wife of the missionary, was the secretary of the Epworth
League, the youth ministry of the nascent church. In 1927 the women's
society in Prague Ječná advertised an invitation for reading evenings in the
church magazine. They founded a library in the church and wanted to build
up a center for "good Czech literature" to combat the "bad literature" that
many consumed. They also viewed this as an important strategy in the cultivation of their native language.[27]

The ministry of two other women missionaries deserves attention. Arrena
Carroll Collyer, born in Dayton, Ohio, graduated from the Wesley Female
Institute in Staunton, Virginia, and Scarritt Bible and Training School in
Nashville, Tennessee. In 1911 she married Rev. Charles Thomas Collyer
of London, England, who had served as a missionary in Korea.[28] She was
appointed to Prague in 1921. More is known about the husband of Mrs. D.
P. Melson than about her service as a missionary.[29] Like Arrena's husband,
Melson's husband also had previous missionary experience in Asia, namely,
in Japan. We know that the two served together in Czechoslovakia for a
decade, from 1923 to 1933, and that Rev. Melson was appointed superintendent to a three-year term in 1924 and functioned simultaneously as
the mission treasurer. From 1924 until their departure Melson served as
President of the Biblical Seminary in Prague where young Methodist Czech
preachers received their training. So Mrs. Melson could have been nowhere
other than in the center of all the pioneering developments of the Methodist
Church. Unfortunately, we know nothing other than this.[30]

On August 2, 1924, Mrs. Bartáková received an official letter from
Mrs. Stephenson, the president of the Woman's Missionary Council,

reporting that the Czech women's societies were approved by the Council and that Mrs. Abiline in Texas was appointed the corresponding secretary. With regard to the financial arrangements for their work, they decided that, from the missions donations, two-thirds should be transferred to the Woman's Missionary Council and one-third earmarked for the work in Czechoslovakia. Profits from bazaars or buffets were to be used for mission work among the congregations.

According to Emilie Dobešová, Bishop Beauchamp appointed her officially as secretary of the Woman's Missionary Society at the Annual Conference in 1925.[31] She described how she had helped to launch and advise the societies, which, according to the report to the Annual Conference in 1930, had grown to 26 with 480 members. In that year they collected 48,778 Kč. Emilie expressed her regrets for not having done as much in missions for other countries; she very faithfully discharged her responsibilities, however, for Czechoslovakia. On April 21, 1930 the women's societies held their first conference in Prague Ječná, at which 22 of 26 delegates from the societies attended.[32] At this conference, the women's societies officially united on the Conference level, electing officers and representatives. Emilie Dobešová was chosen to chair the organization, with M. Vančurová, A. Malačová, and M. Ničková serving as English secretary, Czech secretary, and cashier respectively, and K. Faltová and B. Matěnová appointed at large members.[33]

At the Second Women's Conference, held in May 1931 in Praha-Strasnice, a Czech couple, Hazel and Alexander Reid, who had served in Praha from 1928 to 1929, was approved for missionary service in the Congo. The Woman's Missionary Society had enough funds in hand to suffice for two annual salaries. On June 1, 1932 Mrs. Dobešová reported in the church periodical that the Society had the great joy to have sent financial support directly to brother Reid which would make it possible for them to employ two African pastors. The women contributed 1,200 Kč annually to this project and then raised their support to 1,500 Kč in 1937. The church also worked in the Karpathos-Ukraine, supporting a colporteur with an annual stipend of 200 Kč. Procházková underscored the idea that this mission project was borne by prayers. The women stipulated the second Sunday in February as a "Mission Day" with a special program and all proceeds to support their programs. Most of these efforts supported the social work of the church, such as the orphanage and a residence for the elderly in Horni Pocernice, where Mrs. and Mr. Zloch served as house-parents, and Castle Týn nad Vltavou and Kamp Poste near Bechyne. After the church union in the USA in 1939, which reunited the MEC, MECS, and Methodist Protestant Church, the name of the women's organization was changed in Czechoslovakia to "Christian Service of Sisters."

According to Procházková, the Annual Conferences reports indicate that young Czech women became deaconesses, but they received their education through other Protestant churches. There is no evidence, however, in terms of when this happened or where, specifically, they were trained. According to the statistics for the MECS in Czechoslovakia, the initial increases in membership in the early 1920s was eclipsed by a large decline of more than 7,000 members in 1928. Sledge explains this change in relation to differences in the method of counting members (probationary and full members were separately listed from that year onwards), but he also points to the challenges Czechs Methodists encountered with regard to the traditional lifestyle of their contemporaries. In his view, religious affiliation rather than discipleship tended to be the norm in the Czech culture, and becoming a church member was not taken as seriously as a life-transforming conversion. Moreover, in this context, he concludes that genuine conversion made a person's life much more difficult and isolated. Some who had undergone such radical change were driven from their homes for joining the Methodist Church.[34] The Great Depression must have affected the ministry of the women in the church as well, but information related to both indigenous women and expatriate missionaries beyond this point remains elusive.

Poland

As in the other two countries under discussion, the MECS entered Poland primarily for the purpose of providing relief following World War One because the conditions in the newly founded republic were so appalling. Poland experienced restoration and consolidation after the Paris Peace conference in 1918, having been segmented for about 150 years. Bishop Cannon and his team of observers experienced the dire straits of this country during their visit. The destructive consequences of the war were catastrophic. Cold, hunger, and disease prevailed – millions of men, women, and children were destitute and many were starving. "Cannon was deeply moved," Sledge reports, "by the plight of the Polish people."[35] As with regard to Belgium and Czechoslovakia, the bishop directly contacted the president of the state, Josef Piludski, and "came away very impressed by the man."[36] They agreed that their first priority would be the emergency relief of the stricken nation.

This was not the first exposure of the Polish people, however, to the Methodists. In 1876 the Wesleyan Methodists channeled evangelistic work there through the director of the *Missionshaus* (mission house) in Cannstatt, Germany.[37] Around the same time, as early as 1880, the Church of the United Brethren in Christ (UB) tradition launched a mission effort in Stargard. Evangelism in the surrounding area led to *Stubenversammlungen* (room assemblies), which then grew into a little awakening that spawned a UB community in as many as 14 villages around Beweringen. This evangelistic wave also spread to Stettin, Posen, and other cities.[38] As a consequence of the union of the Wesleyan Methodists with the MEC in Germany, much of this work shifted to the MEC in the late nineteenth century, especially in light of the ongoing political disruptions associated with this region. Tensions were always high between the native peoples and Germans, but when the German territories of Posen and West-Prussia were ceded to Poland in

1920 and 1922, respectively, in addition to Upper Silesia, the Germans left or were expelled.

In 1920, Bishop Cannon of the MECS and Bishop Nuelsen of the MEC coordinated their efforts for a major relief program for Poland partnered with the League of Nations.[39] Sledge reports that "George W. Twynham was the first administrator of the program, assisted from time to time by Josef Dobeš of the Czechoslovakia mission," and simply mentions that the women's missionary societies were enlisted early in these efforts.[40] Boguslawa Puslecka, however, maintains that the mission board actually invited the Woman's Missionary Society to organize these humanitarian efforts for the Polish people.[41] She reports that the MEC and the UB both had branches of women's societies in many of the congregations and also on the level of the Annual Conference.[42] She also explains that Daisy Davies was put in charge of the entire aid agency of the church. Davies was well positioned for this work "as field secretary of the Woman's Board of Foreign Missions, as manager and also field secretary of the Council, and as a member of the Board of Missions," according to Council records.[43]

Puslecka maintains that Davies was absolutely central to the success of this mission and "none of these developments would have occurred without the help of the women in the church."[44] This work entailed a number of critical facets:

> In a campaign directed by Daisy Davies of the Board of Missions, the women sent more than 25,000 letters soliciting clothing and other supplies for Polish relief. This effort garnered more than a million items of clothing at Newport News, Virginia, where the material was stored in a War Department warehouse until it could be packed for shipment by volunteers from the area churches.[45]

A special ship was chartered to transport these material goods to Poland.[46] Davies established a number of strategic locations across Poland that functioned as Methodist relief stations and distribution centers for the poor and needy. Just in the city of Warsaw alone ten soup kitchens were feeding thousands of people daily.[47] The Board of Missions sent Davies twice to this region of the world where she not only spearheaded this relief work, but also had an important role in actually establishing these missions. According to the records, "as an evangelist, she has brought the light, even the Light of the world, to many who sat in darkness."[48]

As was the case in Belgium and Czechoslovakia, the WFMSS had sent a host of women missionaries to Poland in 1920. Margaret Quayle, the daughter of a MEC bishop, worked with Polish girls in Warsaw and the surrounding area. Jessye Branscomb worked in Wilno and "ran a soup kitchen which fed a thousand or more people daily."[49] Her father was the director of the Methodist mission Centenary. On the basis of Branscomb's missionary file, one can see how she would have had great versatility on the mission field, being well-versed in educational, secretarial, and medical skills, and having worked for some time with the Red Cross. In addition to Mrs. M. S. Baker, about whom nothing can be ascertained, three preacher's wives completed this initial cohort of women missionaries: Mrs. H. K. King, Mrs. Charles Morgan, and Mrs. George Twynham.[50] This last missionary was the wife of the man Sledge identifies as the director of the relief efforts and, while no other information is available to us concerning the work of these women, they would have had a major role, one can only assume, in this work alongside Daisy Davies.

In 1921 three more missionaries were added to the original six. Josephine Bartlett served as a nurse in Klarysew, having worked over a year in the US Army as a specialist in surgical dressings.[51] In addition to the responsibilities in health care ministries, she established an orphanage that was serving 120 children before the end of that year. Eunice McKinney, also a nurse, arrived at the same time, so these two must have collaborated in these efforts.[52] Minnie Tiller Woodard, a married missionary, spent nine years in Poland before being reassigned to the work in Belgium in 1930 with her husband, Fred.[53] In 1922, a deaconess, Friede Lentz, arrived. Her qualifications for her role were unique and of special importance since she was a Polish woman with German origins and was bi-lingual.[54] In her account, Puslecka emphasizes the role of Mrs. Berezowska, a native Pole who was employed by the WFMSS as a much needed social worker.

The records of the MECSS Women's Missionary Council related to Poland are generally segmented into the work in Warsaw and in Wilno. Warsaw, perhaps obviously, functioned as the hub of mission operations in Poland. Wilno, on the other hand, was the base of operations for a special mission to the so-called White Russians.[55] A lengthy discussion of this particular group from one of the women missionaries provides great insight into the plight of this particular group and the nature of the work among them:

> They are Ruthenians and are called "White" because they are a white race. The White Russians in Harbin are Russian people and are called "White" in contrast to the Soviet Russian "Reds." The White Russians in Poland have preserved their language in spite of the fact that for centuries they have been dominated in turn by Russia, Germany, Lithuania, and Poland, and each of these have compelled them to use the language of the country. For this reason they do not have a literature, and the whole of the Bible has not yet been translated into their language. They have been so sorely oppressed that they are suspicious of everybody's motives, therefore, our workers have had a hard time to gain their confidence and establish work among them. In their eagerness for a national existence of their own, they resemble the Koreans. They are constantly under the suspicion of the Polish authorities.[56]

It can easily be said that mission service to these White Russians dominates the reports from 1928 onwards. The report of the women's work, delivered at the annual Polish Mission Conference, held in Klarysew in July 1928, documents that the Woman's Missionary Council opened its work in the Wilno District to this group in September 1927.[57] With regard to this effort, five women missionaries stand out: Constance Rumbough of Lynchburg, Virginia (from 1927); Sallie Lewis Brown of Sussex, Virginia (from 1927); Eurania Pyron of Jackson, Mississippi (from 1928); Ruth Lawrence (from 1930); and Dolores Norene Robken (from 1931). The information related to their lives and work is sketchy at best. There are conflicting records and some of the more contemporary accounts seem to be at odds with earlier reports, but a basic portrait of their missionary endeavors can be pieced together from several sources. Constance Rumbough and Sallie Brown were transferred from the Russian-Siberian Mission in Harbin, China, probably early in 1927, with specific instructions to work among the White Russians.[58] They had spent time learning the Russian language, but found it necessary, under the unique circumstances, to learn both Polish and the White Russian dialect as well. Language study, as might well be expected, pervades their early reports back to the Council. It is likely that Eurania Pyron, who we know arrived in Poland in April 1927, rendezvoused with the other two members of this energetic team later in Wilno. She writes:

> I arrived in Wilno in the early morning of August 10 [1927]. From the beginning, the people, the work, and the city of Wilno appeals to me; therefore, I am very happy here. The days have passed so quickly that I can hardly realize I have been here five months already.[59]

She provides this portrait of her life in the White Russian District:

> I have been having Polish lessons daily. Each morning in the week except Monday I study for two consecutive hours with my teacher, and then from two to three hours I study along, thus trying to spend no less than five hours each day in language study. This study consumes the greater part of my time; however, once a week for an hour and a half I give English lessons to our Polish pastor here. Because of the lack of a knowledge of the language I am unable to do active work, but often I do have the opportunity to play the piano for our services in the chapel and also to make occasional talks for our Missionary Society and Epworth League. For all of these opportunities of service for Christ I am most thankful, and my constant prayer is that I may serve Him with all my heart, soul, mind, and strength.[60]

In November 1927 Sallie and Constance began working with a small group of women, organized a Sunday school program, held monthly meetings in the Methodist chapel, and provided a Bible lesson each week.[61] With the church having had earlier difficulties in cultivating indigenous women's leadership, these new missionaries hoped that Polish women involved in these activities would become a core group around which to develop women's societies, and their hope seems to have been well-founded. The first women's society had been founded in Lwow (Lemberg) in 1924 with limited success, but by the end of 1927 there were 12 organized Methodist congregations and seven women's societies with a total membership of nearly 150.[62] By 1930 the societies had grown in number to 21, all of them represented when a conference was held in Wilno that year, and at which event they changed their name to "Women's Service in Poland."[63]

In January 1928 the missionaries opened a school dormitory in Wilno which accommodated 12 girls from the countryside who studied at the White Russian gymnasium. A Mrs. Nausner served as house mother, with Constance Rumbough providing daily spiritual direction for the girls.[64] Soon thereafter they took over the supervision of a similar dormitory that had been set up in Radoszkowicze two years earlier. They visited the girls there once a month, meeting with them on a Saturday evening and providing a chapel service with biblical instruction on the Sunday. As a consequence of these activities, Constance reported: "At least people are not so suspicious of us, and we have found some real friends in this time. Certainly it will be no easy task to interpret Christ through social evangelism here."[65]

At the annual meeting of the women, held in July 1928, the mission requested that that board make provision for another missionary who would be able to give all her attention to the Polish work. Ruth Lawrence, who arrived in 1930, might have been the answer to this prayer.[66] Given the growth of the women's societies and the extension of these ministries, the women missionaries in positions of leadership felt all the more acutely the need for someone to organize all the various facets of the work and to train leaders from among the indigenous women of the churches. Given their successes related to the local schools and the accommodation of students, they opened yet another girl's dormitory in Kleck, a small border village about 75 miles from Wilno in 1931.[67] But their nemesis in this arena was always the weakness of the schools to which these hostels were attached, and when hard economic times fell on the young nation as a consequence of the Great Depression, the dissolution of the schools led ineluctably to the abandonment of the girl's dormitories and those ministries.

Ruth Lawrence and a new missionary, Norene Robken, who arrived in 1931, carried on the work at Wilno in the wake of virtual economic collapse and under serious duress, while Sallie Brown and Eurania Pyron shifted the focus of their attention to Warsaw. In one of her communications, Lawrence confessed that their work "seemed an impossible task, physically and mentally."[68] But she also reveled in small triumphs, reporting that "the most brilliant and capable girl in the *Internat* (dormitory) joined our Church. She is a strong Christian who can brave the criticism and taunts of both acquaintances and school authorities without flinching."[69] Indeed, the 1930s witnessed a marked decline in the Polish mission. Sledge points to a number of causes: the opposition of the Roman Catholic Church, resistance from the atheistic Bolshevists who encroached across the border from the

Soviet Union, and ethnic rivalries which created difficulties among congregations.[70] Like the work of the women in Belgium and Czechoslovakia, the economic decline that swept the world, in addition to the growth of new political forces that disrupted Europe in 1939, wreaked havoc on the life of the Methodist communities.

Women Missionaries of the Methodist Episcopal Church, South Belgium (1920–1933)

Name	Post	Events	Sources
Margaret Quayle	Brussels	assigned (a) 1920	later to Poland
Lucille Burlew	Brussels	a 1920	
Elizabeth Duncan	Brussels	b 1889	UM Archives 1273–1–1:55
		a 1920	
Maude Hayes	Brussels	born (b) 1876	UM Archives 1273–1–1:84
		a 1920	
Blanche Holland	Brussels	a 1920	
		listed (l) 1921	
Mary Tinny	Brussels	a 1920	
Mrs. George Twynham	Brussels	a 1920	UM Archives #69 ID 2318
(Rev. George Twynham)		listed (l) 1920	later to Poland
Minnie Tiller Woodard	Brussels	a 1921	UM Archives #73 ID 2482
(Fred Woodard)			
Byrd Boehringer	Brussels	b 1894	French-speaking
		a 1922	
Edith Clara Rugby	Brussels	a 1922	UM Archives #71 ID2445
		l 1928	
Mrs. W. Thomas	Brussels	a 1922	
(Rev. W. Thomas)		l 1938	
Renee Thonger	Brussels	a 1922	UM Archives #64 ID2271
(Mr. W. G. Thonger)		l 1938	
Mrs. W. G. Wilmot	Brussels	a 1922	
(Rev. W. G. Wilmot)		l 1938	
Elizabeth Dean	Brussels	a 1922	
Ruth McCain	Brussels	born (b) 1894	teacher
		a 1924	
		l 1927	

Czechoslovakia (1920–1938)

Name	Post	Events	Sources
Mrs. M. Bartáková	Prague	born (b) 1888	UM Archives #19 ID 357
(Rev. Joseph Paul Bartak)		appointed (a) 1920	
		died (d) 1953	
Mrs. Emilie Dobešová	Prague	a 1920	
(Rev. Josef Dobeš)		retired (r) 1939	
Mrs. J. L. Neill	Prague	a 1920	UM Archives 1470–5–8:14
(Rev. J. L. Neill)			

(*Continued*)

Name	Post	Events	Sources
Arrena Carroll Collyer (Rev. Charles Thomas Collyer)	Prague	b 1870 married (m) 191 a 1921 f (furloughed) 1923 d 1974	UM Archives #28 ID 658
Miriam P. Draper	Prague	a 1921	
Mrs. Henry Ibser (Rev. Ibser)	Prague	a 1921	
Mrs. D. P. Melson (Rev. Melson)	Prague	a 1923 listed (l) 1928 f 1933	UM Archives 1470–5–4:71
Mrs. Vaclav Vancura	Prague	a 1924	
Hazel Reid (Alexander Reid)	Prague Congo	a 1928 a 1929	

Poland (1920–1939)

Name	Post	Events	Sources
Margaret Quayle	Warsaw	assigned (a) 1920	
Jessye Branscomb	Warsaw	born (b) 1890 a 1920	UM Archives 1273– 1–1:26
Mrs. H. K. King (Rev. H. K. King)	Warsaw	a 1920	UM Archives #46 ID 1382
Mrs. Charles Morgan (Dr. Charles M. Morgan)	Warsaw	a 1920	
Mrs. George Twynham (Rev. George Twynham)	Warsaw	a 1920 listed (l) 1920	UM Archives #69 ID 2318
Josephine Bartlett	Warsaw	b 1895 a 1921	UM Archives 1273– 1–1:14 nurse
Eunice McKinney	Warsaw	a 1921	UM Archives 1273– 1–1:14 nurse
Minnie Tiller Woodard (Fred Woodard)	Warsaw Brussels	a 1921 a 1930	UM Archives #73 ID 2482
Frieda Lentz [Gamble?] [Thomas J. Gamble?]	Lwow	a 1928	deaconess
Mrs. M. S. Baker	Warsaw	a 1923	
Florence May Chambers (Rev. Edmund Chambers)	Warsaw	a 1923	UM Archives #27 ID 600
Mrs. Gaither P. Warfield (Rev. Warfield)	Klarysew Warsaw	a 1924 a 1936	
Mrs. Ruby Pearl Hardt (Rev. Charles T. Hardt)	Warsaw	a 1926	UM Archives 1470– 4–2:26 teacher
Constance Rumbough	Wilno	a 1927	Trans from China
Sallie Lewis Brown(e)	Wilno	a 1927	Trans from China

Name	Post	Events	Sources
Eurania Pyron	Wilno	a 1927	
[Jackson?]	Katowice	a 1933	
Mrs. Willard Cram	?	a 1928	
(Willard Winston Cram)			
Luiza May	Warsaw	a 1928	
Doris Anne Gibson	Warsaw	a 1930	UM Archives 1469–
(Rev. Foye Gibson)			3–5:29
Ruth Lawrence	Wilno	a 1930	
Norene Robken	Wilno	a 1931	
Ellen C. Newby	Warsaw	a 1939	contract

Notes

1 Arbeitsgruppe Frauendienst, *Geschichte des Frauendienstes in den Ländern der Zentralkonferenz von Mittel- und Südeuropa* (Bülach: Schweiz, privately circulated, 2001). Not all the material in this collection conforms to the highest standards of scholarly research and is presented in more of an oral narrative style. Nevertheless, we feel that it is important to include this narrative sourcing with hopes that documentary evidence will be discovered to either confirm or correct aspects of these oral traditions. Comparing this material with other sources at hand, we have been able to confirm much of this information. In a number of cases, however, the stories told here do not have documentary support to confirms the claims, and maybe never will.

2 Ibid., 2.

3 *Twenty-second Annual Report of the Woman's Missionary Council of the Methodist Episcopal Church South, 1931–1932* (Nashville: Publishing House Methodist Episcopal Church South, 1932), 119.

4 For a basic account of Methodist mission in Belgium, see Patrick Ph. Streiff, *Der Methodismus in Europa im 19. und 20. Jahrhundert* (Stuttgart: EmKGM 50, 2003); cf. Robert W. Sledge, "Five Dollars and Myself" in *The History of the Mission of the Methodist Episcopal Church, South, 1845–1939* (New York: GBGM Books, 2005), 369–371.

5 See his account of such a visit, for example, in *Nineteenth Annual Report of the Woman's Missionary Council of the Methodist Episcopal Church South, 1928–1929* (Nashville: Publishing House Methodist Episcopal Church South, 1929), 16. Bishop Cannon proceeded on to Czechoslovakia and Poland, as well, to survey the needs in those countries.

6 Streiff, *Der Methodismus in Europa*, 218.

7 Thonger was born in Paris, France, of an English father and Huguenot mother. Educated at the Sorbonne he received his theological training at the French Reformed Theological Seminary in Paris. By all accounts, he was an outstanding Protestant leader in Europe and a brilliant scholar. Under his supervision, thousands of copies of the Bible and portions of the scriptures were sold by Methodist colporteurs, who were hired to distribute Bibles and other Christian literature in a ministry that took them, literally, door-to-door.

8 Paul Neff Garber, *The Methodists of Continental Europe* (New York: Editorial Department, Division of Education and Cultivation, 1949), 27–28.

9 Administrative Files of the Methodist Episcopal Church, South, The Methodist Archives, Drew University, Madison, New Jersey, File 1273–1–1:84.

10 Ibid., 1273–1–1: 55.
11 Missionaries, both men and women, were also posted to Belgium temporarily to engage in language study before making the journey to their final destination, but this generally meant the Congo (see *Nineteenth Report of the Woman's Missionary Council*, 17).
12 *Twenty-second Report of the Woman's Missionary Council*, 116.
13 Ibid.
14 Ibid.
15 Vilém Schneeberger, "Der Methodismus in der Tschechoslowakei," in *Methodismus in Osteuropa: Polen – Tschechoslowakei – Ungarn, Friedrich Hecker, Vilém Schneeberger, and Karl Zehrer* (Stuttgart: EmKGM 51, 2004), 30–166. The chapter is based on two Festschriften about Methodism in Czechoslovakia – for the tenth and fiftieth anniversary. The last was duplicated and circulated as well. He also used some sources from church periodicals and scattered material. In 1993 Czechoslovakia was divided into the Česká republika (the Czech Republic) and Slovenská republika (the Slovak Republic).
16 Schneeberger mentions that Pázdral's studies and ordination are undocumented ("Der Methodismus in der Tschechoslowakei," 34). It is not exactly clear which "American board" is suggested, but it is most likely the American Board of Commissioners of Foreign Mission that worked in Eastern Europe and also together with Methodists.
17 Garber, *Methodists of Continental Europe*, 29.
18 Sledge, *Five Dollars and Myself*, 364.
19 Miroslava Procházková, "Frauendienst in Tschechien und in der Slowakei, Bratislava, im März 2000," in *Arbeitsgruppe, Geschichte des Frauendienstes*, 17–19.
20 Email from Pavel Procházka to Ulrike Schuler, October 8, 2015; cf. ibid.
21 Discussions in this material include Křestanský Buditel, Metodista, Oběžník, Slovo a život, Ohnisko. These sources are all in Czech or Slovene languages. While this material will be helpful for future research, the scholarly standards are insufficient for proper documentation and are difficult to validate.
22 Josef Dobeš was born on February 23, 1885 in Prague. He died on November 13, 1957 in Prague. Dobeš had migrated to the USA before World War One, joined the MECS, and served congregations in the Czech-speaking regions of central Texas. He was appointed 1920 to 1939 when he retired. December 10, 1939 the Dobeš couple retired and went back to the USA to stay with their children.
23 Procházková, "*Frauendienst in Tschechien und in der Slowakei*," 18.
24 Mission Biographical Files of the Methodist Episcopal Church, South, The Methodist Archives, Drew University, Madison, New Jersey, File #19 ID 357, and Administrative Files, MECS, Methodist Archives, File 1470–5–8:14.
25 J. P. Bartak (1887–1964), a naturalized US citizen from Czechoslovakia, was educated at Southwestern University (BA), Vanderbilt School of Theology (BD), and the University of Chicago (MA). In 1925 Southwestern University conferred the honorary degree of Doctor of Divinity upon him. He served as superintendent in Vienna, Austria, and Prague. He was arrested by the German Gestapo when the war with the USA was declared, but was later exchanged under the articles of war, arriving in New York on the "diplomatic ship," Drottningholm, on June 1, 1942 (ibid.).
26 Procházková speaks of 6,000 Kč for a church building and 500 Kč for the preacher's fund but not saying when and where ("*Frauendienst in Tschechien und in der Slowakei*," 18).
27 Procházková, "*Frauendienst in Tschechien und in der Slowakei*," 18.

28 Mission Biographical Files, MECS, Methodist Archives, File #28 ID 658.

29 Administrative Files, MECS, Methodist Archives, File 1470-5-4:71.

30 We have not been able to recover any information concerning the other four women assigned to Prague by the MECS Mission Board (see list of missionaries at the close of this chapter) and have no way to determine the nature of their service.

31 This is an English translation by Ulrike Schuler of the citation that Miroslava Procházková himself translated from a Czech source into German. It is doubtful that "elected" is correct.

32 Listed are Bratislava, Jihlava, Ostrava, Praha-Strašnice, Praha-Vršovice, Vrútky, Klatovy, Litoměřice, Most, Plzeň, Praha, Ústí nad Labem und Lovosice, Velvary, České Budějovice, Lomnice nad Loučnicí, Protivín, Sedlčany, Sedlec, Stráž nad Nežárkou, Týn nad Vltavou (Procházková unpublished paper sent by Pavel Procházka).

33 She remained in this position until 1940 when Mrs. Matěnová was elected.

34 Sledge, *Five Dollars and Myself*, 367.

35 Ibid.

36 Ibid., 368.

37 Streiff, *Der Methodismus in Europa*, 218.

38 See Karl Zehrer, "Der deutsche Methodismus im heutigen Polen von den Anfängen bis 1945," in *Methodismus in Osteuropa*, 9. For the origins of Methodism in Poland, see the full chapter, 9–29.

39 See Chapter 5 for information on Nuelsen. Cf. John D. Nuelsen, Theophil Mann, and J. J. Sommer, eds. *Kurzgefasste Geschichte des Methodismus* (Bremen: Verlagshaus der Methodistenkirche GmbH, 1929). The MECS assumed continuing responsibility for those districts that were mainly German (Posen, Kolmar, Graudenz, Danzig) through the North German Annual Conference (see Zehrer, "Der deutsche Methodismus im heutigen Polen."

40 Sledge, *Five Dollars and Myself*, 368.

41 Boguslawa Puslecka, "Frauendienst in Polen," in Arbeitsgruppe, *Geschichte des Frauendienstes*, 13–16. Puslecka became president of the Women Service in Poland in 1991.

42 Ibid. These societies, of course, became part of the MECS work in 1920 when the southern Church was given responsibility for this arena of mission service.

43 *Nineteenth Report of the Woman's Missionary Council*, 148. Davies had represented the Council at the World Missionary Conference in Edinburgh in 1910 and was held in high esteem among the leadership of the various Methodist church families.

44 Ibid.

45 Sledge, *Five Dollars and Myself*, 368.

46 Garber, *The Methodists of Continental Europe*, 29.

47 Ibid.

48 *Nineteenth Report of the Woman's Missionary Council*, 148.

49 Administrative Files, MECS, Methodist Archives, File 1273-1-1: 26.

50 See Mission Biographical Reference Files, Methodist Archives, #69 ID 2318 and #46 ID 1382.

51 Administrative Files, Methodist Archives, 1273-1-1: 14. Josephine was highly education, an amazing linguist who had studied Latin, Greek, German, and French. She trained as a nurse at St. Thomas Hospital Training School in Nashville, Tennessee, before having been deployed by the Army in the Medical Corps. A note in her file, written by her nursing superintendent, reflects something of the "backdrop" related to women in mission after World War One: "Bartlett," she writes, "has recently undergone a heavy sorrow, by the death rather suddenly, of

the one she intended to marry, and this has brought her on a depression which might be too great under a heavy strain." Klarysew is about ten miles outside the capital city of Warsaw.

52 Ibid. Material on McKinney is actually included in Bartlett's file.
53 Mission Biographical Files, MECS, Methodist Archives, File #73 ID 2482.
54 Puslecka, "Frauendienst in Polen," 14.
55 Present-day Vilnius in Lithuania. The city was known as Vilna among the Russians and Jews, but is Wilno in the Polish language.
56 *Nineteenth Report of the Woman's Missionary Council*, 62.
57 Ibid., 321.
58 Ibid., 61–62. The understanding of the Board of Mission, apparently, was that they were simply shifting funds from one section of the world to another to support the same people, which proved to be an erroneous assumption.
59 Ibid., 321.
60 Ibid.
61 This information, as well as that which follows, is drawn from their report in Ibid., 321–322.
62 Present-day Lviv, the largest city in the western Ukraine; Lwow is the Polish spelling of this Ruthenian capital.
63 Puslecka, "Frauendienst in Polen," 15 cf. *Twenty-second Report of the Woman's Missionary Council*, 119.
64 Sledge reports that this enterprise flourished for a time in spite of considerable opposition from the community. "But changing ethnic populations in the area," he observes, "eventually led to it being abandoned after about ten years" (*Five Dollars and Myself*, 369).
65 *Nineteenth Report of the Woman's Missionary Council*, 322.
66 Two women were appointed to Poland in 1930, but the other, Doris Anne Foye, was sent to Warsaw to assist her husband, Rev. Gibson Foye, in his pastoral responsibilities. See Mission Biographical Reference Files, Methodist Archives, 1469-3-5: 29.
67 See the report of Eurania Pyron in *Twenty-second Report of the Woman's Missionary Council*, 255.
68 *Twenty-second Report of the Woman's Missionary Council*, 256.
69 Ibid.
70 Ibid.

Sources

"Administrative Files of the Methodist Episcopal Church, South." The Methodist Archives. Madison, NJ: Drew University.

Arbeitsgruppe Frauendienst. *Geschichte des Frauendienstes in den Ländern der Zentralkonferenz von Mittel- und Südeuropa*. Bülach: Schweiz, privately circulated, 2001.

Garber, Paul Neff. *The Methodists of Continental Europe*. New York: Editorial Department, Division of Education and Cultivation, 1949.

Hecker, Friedrich, Vilém Schneeberger, and Karl Zehrer. *Methodismus in Osteuropa: Polen – Tschechoslowakei – Ungarn*. Stuttgart: EmKGM 51, 2004.

"Mission Biographical Files of the Methodist Episcopal Church, South." The Methodist Archives. Madison, NJ: Drew University.

Nineteenth Annual Report of the Woman's Missionary Council of the Methodist Episcopal Church South, 1928–1929. Nashville: Publishing House Methodist Episcopal Church South, 1929.

Nuelsen, John D., Theophil Mann, and J. J. Sommer, eds. *Kurzgefasste Geschichte des Methodismus*. Bremen: Verlagshaus der Methodistenkirche GmbH, 1929.

Procházková, Miroslava. "Frauendienst in Tschechien und in der Slowakei, Bratislava, im März 2000." In *Geschichte des Frauendienstes in den Ländern der Zentralkonferenz von Mittel- und Südeuropa*. Bülach: Schweiz, privately circulated, 2001.

Puslecka, Boguslawa. "Frauendienst in Polen." In *Geschichte des Frauendienstes in den Ländern der Zentralkonferenz von Mittel- und Südeuropa*. Bülach: Schweiz, privately circulated, 2001.

Sledge, Robert W. "Five Dollars and Myself:" In *The History of the Mission of the Methodist Episcopal Church, South, 1845–1939*. New York: GBGM Books, 2005.

Streiff, Patrick Ph. *Der Methodismus in Europa im 19. und 20. Jahrhunder*. Stuttgart: EmKGM 50, 2003.

Twenty-second Annual Report of the Woman's Missionary Council of the Methodist Episcopal Church South, 1931–1932. Nashville: Publishing House Methodist Episcopal Church South, 1932.

Part II
Portraits of pioneer women

Mary Matthews, Methodist Missionary in Macedonia

7 Baroness Amelie von Langenau
Pioneer of Methodism in Austria

Michael Wetzel

Frau von Langenau
und die vier erſten Schweſtern des M. M. Vereins in Wien
1894.

Baroness Amelie von Langenau and Deaconesses

Baroness Amelie von Langenau died on August 24, 1902 in Bangor, Wales, during a holiday trip. Her burial in England was organized according to her last will that declared her wish to be buried in "English soil." Relatives insisted, however, that her body should rest finally in the family tomb at Matzleindorf Cemetery in Vienna. An obituary, emphasizing the uniqueness of Amelie von Langenau's last journey, as well as her many contributions to Austrian society, appeared in Vienna's popular newspapers; likewise, the Methodist press did not hesitate to praise her as the founding mother of Austrian Methodism.

Regardless, the Baroness remained a little-known figure until the Methodist pastor Paul Ernst Hammer (1902–1992) began extensive research on her life and work. Unfortunately, having compiled detailed information about her biography, he was not able to secure a publisher for his manuscript.[1] In 2001 an extract from Hammer's work, printed on the initiative of Helmut Nausner, opened her life more fully, at least to the Methodist reader.[2] Even today, most people have no clue about the leading role the Baroness once played in early Austrian Methodism. Her life and work clamor for attention as Amelie von Langenau belongs to the circle of Methodist women pioneers in Europe.

Amelie von Langenau was a descendant of the Haffner family that once lived in Alsace. Probably in 1686 when re-catholicization began in this territory, some of the Protestant family members emigrated to Denmark where Amelie's grandfather obtained Egholm manor in 1812. In Denmark the Haffners started a remarkable career. Amelie's father, Wolfgang von Haffner (1810–1887), was considered a highly decorated military leader. In 1869 he even became Minister of Domestic Affairs, and from 1870 to 1877 he served as Minister of War and Marine Affairs. His wife, Sophie, was the daughter of an admiral in the Danish fleet.

Early life

A veil of uncertainty shrouds Amelie's birth. While official documents declare 1833 the year of her birth, Amelie always referred to December 28, 1830 as the beginning of her life. Some speculate that the official records may have been forged in order to extinguish the suspicion of an extramarital birth. Decades later Amelie cryptically spoke of "incongruities in my parents' house." Her confidante, the Methodist pastor, Friedrich Rösch, concluded that a lack of mother love in childhood contributed, as a main factor, to what he described as Amelie's deeply injured soul.[3] On April 27, 1856, Amelie married Ferdinand von Langenau (1818–1881). A renowned officer in the Austrian army, her husband's high expectations collapsed tragically in 1849 when he was severely wounded in a battle against Hungarian nationalists. Only 32 years old, Ferdinand was not willing to spend the rest of his life as an invalid. He applied for a post in the Austrian diplomatic corps and, as a non-Catholic, received appointments to several Protestant courts in Germany.

In 1851 Ferdinand was posted to Sweden where he later met Amelie, and they started their family together. In 1858 they celebrated the arrival of a son, named after his father. But at the rare age of 13 her son died tragically, leaving behind his mother, broken-hearted and in deep despair. Still under the shadow of this horrific event, in 1871 Ferdinand became the Austrian envoy to Russia. The Russian capital, St. Petersburg, meant a bright stage and opulent living conditions to an eloquent and cosmopolitan lady like Amelie, which proved to be a distraction for some time. The Baroness was often seen in the salons of the aristocracy, taking part in aesthetic conversations. During her time in Russia, however, Amelie experienced a rather amazing transformation with regard to her view of life and a way to navigate her own grief. A unique influence, in fact, provided the impetus for the empathy which later characterized her life and the social activism in which she engaged so eagerly.

Russian literature – with its depth of pathos – helped her develop a strong consciousness of how thoroughly poverty, proletarianization, social exclusion, and the lack of education harmed the poor across the European continent. She familiarized herself with the prosaic and religious works of Fjodor Dostojevsky, Ivan Turgenev, and Leo Tolstoi.[4] She read the novels *War and Peace* and *Anna Karenina* which provided tremendous insight, in her view, with regard to the ambiguities of Russian social life. From Leo Tolstoi, in particular, she learned to value charity and held the virtues of asceticism and non-violence in high esteem. She also took special note of Tolstoi's critical attitude toward all forms of social injustice, monumental concerns that were real – not imagined – problems among the poor. She witnessed the extent to which social tensions generated malevolent acts against those in power. In the development of her thinking, and under the influence of these important literary works, her thoughts about social responsibility had already gained ground when Amelie was called to navigate the deepest crisis of her life.

On January 19, 1881 Ferdinand died after an illness of only four days. Now none of her possessions or aristocratic networks counted for anything. Instead, the Baroness felt the unbearable burden of loneliness and emptiness and the only way to find ease for this burden was pastoral care. She returned to Austria and met the Lutheran pastor, Dr. Paul von Zimmermann, in Vienna. Apparently, Zimmermann was the sort of pastor to offer hasty advice, and he immediately commended social activity to Amelie as a means of distraction.[5] She took his advice to heart and became involved in several arenas of Protestant social work in Vienna. For a noble woman to engage in this kind of activity raised the suspicion of many and proved to be quite challenging. Moreover, the Protestant Church in Austria represented only 6 percent of the population among a vast majority of Catholics who found it difficult to make sense of her intentions. Nevertheless,

Amelie's outstanding generosity made her an often praised and frequently consulted person whose donations actually lifted the quality and quantity of the granted aid to a much higher level.

Work among the Methodists

Amelie's first recorded donation came in 1882 with her funding of an orphanage and a hospital in a rural area. Six years later she gave the almost incredible amount of 12,000 florins to establish an asylum for epileptic and mentally ill people. Many not only recognized her generosity but appreciated her skills and she was appointed chair of three different associations, all under the jurisdiction of the Evangelical Union of Inner Mission in Upper Austria. In all of this activity, however, Amelie did not find what she was seeking. She was trying to salve the wounds of a broken heart and the emptiness she felt inside with frenetic efforts to do good. She soon discovered the importance of spiritual needs she had left unattended in her life. Friedrich Rösch, the Wesleyan minister who served a small congregation in Vienna from 1888 to 1895, provided the spiritual guidance she needed to find deeper healing.

In his memoirs Rösch recalls his first encounter with the Baroness:

> To the astonishment of both, the preacher and the small congregation of no more than 20 to 25 plain people, the Baroness joined their evening service, that was celebrated on November 10, 1889 in a rather shabby room on the 4th floor of an ordinary tenement. During the following weeks she kept on attending the meetings.[6]

Later Amelie would explain that she was given advice to do so by a British missionary who worked among Jews. There can be no doubt that the way Rösch testified to the gospel of Christ began to touch Amelie's heart. For years she had been a fairly faithful member of the church and a reader of numerous sermons without being able to discern the relevance of biblical texts to her personal needs.

Precisely this insight occurred when Rösch was preaching a sermon on the Lord's Prayer on February 2, 1890. He drew an intimate portrait of the heavenly Father and emphasized that his beloved children are given unreserved access to his heart. This message laid bare Amelie's hidden yearnings. Rösch observed that "On that Sunday afternoon the Lord acted on her as much as on Lydia's heart."[7] Two days later he received an invitation to Langenau Palace where the Baroness wanted to converse privately with him, and this conversation helped spur on her spiritual awakening. As she often confessed, in that moment she had laid away all of her self-righteousness. "I started trusting in Christ and a wonderful peace, that I had never experienced before, filled my heart. I vowed to dedicate my whole life to the service for my Lord."[8]

This breakthrough, indeed, changed Amelie's life as much as it offered a new arena of opportunity to the small Methodist congregation in Vienna. Completely unexpectedly, the multiply hampered and underfinanced work of the Wesleyan Methodist Church (WMC) in Austria had gained a powerful supporter.[9] No one could ever have predicted this extraordinary and presumably unique action, that a noble woman would sign up for membership in a religious community that found itself on the periphery of society. As might well be expected under these circumstances, the established Catholic clergy led a campaign in the newspapers, vilifying the Methodists for the way in which they had led the Baroness astray.[10]

Amelie showed herself unimpressed by diatribes of this kind. She began to open her palace to the public. On April 3, 1890 Rösch had the privilege of proclaiming the gospel to over a hundred visitors who listened intently to the preacher in her Big Salon. In 1891 John Cook Barratt, general superintendent of the WMC in Germany, gave a report to the Mission Committee in London outlining the remarkable extension of the Methodist work in Vienna due to "a divine ray of light that had broken into our darkness."[11] Actually, Amelie's social rank and wealth enabled her to shelter and to promote the Methodists tremendously. When public gatherings were prohibited by the Austrian government in 1891, the Baroness provided her home for about 15 months for the purpose of weekly prayer meetings and services there. Moreover, she considered it her duty to fight for the full legal recognition of the Methodists. In her letters she sometimes compared her struggle with Jesus' parable of the persistent widow and the unjust judge (Luke 18:1–8). In times of particular difficulty, the Baroness sought audience with the Minister of Religious Affairs. She also activated her good contacts with the British ambassador to Austria whom she considered to be well-disposed towards the Methodists. Eventually, the Baroness obtained access to the Prime Minister, Count Kasimir Felix Badeni, who abolished the ban against the Methodists in 1897.[12]

Another important issue that raised Amelie's interest immediately following her conversion was the adequacy of Methodist properties. She believed that the future growth of the Methodist movement depended on the purchase of property. Due to her unrelenting efforts a house in excellent location not far from Vienna's main road was obtained in 1891. Much delighted, Amelie wrote to the Wesleyan Methodist Mission Committee in London:

> A notable attorney . . . gave us the hint, that we would gain greater attention if we owned a house. . . . After numerous prayers and deliberations with Mr. Rösch we set out looking for an appropriate building. I regard it a sign of the Lord, that the house we inspected second, has met our taste thoroughly.[13]

In the eyes of the congregation it was an unbelievable gift when the Baroness supplied the full purchase price of 90,000 florins and another 5,000 florins for reconstruction. After some renovation the multi-story structure included a spacious chapel with the capacity of about 150 seats, the preacher's apartment, and several lodgings.[14] The opening of the chapel on July 5, 1891 must be considered a milestone in early Austrian Methodism. The event also shows evidence of the fruitful cooperation between the Baroness and Rösch. They can be identified as the two main figures who advanced the Methodist movement in Vienna decisively.

Methodist social work

Not only congregations benefited from Amelie's generosity. In line with her earlier efforts in the arena of social service, she soon launched new projects under the auspices of the Methodists. Not all of her campaigns turned out to be successful or sustainable. Obstacles frequently stood in the way of her plans. A hostel for Protestant housemaids, for instance, was just on the threshold of opening when the municipal court of Vienna denied the necessary permits "because the hostel is an affiliate to the illegal Methodist congregation."[15] This intervention hit the Baroness hard, since she had already recruited the staff for the hostel.[16] Due to her strong and vivacious character, she never gave up. If it was ever necessary to abandon a plan, as in this case, new ideas immediately popped into her mind.

One of her most successful foundations, still in existence today, roots back to the year 1891. From May to July 1891 the World Postal Congress was held in Vienna. Besides the official agenda the British delegate, Sir Arthur Blackwood (1832–1893), advocated an increased awareness of the social and spiritual needs of postmen and their families. He discovered an avid advocate in the Baroness who shared his vision. So the decision was made to have a gathering in Langenau Palace as the initial step towards the foundation of a so-called "Postmen Mission." More than 50 postmen attended that first convention.[17] Soon a monthly evangelistic journal with the title *Der Briefbote* was printed and distributed. From 1894 to 1896 the Baroness herself edited the periodical. These beginnings in Vienna also inspired the foundation of the German Christian Post Association in 1901.

Most of her endeavors met with considerable success and impacted many communities. Nevertheless, to broaden her sphere of activities the Baroness urgently sought to align herself and her influence with major professional institutions. She entered into a fruitful collaboration with the *Martha-Maria-Verein für allgemeine Krankenpflege* (Martha Maria Society for Medical Care and Nursing), the Methodist deaconess establishment in Nuremberg, Germany. This partnership resulted in one of the most remarkable developments in European Methodist history. The association had experienced a lot of turbulence at its foundation. Several attempts failed to integrate the deaconess movement into the WMC synod. The synodical leaders were not willing, however, to take the financial risk, so the association was established outside the official structure in 1889.[18]

Amelie was not fully aware of all these complexities when she asked for a young Methodist deaconess to be sent to Vienna. She actually visited the *Martha-Maria-Verein* headquarters in May 1890 and had left deeply impressed by the passionate service the deaconesses were carrying out despite their poor working and living conditions. She appreciated that kind of dedication and contributed the high sum of 40,000 florins for a well-equipped mother house.[19] Later she donated another 20,000 florins to build an affiliate foster home in Magdeburg, Northern Germany. In recognition of and appreciation for this support, the association sent four nurses to Vienna. The year 1890, therefore, marks the beginning of the Methodist deaconess movement in the Austrian capital.[20]

Under the patronage of the Baroness the sisters looked after sick people and cared for destitute children. Because of her special concern for these children, Amelie established an orphanage with the aim to provide shelter and education to those who had come to grief. In Vienna these poorest of the poor became famous as the so-called "red children," since they always wore red uniforms and hats. The orphanages provided a solid education, including English, French, and stenography. The Baroness put high value on these subjects, in particular, as she knew these would be important in her later efforts to procure good jobs for them as officials or secretaries. She often became directly involved in their education, teaching these subjects to them herself. Working among them, she exemplified virtues such as reliability, orderliness, and a sense of duty, combined with the strong intention to make "her" children disciples of Christ. The life stories of the children reveal the lasting influence the Baroness had on her wards. Two of the "red children," for example, became deaconesses of the *Martha-Maria-Verein*, another married a Methodist preacher and served the church faithfully as a pastor's wife. Once questioned why she had surrounded herself with dirty street kids, Amelie simply replied, "This fellowship is the joy of my heart."[21] In this manner she unequivocally testified her genuine Methodist spirit – a way of life that always finds expression in the loving care of the poor.

Because of her deep commitment to the Methodist deaconess work and the financial support she had provided, the Baroness was appointed to the supervisory board of the *Martha-Maria-Verein*. According to the board minutes, she joined the first session in September 1891 and missed no board meeting until 1895. Although an esteemed member of the board, she soon found herself vulnerable as a consequence of her visionary thoughts. A grave quarrel arose in 1895 when she carefully read the statutes of the *Martha-Maria-Verein* for the first time. She openly criticized the loose ties between the WMC synod and the *Martha-Maria-Verein* and suggested a modification of the statutes. She also disagreed with the extensive rights the statutes conceded to the chairman, Jakob Ekert (1859–1906), whom she once bitterly had denounced as an "almighty autocrat."[22] The more intransigent Ekert became with regard to Amelie's concerns, the more her annoyance grew until she withdrew herself from the supervisory board later that year and subsequently suspended her financial support.[23]

Connections with the Methodist Episcopal Church

In light of these developments, her interest turned increasingly in the direction of another segment of the Methodist family in Europe, the Methodist Episcopal Church (MEC) in Germany. Unlike the Wesleyan Methodists, who had come directly from England to Southern Germany, disseminating its influence from there since 1830, the MEC established its base in the Northern German seaport of Bremen, where the American Methodist, Dr. Ludwig Sigismund Jacoby, became a missionary in 1849.[24] The church structures as well as the social institutions of the MEC attracted the Baroness mainly because of what she considered to be their pure spirit. Here, in her opinion, acceptable hierarchies were to be found. In particular, the mission plan developed by the superintendent, Karl Schell (1852–1920), smoothly fit Amelie's understanding of Methodist evangelization. Schell intended to send a couple of preachers to the far eastern regions of Germany (later to become Poland). This pioneering work contributed to the rise and expansion of Methodism in cities like Stettin (today Szczecin, Poland), Danzig (Gdansk, Poland), and Königsberg (Kaliningrad, Russia) in the 1890s and 1900s.[25] The Baroness did not hesitate to support this program with her financial support. Several congregations remember her fondly as she furnished a number of chapels and equipped them with Communion sets and other sacred items.

The more intimate her relation to the MEC, the clearer her vision of a united church, binding together the WMC and the MEC became. A dialog about the advantages and disadvantages of such a fusion had already begun when the Baroness allied herself with the Methodist Episcopal tradition. The Wesleyan synod and the Methodist annual conference were discussing the matter carefully, but it was the Baroness who really drove the deliberations in a promising direction. In 1892, as a sign of good will, both ecclesial communities decided to send delegate observers to their respective assemblies. Unification committees were set up in order to determine priorities and to clarify any contentious issues. In the midst of these developments, the highly esteemed WMC leader, Christian Dieterle, began to agitate against any form of consolidation or union.[26]

As might well be suspected, the committees got caught up in concerns about the transfer the properties of the WMC into a united corporation, with the Wesleyan Methodist Mission Committee in London insisting on financial compensation in this case. This muddled situation elicited one of the most important moments in Amelie's life. All previous acts of generosity were eclipsed by the action she felt compelled to take in the midst of this impasse. Her financial circumstances enabled her to satisfy the claims of the Wesleyan Methodist Mission Committee completely by a contribution of

250,000 Marks.[27] Even for a wealthy aristocrat, such an amount entailed considerable sacrifice. Her intervention removed the last obstacle, and the unification documents were soon signed, enabling the church union to become effective as of June 1897. The first joint Northern German Annual Conference (including Amelie's congregation in Vienna) was held in Kassel from June 23 to 28, 1897.[28] Methodist newspapers reported that Baroness Amelie von Langenau proudly participated in the celebration of this important event. She addressed the conference expressing her deepest joy and satisfaction.

She had already become something of a public figure within Methodism. She loved to travel and visited many congregations, synods, and Methodist conferences as a guest. In 1896, for example, she had participated in the General Conference of the MEC in Cleveland, Ohio and filed a report for the Methodist periodical, *The Christian Advocate*. Although she had neither voice nor vote in many of these kinds of assemblies, she must be regarded a leading figure in Methodist church politics between 1890 and 1900. She frequently conversed with bishops and preachers, creating a remarkable human network; but sometimes it was simply her money that opened doors.

Apologetic writings and international connections

A woman of many gifts, the Baroness also contributed to the writing and promotion of good Christian literature. She produced written testimonials of her own faith narrative which can be found in several American, English, and German Methodist periodicals such as *The Christian Advocate*, *Der Christliche Apologete*, and *Der Evangelist*. These publications demonstrate her ability to use different genres in the proclamation and promotion of the gospel. She often published her letters, addresses, and reports, as well as poems and short stories, anonymously or with the cryptic moniker, "A. L." While none of her literary works would be considered of the first order, they were all honest and sincere attempts to digest her personal insights using a rather plain language that found its way into many hearts. Two recurring themes pervade her among literary works: personal faith and a sanctified life.

Her most popular short story with the title "The Poor Rick" was published in *Der Evangelist* in a series of five pieces from November 13 to December 11, 1897.[29] The heart-touching story, possibly adapted from an English anecdote, is worth to be briefly summarized here, since some of its content is derived from the Baroness's own experience with the street children of Vienna and her Sunday school teachings. Rick, a poor orphan, who lives in the streets of an undetermined English industrial city, is used to stealing food in order to survive. An older companion often beats him and takes away what Rick had in order to eke out an existence. Rick is invited to a Methodist Sunday school where he not only gets fed, but also learns of Jesus and the power of forgiveness. One day in winter when it is bitterly cold, after a hard week of starvation, Rick practices this forgiveness, handing over his unexpended food vouchers to his hostile companion as a free gift. While the one he has befriended survives the cold night, Rick's frozen body is found the next morning. Amelie wrote this story to portray the power of unparalleled self-dedication that results from the internalization of Christ's love. In this respect her personal experience and the essence of her own character glimmer through the text.

Amelie was well gifted by the knowledge of many different languages. Her skills enabled her not only to contribute to various magazines, but also to translate English literature into German. She proved, in this way, to be a bridge across cultures and even continents. She popularized the ideas of the visionary British Wesleyan Methodist, Hugh Price Hughes, among her German readers.[30] His concept of the inseparability of evangelism and social action had inspired her and guided her own life. In 1893 the Baroness translated his brand new book, *Ethical Christianity*, and organized its printing and distribution on the Continent. In fact, she had very carefully selected this book from a long list of others because of her deep admiration for Hughes's Wesleyan perspective. This work, in particular, mirrored of her own plans and intentions. The Baroness convinced Adolf Stöcker, the former preacher at the emperor's court of Wilhelm II (1859–1941) in Berlin and head of the Berlin City Mission, to write the preface.[31] The connection to Stöcker is a good example of the interdenominational dialog in which the Baroness engaged. Stöcker oriented his own social vision along the same trajectory of Hughes and von Langenau. On October 31, 1892 she invited Stöcker to Langenau Palace in Vienna where he delivered a lecture on the principles of Protestant social work under the conditions of a growing social diversity in the urban centers of Germany.

She extended a long list of invitations, in fact, to other famous visitors to Langenau Palace who also presented lectures and engaged in public dialog. Georg Müller of Bristol, England, outlined his charity work and orphanage promotion in England's well-known seaport.[32] Dr. Friedrich Wilhelm Baedecker explained his work of evangelization in Russian prisons.[33] James Hudson Taylor and Dr. Emil Lühring provided reports on their mission trips to India, China, and Singapore.[34] Ernst Gebhardt performed his sacred songs and music.[35] All in all, Amelie's home became a location of spiritual exchange bringing together the rich and the poor as well as Methodists and non-Methodists, literally, from around the world. For her own part, the Baroness played her own unique role as a pioneer of the German Evangelical Alliance, founded in Bad Blankenburg, Germany, in 1886. As often as possible she visited the Alliance meetings there. One of her last activities was her participation in the Ecumenical Methodist Conference in London in 1901 as the delegate of the European Methodist Women's Association. One can only imagine the deep sense of loss occasioned by her sudden death on August 24, 1902. Not only did this devastate her Methodist congregation in Vienna, but felt like a seismic shock throughout the entire church and the Austrian society.[36]

The legacy of Baroness Amelie von Langenau

This survey of Amelie's life demonstrates just how widespread her influence was with regard to the development of nascent Methodism in Austria over such a short period of time, from her religious awakening in 1890 to her death in 1902. Her partnership with the Methodist cause proved to be a mutually beneficial adventure of large proportion. On the one hand, Amelie's connections with Methodism led to her own spiritual renewal and created channels for her amazingly generous spirit. Within Methodism she experienced the healing that brought wholeness to her life, obtained the identity she had long sought, and engaged in a quest for sanctification – a holiness of heart and life that revolved around love. On the other hand, the Baroness was able to give back so much. Her strong will, tireless effort, intense missional vision, useful social contacts, and lavish generosity helped strengthen the Methodist movement in Austria and Germany in ways that could never have been imagined. Her advocacy for Methodist unification in the German-speaking countries of Europe gives her a place among the most meritorious figures in European Methodist history and her interdenominational engagements anticipated the modern ecumenical movement.

She knew all too well that money alone could never guarantee success. Some even perceived a kind of naïve gullibility in her character, the product, perhaps, of an aristocratic lifestyle that separated her from the world of ordinary people for years. The fact of the matter, however, is that she had a sympathetic heart and of ardent enthusiasm to relieve the misery of others. To assess her social activism properly, it is essential to recognize the inseparable connection between her charity and the gospel of Christ – a vision of faith working by love that arose out of a newly defined relationship to God. After her conversion Amelie fully affirmed the Methodist doctrine of sanctification and constantly strove for selflessness in imitation of Christ. The Good Shepherd who gave his life for the sheep (John 10:11) was the One she sought to follow and exemplify in all she did. In the late 1890s, those within Austrian society admired many benefactors, but a clear Christian motivation could not always be attributed to them. The friendship, social work, and philanthropy of the Baroness were, in and of themselves, the way in which she shared the gospel of Christ with others.

Langenau Palace was sold right after her death and most of the memorabilia associated with the life of Baroness Amelie von Langenau remain untraceable. The collective memory of her influence, however, particularly as a pioneer of Methodism, remains. On the occasion of what would have been her 100th birthday in 1930, a memorial plaque was affixed at the wall of Vienna's main Methodist chapel as a reminder: The Methodist churches in Austria and also in Germany do owe the Baroness a lot.

Notes

1 Paul Ernst Hammer's manuscript is preserved in the Central Archives of the United Methodist Church in Germany in Reutlingen.

2 Paul Ernst Hammer, *Amelie von Langenau* (Vienna: The Methodist Church in Austria, 2001). Details concerning her life are drawn primarily from this document.

3 Friedrich Rösch, "Baronin Amelie von Langenau," *Der Missionsbote* (1902), 8. Rösch was a WMC preacher in Vienna (1888–1895) who died in 1931.

4 Fjodor Michailovich Dostojevsky, born in 1821, Russian novelist, short story writer, essayist, and philosopher, one of the greatest psychologists in world literature, died in 1881. Ivan Sergeyevich Turgenev, born in 1818, Russian novelist, short story writer and playwright, died in 1883. Leo Tolstoi, born in 1828, Russian novelist, short story writer, playwright, essayist, one of the greatest writers worldwide, died in 1910.

5 Hammer, *Amelie von Langenau*, 16–17.

6 Friedrich Rösch, *Erinnerungen an Wien: Aus dem Leben eines Methodistenpredigers* (Bremen: Anker Verlag, 1931), 8.

7 Ibid. See Acts 16: 14–15.

8 Christian Golder, *Geschichte der weiblichen Diakonie* (Cincinnati: Jennings & Pye, 1901), 137.

9 Helmut Nausner, "Die Methodistenkirche in Österreich bis zum Jahre 1920," *Mitteilungen der Studiengemeinschaft* 20 (1999): 3–21.

10 Rösch, *Erinnerungen*, 31.

11 Ibid., 12–13. John Cook Barrat, born in 1832, WMC missionary to Germany, General superintendent in Cannstadt near Stuttgart, died in 1892.

12 Kasimir Felix Badeni, born in 1846, Polish aristocrat, Austrian statesman, Prime minister of the Cisleithanian half of Austria-Hungary 1895–1897, died in 1909.

13 Hammer, *Amelie von Langenau*, 62.

14 Rösch, *Erinnerungen*, 35–36.

15 Hammer, *Amelie von Langenau*, 44–45.

16 John L. Nuelsen, Theophil Mann, and J. J. Sommer, eds., *Kurzgefaßte Geschichte des Methodismus* (Bremen: Verlagshaus der Methodistenkirche GmbH, 1929), 281.

17 *Festschrift zur Feier des Fünfzigjährigen Bestehens der Methodistenkirche in Wien am 8. Dezember 1921* (Wien: Selbstverl. der Bischöflichen Methodistenkirche, 1921), 21.

18 Georg Rexroth, *Jakob Ekert* (Winnenden: nd), 53.

19 Martha-Maria-Verein für allgemeine Krankenpflege e. V. Nürnberg: Denkschrift zum 40 jährigen Bestehen des Vereins, 1889–1929 (Düsseldorf: Selbstverlag des Vereins, 1929), 13.

20 Mareike Bloedt, "Ein Leben des Dienens: Die Anfänge des Diakonissenamtes in den methodistischen Kirchen in Deutschland," *EmK Geschichte* 2 (2015), 31.

21 Hammer, *Amelie von Langenau*, 57.

22 Letter to Jakob Ekert, October 16, 1895, Central Methodist Archives, Reutlingen. On his life and work, see Paul Nollenberger, Jakob Ekert, *Eine Pioniergestalt der Diakonie* (Stuttgart: Christliches Verlagshaus, 1988).

23 *Annual Report of the Martha-Maria-Association* (Nürnberg: np, 1895).

24 Ludwig Sigismund Jacoby, born in 1813, Methodist clergyman of Jewish extraction, emigrated to Cincinnati in 1838, presiding elder and superintendent of the MEC in Germany (1849–1872), died in 1874.

25 Nuelsen, *Kurzgefaßte Geschichte*, 636–637.

26 Christian Dieterle, born in 1843, WMC preacher, separated himself from the church in 1897, died in 1911.

27 Hammer, *Amelie von Langenau*, 112–113.

28 Patrick Ph. Streiff, *Methodism in Europe: 19th and 20th Century* (Tallinn: Baltic Methodist Theological Seminary, 2003), 107.
29 *Der Evangelist* 46 (1897): 362–363; 47 (1897): 370–371; 48 (1897), 378–379; 49 (1897): 386–387; 50 (1897), 394–395.
30 Hugh Price Hughes, born in 1847, Welsh protestant reformer, organized the West London Methodist Mission, great orator, superintendent, and editor of the *Methodist Times*, died in 1902.
31 Adolf Stöcker, born in 1835, German Lutheran theologian, court chaplain in Prussia, founder of the Christian Social Party, died in 1909.
32 Georg Müller, born in 1805, German evangelist, Director of the Ashley Down orphanage in Bristol/England, established 117 schools for Christian education, died in 1898.
33 Friedrich Wilhelm Baedecker, born in 1823, missionary in Russia among prisoners, one of the founders of the German Evangelical Alliance, died in 1906.
34 James Hudson Taylor, born in 1832, missionary in China, founder of the China Inland Mission, died in 1905. Emil Lühring, born in 1863, missionary and colonist in South East Asia, sent to Singapore in 1889, spoke 24 languages, died in 1937.
35 Hammer, *Amelie von Langenau*, 48–59. Ernst Gebhardt, born in 1832, German Methodist preacher, famous song writer of the holiness movement, editor of several Methodist periodicals, died in 1899.
36 See the obituary written by preacher Theophil Mann in *Der Evangelist* (1902), 301–302.

Sources

Annual Report of the Martha-Maria-Association. Nürnberg: np, 1895.
Bloedt, Mareika. "Ein Leben des Dienens: Die Anfänge des Diakonissenamtes in den methodistischen Kirchen in Deutschland." *EmK Geschichte* 2 (2015): 5–37.
Der Evangelist. Dezember 1921. Wien: Selbstverl. der Bischöflichen Methodistenkirche, 1921.
Festschrift zur Feier des Fünfzigjährigen Bestehens der Methodistenkirche in Wien am 8 Dez. 1921. Wien: Selbsverl. der Bishoflichen Methodistischenkirche, 1921.
Golder, Christian. *Geschichte der weiblichen Diakonie*. Cincinnati: Jennings & Pye, 1901.
Hammer, Paul Ernst Hammer, *Amelie von Langenau*. Vienna: The Methodist Church in Austria, 2001.
Martha-Maria-Verein für allgemeine Krankenpflege e.V. Nürnberg: Denkschrift zum 40 jährigen Bestehen des Vereins, 1889–1929. Düsseldorf: Selbstverlag des Vereins, 1929.
Nausner, Helmut. "Die Methodistenkirche in Österreich bis zum Jahre 1920." *Mitteilungen der Studiengemeinschaft* 20 (1999): 3–21.
Nollenberger, Paul. *Jakob Ekert: Eine Pioniergestalt der Diakonie*. Stuttgart: Christliches Verlagshaus, 1988.
Nuelsen, John L., Theophil Mann, and J. J. Sommer, eds. *Kurzgefasste Geschichte des Methodismus*. Bremen: Verlagshaus der Methodistenkirche GmbH, 1929.
Rexroth, Georg. *Jakob Ekert*. Winnenden: nd.
Rösch, Friedrich. "Baronin Amelie von Langenau." *Der Missionsbote* (1902): 8.
Rösch, Friedrich. *Erinnerungen an Wien: Aus dem Leben eines Methodistenpredigers*. Bremen: Anker Verlag, 1931.
Streiff, Patrick Ph. *Methodism in Europe: 19th and 20th Century*. Tallinn: Baltic Methodist Theological Seminary, 2003.

8   Anna Eklund
Methodist pioneer in Russia

S T Kimbrough, Jr.

Anna Eklund, Methodist Pioneer in Russia

Anna Eklund was born of Swedish parents in Turku, Finland on May 25, 1867.[1] In her youth she was very interested in the theater for which she had many gifts. The religious awakening of the 1880s that swept across many of the countries of Scandinavia and the Baltic States, however, captivated her spirit and she determined to do something else with her life in service to God and others. Therefore, she joined the Methodist congregation in her home town of Turku. At that time and still today there is a significant constituency of Swedish heritage in Finnish Methodism.

Deaconess training and ministry

Convinced that God had called her to a life of Christian service, she applied to the deaconess training center, the Bethany Deaconess Home, known as *Bethanien*, in Hamburg, Germany, and was accepted. After completing her education and training, part of which was spent at the deaconess training center in Frankfurt, Germany, as well, she was consecrated a deaconess in 1886 at the annual meeting of the Finland and Russia Mission Conference. When she returned to Finland, however, there was no place for her to work on behalf of the church. Since she had to seek private employment, it was fortunate that she was trained in therapeutic gymnastics and as a masseuse. She would have to wait until the fall of 1908 for an appointment by Bishop William Burt to the Methodist Episcopal Headquarters in Petrograd, Russia.

Methodist work had begun in St. Petersburg by Swedish lay preachers in the 1880s, and it had continued primarily among Swedish and Finnish expatriates in the city and surrounding area. It was not until 1907, however, that the work received the impetus, which would make it an effective and a growing work in the Methodist Episcopal connection. In the spring of that year Bishop Burt appointed The Rev. Hjalmar Salmi, a Finnish citizen born in St. Petersburg and graduate of the Methodist theological school in Helsinki, to St. Petersburg. In the fall of the same year he also appointed Dr. George A. Simons, a native of New York State and a graduate of Drew Theological School, as superintendent and treasurer of the Russia Methodist Episcopal Mission in St. Petersburg. These two men were Anna Eklund's coworkers when she arrived there in 1908.

In a letter to the Board of Foreign Missions of the Methodist Episcopal Church dated December 12, 1907, George A. Simons describes the context into which Sister Anna came.[2]

> The claim is made, and I am inclined to believe it, that in no other city in Europe are the rents and cost of living so high as in Petrograd. Hence I have deemed it the best policy to wait with the establishing of our headquarters until we can secure a suitable house, with room for a commodious chapel, book depository, apartments for the Superintendent, pastor, etc. Brother Salmi and I spent several weeks looking around for such a place, but none was to be found that was desirable in point of location, rental, etc. Finally we hired a hall in that part of the city

known as Vassilli Ostroff, which is not at all centrally located. The hall
is in an old dilapidated building, which the City Mission of the German
Lutheran Church of Petrograd is using. We are renting the hall from
them, paying sixty rubles a month ($30). The hall has a seating capac-
ity of about 250, is furnished with organ, electric light, porter, etc. We
are entitled to it three evenings during the week and have it nearly all
day Sunday. We are preaching to the Russians, Finns, and Swedes, and
shall soon hold services also in German and English. It is our purpose
to carry on a strong, evangelistic, thoroughly Methodist work, but are
laboring under great difficulties. . . .

For twenty years Methodism has been trying to gain a foothold in
Petrograd and has not succeeded. Hitherto we have had but a handful
of Swedes here, who were not members of our church, and these were
taken care of by an old local preacher. These dozen souls have constituted our "Methodist Society" in Petrograd, existing at a "poor, dying
rate." Nearly all of them are poor and advanced in years. Now if we are
to work here at all, we must have the right leaders, suitable property,
strong Methodistic literature and sufficient funds. . . .

On the first Sunday in November we began holding services at the
"First Methodist Episcopal Society of Petrograd." There were only a
few persons present. Since then the attendance has had a steady increase.
Last Sunday we held four services: at 10 a.m. for the Finns, 30 being
present; at 3:45 p.m. for the Russians, 50 being present; at 5:15 p.m. for
the Swedes, 30 being present; at 7 p.m. for the Finns, 20 being present: a
total attendance of 130 for the whole day. Our services during the week
are also gaining. Up to this time no collections had been taken in our
meetings. Last Sunday I suggested to Bro. Salmi that we initiate the people into this time-honored, genuinely Methodistic means of grace, and
they responded with collections amounting to three rubles, i.e. $1.50, a
most gratifying beginning. A few days ago the church, Sunday school,
and Quarterly Conference Records, which I had ordered from New
York, arrived. We mean business, brethren!

Pastor Salmi is a linguistic genius. He preaches fluently in Finnish,
Russian, and Swedish, besides being able to converse in English. Before
I came to Petrograd he had been devoting his attention to the Russian-
Finnish settlements just outside of the city and there 150 souls have
been soundly converted under his preaching. It is just a year since he
began his work among those dear people and already we have a following of nearly 500 persons, who will join as soon as we build a church.
We are preaching in seven villages and ought to have a chapel in each
of them.

The Methodist Episcopal Church has a great mission in Petrograd
and all Russia. But if she is to accomplish anything here, she must have
such a headquarters as shall command the respect and confidence of
both the *best* and the *worst* people in this Empire.

When Sister Anna arrived in St. Petersburg on September 30, 1908, there were no funds to begin the deaconess work, except for $100 given to her for that purpose by Bishop Burt. Nevertheless, not long after her arrival a Bethany Deaconess Home was opened with five young, dedicated women, each of whom could speak two or more languages. She had an untiring spirit and drive to make the deaconess home effective. There seemed no other way than to use her own furniture to equip it and give the young deaconesses clothes from her own wardrobe.

It was clear from the beginning that Sister Anna would rush to the aid of the humblest person in need and it was not long before she and the other deaconesses were known for helping the marginalized of the city. One would often find them working in the hospitals of the city. On many occasions Sister Anna even persuaded some of the local bakers to supply bread for the poor. She and the Sisters working with her did everything they possibly could from soliciting funds to holding bazaars at the Bethany House to raise support to help the less fortunate.

Not long after she came to St. Petersburg, she began developing work among the children of the city. In 1908, on her first Christmas in Russia, she and her fellow deaconesses in training prepared a celebration for some 150 street children. They gave them clothes they had collected to replace their worn and unclean rags. Thus, the Methodist deaconesses in St. Petersburg aided the poor and needy on behalf of Christ and the church. Dr. George A. Simons, the superintendent, also invited them to preach in St. Petersburg and in the surrounding villages where Methodist chapels had been built.

The years between 1908 and 1914 leading up to World War One were particularly difficult for Sister Anna and the other sisters. They were called upon to care for the wounded, which they did most willingly. There was a hospital primarily for the Finnish Regiment of the Russian Army to which one of the sisters was assigned. During their faithful war-time service three of the sisters died.

Sister Anna was asked to assist in the clinic of the Red Army, which she did willingly. Other members of the Methodist Episcopal Church of Christ Our Savior in St. Petersburg also helped at the clinic. When Sister Anna was not found there or in the hospitals, she could often be seen helping in the city orphanages that were filled with homeless, poor children. After the war in 1919, she was asked to assist at the Peter and Paul Hospital where Swedish Communist patients were suffering from typhoid fever. This was a natural and welcome task for her, since most of them did not know the Russian language and Sister Anna could speak with them in Swedish.

At the end of World War One, among the soldiers gradually returning home, there were some Methodists. One of them, Oskar Pöld, arrived in March 1921, and began serving as Sister Anna's coworker in ministry. In 1909 the governor of the region, which included St. Petersburg, issued a document, which legalized the Methodist Episcopal Church of St. Petersburg, with full rights to operate in the entire province or regional government. In 1912 a superb property and building at 58 Bolshoi Prospect were purchased and the Methodist Episcopal congregation finally had its own place of worship and outreach. The church was named "The Church of Christ Our Savior."

Sister Anna had been in St. Petersburg just four years when Dr. Simons was able to purchase a two-story frame house as the Methodist Episcopal headquarters and place of worship. It was named "The Church of Christ our Savior" and located on the Vassilli Island. There was a sizable yard in the front and some buildings in the rear, which were formerly used as a barn and stable. The house was previously a private residence. By removing some of the partitions, an auditorium was created that would seat about 300 persons. In addition, there were rooms for study classes, a library, and a sleeping room occupied by two young girls, candidates for deaconess work. On the upper floor are the apartments of Dr. Simons, his sister, Sister Anna, and the present Pastor, Rev. Pöld, as well as an office and two large rooms used for social outreach. Poor people and children were received in these rooms; meals and clothing were distributed, and a beginning was made to give sewing lessons to young girls.

Revocation of the government registration of the Methodist Episcopal Church in St. Petersburg

Sister Anna would discover in those early years of her residence in Petrograd that the struggle for the existence of the Methodist Episcopal Church in Russia would not be an easy one. For example, in 1913, in spite of pleas to the mayor of St. Petersburg, the Ministry of Interior, and the governor, it was declared that the registration of the congregation issued by the governor in 1909 was not in accordance with the law under which it was issued. Therefore, all services and activities at the church were suspended for five weeks until Dr. Simons could secure legal permission for holding meetings as a Methodist Society. Christmas fell within the period of suspension, hence the annual Christmas Festival for children could not be held. Nevertheless, Sister Anna and her coworkers prepared some 900 bags of candies and gifts and distributed more than 700 of them from the Deaconess Home. The remainder went to the Sunday schools in the three villages near St. Petersburg: Sigolovo, Handrovo, and Haitolovo. Thus began a period of religious repression throughout Russia, which was not limited to any one group and was to take a tremendous toll on the faith communities of that vast country.

The Methodists faced many hardships and difficulties. The year 1918 was horrendous: hunger and starvation were ravaging the entire country. During August most citizens received only one-eighth of a pound of black bread for the whole month. Sister Anna altered her clothes time and again. Dr. Simons lost some 40 pounds and his sister over 50.

In the fall of 1918 the American government ordered all Americans to leave Russia. Dr. Simons and his sister were most reluctant to leave, but, as Americans they had no choice. Sister Anna bid them depart and told them:

"It is far better that I remain and die if God so wills, than that all three of us should starve to death. God will take care of me. I am not afraid."

On October 6, 1918, Dr. Simons and his sister bid goodbye to Petrograd, the congregation of the Methodist Episcopal Church of Christ Our Savior, and Sister Anna, leaving the congregation and the property in her care. All administration, indeed the entire work of the Methodist Episcopal Church in Russia, was now placed under her supervision.

It is difficult to imagine all that Sister Anna, this saint of God, endured in the ensuing years, until 1931, when she was finally forced to leave Russia. Sister Anna, along with the assistance of the Rev. Oskar Pöld, literally held the work of the church together by God's grace and the persevering faith of the congregation. She managed to maintain the Sunday school and in all those years from 1918 to 1931 the Methodist Episcopal Church in Petrograd was never closed for public worship services. In 1922 Bishop John L. Nuelsen officially appointed Rev. Oskar Pöld as pastor of the church in Petrograd. He was 25 years of age, young, and inexperienced, but he was the bishop's only viable choice at the time. An Estonian by birth, his parents were living in Riga, Latvia at the time. He had wanted to study at the Methodist seminary in Frankfurt, Germany, but was drafted into the Red Army. After he was discharged he went to Petrograd, made a connection with Sister Anna, and began working with her there. He spoke fluent Estonian, Russian, and German and had a reasonably good knowledge of English and Swedish, but without the keen, competent, and mature leadership of Sister Anna, Pöld might not have survived long in the position as pastor.

This was an extremely difficult period for the people of Petrograd and elsewhere in Russia. It was an horrendous time of humiliation and oppression. There were unannounced house searches at night, thousands of arrests, innumerable executions, hundreds left impoverished and languishing on the streets of the city, thousands were dying of starvation, cholera, other death-causing diseases that were rampant, and with little or no medical care. Sometimes houses of wood were torn down and used for fuel. The only way Sister Anna was able to save the Methodist Episcopal Church of Christ Our Savior, a wooden structure, was by negotiating with the government officials that only a certain number of planks would be taken from the outside of the building for fuel. How glad she was they accepted her suggestion.

So it was that Sister Anna taught, preached, nursed, buried the dead, and performed innumerable other pastoral duties, long before women were officially allowed to do those things in Methodism. Though I am confident John and Charles Wesley would have approved.

Sister Anna's own words

Sister Anna's own letters and those of others describe best the difficulties she endured and the quality and breadth of her service to Christ, the church, and humankind.

Dear sister and brother! [George & Ottillie Simons][3]

I rejoice unceasingly over the beautiful and blessed work in our parish. The best of all is that God is with us! In our most difficult days, when I had heard nothing from you, I found solace in speaking of you with our congregation. An inner voice said to me, "Yes, you are completely involved in the work of God's Kingdom," and I had not been mistaken. Even though separated at a distance from one another, we were united in prayer. "Which of Job's sufferings have I not endured in these difficult times!" How often I had to explain to our friends, who wanted to doubt, that we were not there for our own purpose, rather it was only for God's purpose that we must take a stand and endure, and if necessary, place the seal of death on our own cause. Thanks be to God, who has helped us through the most difficult hours! There are friends who have faithfully stood by me, and who were not afraid to enter their names in our new church registry. It will be a blessed day, when I can come to you with a small band of them! God, let this day come *soon*!

Up to the present day not one Sunday has passed when God and the divine cause have not been served, which not every Protestant church can say! And I thank God on my knees for all the encouragement I have received from the organization here. Our work here was, is, and will always be for the suffering *land* and *people*. And in my most difficult hours I have always known this and we may *never* forget it; and furthermore, that many of our brothers and sisters have fallen, and that others remain faithful in their tasks, as our small congregation works mightily to the glory of God, each according to one's own strength.

When we had our first church meeting with officials present, the joy with which the New Testaments were received is indescribable. The one who gave us the Testaments was greeted with kisses and he wished us God's blessing for our work . . . Please, send me three or four Russian Bibles for our officials here.

Your ever-true Russian Sister Anna

Cooperation with the Russian government

A position in which Sister Anna remained steadfast was her desire to cooperate with the government of Russia and government officials, which was not always easy, nor popular with Methodists outside of Russia, especially in the USA. If Sister Anna had not maintained such a posture in her work, her witness within the sphere of government and its officials would have been greatly weakened. Her dynamic Christian love and concern were strongly experienced by many in those circles with whom she came in contact. This is eloquently indicated in the following letter. One notices the genuine pastoral concerns she has for everyone and what she endures merely to fulfill some of them.

My dear sister and brother![4]

Today I paid a visit to the officials and brought the same papers, which we have to bring each month according to the agreement. The head representative was extremely grateful for the contribution. He took me to another gentleman, whom I have met once before and who greeted me with the words, "Your face," he said, "is *novaya Zhisn*" [new life]. He then spoke with me in German and expressed sincere interest in our church. He said further, "Thank God that the old God is still alive." He was surprised that, although we are living at Vassilli Ostroff, he had never heard anything of us. I told him about you and both gentlemen are most interested to make your acquaintance. He promised to visit me as soon as he has the need for new courage to live.

On December 9, 1920, her birthday, Sister Anna wrote to George A. Simons and his sister expressing her gratitude for a box, which they had sent with all sorts of things for anyone in need. It arrived a day or so before her birthday. The following letter reveals that the way she spent her birthday was the way she spent her life – in service to others.

My dear sister and brother![5]

Today is the 9th of December, Anna's day! On Monday at one o'clock the box was brought to my house. It was opened and everything sorted and put in order. Today began with the distribution. Those who were in great need received butter, meat, and underwear. For example, the large shoes I gave to Mr. S – e; he had no boots and has just had to endure a lot. . . . The two small pairs were given to Alexandra and Katie, who had not had the good fortune to get shoes anywhere and were in great need. But hardly anyone in Petrograd has been without shoes in the way I have. Yesterday with great difficultly I parted with my old, ripped boots, which had served me in so many good ways and burned them in my oven. O, how happy I am with my new shoes!!!

In a letter from Petrograd to Dr. Simons dated January 16, 1921, Sister Anna writes: "One writes so much about hunger; but they should see how they hunger for God's Word." With all of her concern for the social and humanitarian outreach of the gospel, she understood that the fulfillment of such needs is no substitute for the desire to feed on God's Word. Indeed, in the truly Wesleyan sense she understood that personal and social holiness go hand in hand.

In the same letter she writes of the hunger for the Word even among government officials.[6]

Even in the government there are souls who hunger for the Word of God. Many of them tried to serve God in their youth but they could not do it in their church. Now that they are well acquainted with our free-church system, they also await the Doctor and are desirous of hearing your sermons. How many have already come to me in very serious discussions and see in *us*, so to speak, the fulfillment of their hopes. Also, I have been called to families where I could bring solace with spiritual encouragement. This is how it goes from morning until evening . . . one can say of me: she died with great love for poor, seeking souls, who needed spiritual aid . . . May our dear God . . . bring us help for our spiritually starving souls. "The world is indeed our parish," and Russia belongs also to the world.

Your faithful Russian sister, Anna

Famine and human desperation

The winters and famines of 1920–1921 were the worst possible times. Still Sister Anna endured and the boxes of goods, which Dr. Simons was able to send to her on behalf of Methodist European Relief via the Red Cross, as well as personal packages from him and his sister, were welcome indeed. She took great care in distributing them to those in need and kept a careful record in a narrative form that is both informative and moving. Not only did she distribute the things received, keeping little or nothing for herself, she sold her own belongings so that others could have food and clothing.

My dear brother and sister![7]

Now I have unpacked the fourth box. *Thank you so much for everything.* I will once again be in the position to help many people. I distributed the contents of the third box already before Christmas and I was so eager in the distribution that I was almost embarrassed, especially as regards my fellow lodgers, if I had not been saved by a small but richly filled box from Sweden. So far as your personal things are concerned, during the winter after your departure, I had already helped a number of people. For example, Brother Tartarinovitch received your beautiful boots and various warm clothing in order to ease his great need. The overcoat and cap I later gave to Brother Metso, who remains faithful in our work. Diverse older shoes, books, and various other things of Ottillie I gave to Miss Tecklev and Bergmann and A. K. Many came daily to me in the classroom, where they warmed themselves and received tea and soup from me. Poor people came to me during the winter almost in bare feet. Their feet were bound in rags and many of them had no soles on their shoes at all. Our older Brother Seligmann was also a daily guest. It was moving how he also gave us God's blessing. His feet were already so swollen then that I gave him the big boots. Yes, the need was tremendous. At Easter I sold my sewing machine and gave the money to Madame Ragozine.

Then [I sold] part of my bed and all the covers one after the other. The money went to those in greatest need. I know you understand – thank

God that I had things that I could give in this way. I saved nothing, even parted with my twenty-fifth anniversary silver-service. . . . I gave the things from our sick bay – beds, covers, pillows – to institutions with which I came in contact through our church officials and which knew of our social work. Everything was received with deepest gratitude. Whatever else I gave, came from my own clothing and various things.

Yes, dear brother and sister, rejoice with me; our church has really labored!

Come as soon as possible!

Your Sister Anna

In the words of others

One of the most moving descriptions of the desperate situation in Russia during the famine of 1920–1921, the utter lack of food, warm clothing, fuel, medical services, and medicines is found in a letter from the Rev. Hjalmar Salmi written from Tallinn, Estonia on October 14, 1921.[8]

My dear Dr. Simons:

After having secured from the Soviet Government in Moscow the needed permission for entering Russia for distribution of the METH-ODIST EUROPEAN RELIEF supplies, a total of 543 boxes of food, clothing, shoes, medicines, New Testaments, hymnals, and *Poborniks*, I left Viborg on the morning of Aug. 26th, 1921. At Rajoki on the Russian border the goods had to be reloaded in Russian cars in the presence of Russian Custom[s] and "Tcheka" authorities, almost every box being opened and the contents studied. Nothing was taken and the cars were sealed, locked and taken over the border at 7 o'clock in the evening of the 27th of August. I was invited to take a seat in the engine and so I crossed the border in the company of about ten of the most spoken of men of our time, having no other feelings than a great satisfaction that at last the long-cherished wish was to be realized and the greatly needed supplies come into the hands of the needy in Petrograd. It was Sunday morning at six when I reached Petrograd. The church-bells were ringing while I walked through the streets, there being no droskies to be had and no street cars were running on Sabbath days. Walking through the streets of Petrograd, especially through those leading to a railroad station, one who enters Petrograd shall be astonished by seeing the people sitting on the ruins of buildings or on the sidewalks, or in gardens and parks. Most of them are refugees from the famine-stricken region of the Basin of the Volga river, i.e. from the Governments of Samara, Saratov, and Nishni-Novgorod. The citizens of Petrograd are not begging for their living, except some very few old women and invalids, who fill the streets with their luggage, selling and buying, and thus trying to make their living.

When I entered the Methodist Church "Tserkov Christa Spasitelya," I found the congregation, about forty to fifty people, on their knees. Brother Oskar Pöld had conducted the regular Sunday morning service and now they were praying for immediate help. Dear Sister Anna Eklund had noticed me coming and stood in the opening of the door with tears in her eyes bidding me welcome. I had the privilege of giving the congregation, most of them being old Methodist people and personally known to me, your regards and told them that I was sent by the Mother Church with the Relief Supplies. I shall never forget the earnest prayers and thanksgivings that were sent up to Almighty God that morning. It was not so much what I had brought with me that made them rejoice as the assurance that the Mother Church . . . had not forgotten them and that now again the connection was established.

You must also hear the testimony of others about this saint of God, Anna Eklund. Most of them were members of the congregation in St. Petersburg whose letters have been preserved in the Archive of Bishop John L. Nuelsen. Karin Sante, the secretary left in charge of the American Embassy offices in Petrograd. Soon after the Embassy staff left Russia the place was confiscated by the "Reds" and everything looted. Miss Sante was arrested and kept in prison for many months. Later on her father and brother were also imprisoned. All were later freed:[9]

O, and you know Aunt Anna just comes like a little angel from time to time and brings us such excellent things and usually just when it is hardest for us. You really are a dear! Today Aunt Anna brought us again such a nice parcel, and among others a pretty little coat and such dear tiny little shoes. My friend is going to get a little baby (perhaps it is born already; I haven't seen her for a few days) and she had asked me to be godmother. I had told Aunt Anna about it and she, who never seems to forget about anything, brought me those sweet little articles today. I was so glad that I did almost dance; imagine to have such nice presents for my friend. I would not have been able to buy her anything of that kind, and how she will be happy.

Magdalena von Ustinov:[10]

Nobody who has not been in Petrograd these last few years can realize what the misery is. Thank God, that you have good news from Sister Anna, . . . She is surely a heroine; the love for her church made her often act like a lioness protecting her young ones, and with pride she told me when last I saw her that she would not quit her post till the end. Poor Sister Anna has suffered like all of us from hunger and many a time we came together when not the one or the other had a crust of bread to eat. But through all that God has helped us wonderfully, in some way or other we obtained a piece of extra bread, which we enjoyed as if we had the finest cake.

. . .

How many of Sister Anna's clothes and knick-knacks went on the market, and how happy she was when I brought her some money for them! On several occasions she told me that that morning she had no money whatever left, etc., and then how wonderful God heard her prayers. O, I could go on telling you of these dark and dreary times.

There is a letter dated November 6, 1921, from a person, known only as A. K., who had been a member of the St. Petersburg congregation from its inception. He or she has left one of the noblest tributes ever paid to Sister Anna. The letter was apparently written on the occasion of a celebration of the first 13 years of Sister Anna's ministry in Russia:[11]

Dear Members and Friends,

We have gathered today in our church for a special festive and divine service. What is the reason for such a celebration? Thirteen years ago the "Bethany Deaconess Home of the Methodist Episcopal Church in Petrograd" was founded. The founder of said Home was our esteemed and dear Sister Anna Eklund.

Sister Anna comes from a well-known Swedish family in Finland and committed herself at a very young age to Christian service. She left her native country and home, her beloved family, all her friends, and went to Germany, where she studied in the Bethany Deaconess training center. Having finished her course, she worked from the year 1888 for the good of suffering mankind in different cities of Europe, until Bishop Burt sent her in the year 1908 to the Methodist Mission in Petrograd.

It is thirteen years since Sister Anna came to our city in order to work together with our dear Pastor, Dr. Simons, for the benefit of the Russian nation and the glory of God.

She had a hard time at first in this strange place, not knowing even the Russian language, which is not easy for foreigners to learn. But Sister Anna possessed another language, the language of love for suffering mankind. The poor, sick, and distressed understood her very well. Nationality and creed make no difference. She is one and the same to everybody. Everywhere she goes she wins the hearts of the people through her patience, love, and good temperament. Who does not know Sister Anna? How many poor has she visited, how many sick has she helped, how many unhappy has she comforted, and how many tears has she dried? Her work was very hard, but God wanted her to do some more.

Then began the World War, then started the Revolution, and our dear pastor, Dr. Simons, being an American citizen, had to leave Russia and his beloved work in Petrograd. To whom shall he entrust his work and church? He does not hesitate a moment and hands everything over to Sister Anna.

Here begins the hardest time of all for Sister Anna. All communications with America are broken. Many of the congregation have to leave. The finances of Sister Anna come to an end.

How will she keep up the church, how will she help the poor and sick of our congregation, and how will she herself exist? She does not get anything from anybody. Without hesitation she sacrifices her own things and tries to help others who have less than she has. But that isn't all.

She also has to suffer from hunger and cold, but she does not lose her faith in God and better days. Though the congregation grows less and less through death and departure from Petrograd, and many friends disappear, she is still surrounded by a little group of friends.

How difficult it has been for her to save our little church! But God did not leave her alone in this hard time, and she surmounted all difficulties and danger.

She was trusted and esteemed even by the Soviet and Commissariats, to whom she was obliged often to go in connection with church affairs. Thirteen years of very hard but also very blessed work of this self-denying worker in the vineyard of the Lord! May God bless her in her further work and save her for us for many, many years.

A member of the congregation,

A. K.

A group of nurses who had worked alongside Sister Anna expressed their deep appreciation for her witness and that of Pastor Pöld in these words:[12]

Sister Anna and Pastor Pöld, have helped some of us through the greatest difficulties and given us back trust in God and the courage to live, be it in the elegant and warm words of Pastor Pöld on Sunday that touch our hearts, or through the rich gift of love which Sister Anna shares with such affection and warmth that it is so easy for all to receive it, because it is heartfelt love of others that she offers us.

Thank you, honorable pastor, for this tremendously warm, truly "international" love of people. God bless you and lead you back to us soon.

A group of employees of the Alexander Hospital at Vassilli Ostroff send you greetings and wish you a blessed Easter festival.

Signed by a dozen nurses

A New Year's greeting from Russia

The New Year's greeting sent out as a broadsheet by Oskar Pöld and Sister Anna at the end of 1922 summarizes some of the highlights of the work they conducted during that year in Petrograd. The sense of gratitude and the testimony to Christian witness and service, which emerge in this brief document are worthy of Christians in any time or place.

Petrograd, December 5, 1922

To the Kind Friends Everywhere:

In sending this brief message we find ourselves embarrassed because human language is not adequate to fully express what is on our minds and in our hearts. O, how we wish you could see with your own eyes what we have been witnessing in our daily routine of relief activities among all classes, conditions, and ages, and to hear the heart-gripping expressions of grateful people, or to read some of the many remarkable letters that emphatically exclaim: *"You have really saved our lives."* Such tokens of profound thankfulness are an eloquent example of the *shirokaya russkaya natura,* the broad Russian nature.

While our hearts ache because we are not able to do all that we should like, having but modest resources at our disposal, nevertheless the personal touch and the Christian atmosphere in our relief work, as well as the fact that everything passes through our hands and is given in Christ's name, mean unspeakably much to the recipients. Many fall upon their knees, kiss our hands and invoke God's blessing to rest upon us, our work and the countless friends who are making this beneficence possible. Indeed, we have abundant opportunity to observe the deeply religious soul of the dear Russian people.

Another winter with much suffering, due partly to unemployment, has already begun. May God help us all to now bear one another's burdens and thus fulfill the law of Christ!

We are about to bring in a shipment of one thousand pairs of children's shoes of best Finnish quality, which are to be distributed at Russian Christmas among the poor boys and girls, many of whom are actually barefoot and unable to leave their unheated homes. We have been helping during the past year thousands of children in the Soviet institutions, and have enjoyed absolute freedom in all our work. The Soviet officials have been very courteous and helpful to us everywhere. The Government authorities have requested us to do something special among the poor and sick children this winter. Likewise our help is greatly needed among the sadly forgotten inmates of the prisons, many of whom are clamoring for our visits. We have open doors everywhere, and are welcomed as Good Samaritans. But we should not go empty-handed.

We recently opened a Free Medical Dispensary with five beds for emergency cases, chiefly for the employees in the large factories of our section.

. . .

With best wishes for the New Year, we remain,

Ever gratefully and faithfully yours,

Oskar Pöld, *Pastor*
Sister Anna, *Deaconess*
Methodist Episcopal Church
Vassilli Ostroff, Bolshoi Prospect 58
PETROGRAD, RUSSIA

Women precursors of Methodist clergy

Long before women were allowed to be ordained and serve as pastors, superintendents, or bishops in Methodism Bishop Nuelsen reported, "Thus far, Sister Anna has virtually been the Superintendent of our work in Russia. They all look to Sister Anna. She is one of God's elect women."[13] Fortunately Bishop John L. Nuelsen has preserved in his book, *Kurzgefasste Geschichte des Methodismus von seinen Anfängen bis zur Gegenwart*, a report from Rev. Oskar Pöld on the occasion of a celebration of Sister Anna's 60th birthday.[14] It sheds considerable light not only on her life but on that of the church in Leningrad.

On May 25, 1927 the Methodist Episcopal Church celebrated the sixtieth birthday of the heroine and Head Deaconess, Anna Eklund. The Church of Christ Our Savior in Leningrad had the extraordinary joy to sponsor this celebration in her honor. The altar was richly decorated with flowers. In the evening there was a festive worship service. Numerous telegrams and letters were received from many countries, with which Sister Anna has contact, primarily from America, Germany, Finland, Sweden, and the Baltics.

Bishop John L. Nuelsen congratulated Sister Anna via letter and telegram. Many leading persons and coworkers of our church from various countries, thanks to the great trust which Sister Anna enjoys with the Soviet government, have been able to visit the Soviet Union and have shown great interest in the work of evangelization in Russia.

Our valued Head Deaconess, dear Sister Anna, can look back over a rich and blessed life. After receiving her training at the Bethany Deaconess Hospital and training center in Hamburg, Sister Anna has now served thirty-five years as a deaconess. When she was a delegate from Russia two years ago at the Middle Europe Central Conference of the Methodist Episcopal Church at a celebration in Frankfurt she received the Jubilee Cross of the Bethany Deaconess organization for twenty-five years of extraordinary service.

Sister Anna has already been working in Russia for nineteen years and during the last nine years (1918–1927) she has been serving without the usual, ongoing presence of a superintendent. During the first ten years (1908–1918) she served under Dr. George A. Simons, who is now leading the work of the Methodist Episcopal Church effectively in the Baltic states.

In spite of the complicated situation of the church in Russia and the particularly difficult financial conditions, Sister Anna has succeeded with God's help in sustaining the work and the church, and to bring the outreach of the church forward, which is underscored by some forty preaching stations today in Russia. As the leader of the Methodist Church in Russia, Sister Anna is a wise and dear mother of young pastors and deaconesses, who are working effectively in our congregations among the Russian people and who are the sons and daughters of Russia. At the same time under Sister Anna's leadership the blessed assistance for children has gone forward and in the course of this entire year has had particularly joyful success.

In 1931 Sister Anna returned to Finland to recuperate from a series of serious health problems. The Wrede family once again graciously received her and Baron Wrede suggested in March that she go to the Hyvinge Sanatorium for treatment and convalescence. She did so and stayed there for at least a month, steadily improving. Her intent all along was to regain her strength and to return to Leningrad by September. Her health problems, however, necessitated a later return.

At the beginning of June Sister Anna and Oskar Pöld received approved papers to travel to the Finnish border. This would put them closer to Leningrad and make it more readily possible to organize aid for the congregation and the city. From the Finnish border she wrote to Dr. Simons:

> In September, as God wills, I intend once again to travel back to Leningrad. On July 22, we will attend the annual meeting in Kristinestad, Finland in order to confer with Bishop Wade about the extremely difficult situation.
>
> The report of July 12 from Leningrad was terrifying, namely, we became aware that our dear Sister Pauline was arrested during the night of July 7/8 by the G.P.U. At the same time there was an inspection of the church. We hope that the arrest of Sister Pauline does not have any serious consequences, since there could be no reasons for her arrest.
> . . .
> Our position remains fast: to work for Russia; therefore, in spite of everything we want to stand by the people.

Sister Anna finally returned to Leningrad in the fall of 1931. As best she could, she tried to keep in contact with the remaining members of the church. She continued to garner aid for them in any way that she could. But finally the Soviet government of Leningrad confiscated the property and closed the church and the Methodist Episcopal Church of Christ Our Savior continued to live on only in the lives of those who remembered that it once was on the corner at 58 Bolshoi Prospect and had served Christ and the people of the city. Sister Anna was forced to return to Finland.

The last years of her life Sister Anna lived in Helsinki, Finland. Her obituary in the Finnish Christian Advocate, *Nya Budšraren*, states:

> In the spring of 1948 she became very ill and did not recover. At times
> she was troubled by debilitated heart activity that mostly kept her in
> bed. Even her sight was getting worse and she eventually became blind.
> She kept her faith in God, although she had gone through sufferings
> and darkness. On the third day of Christmas [December 27, 1949] she
> passed away.

As did the Christ whom she followed, Sister Anna gave her life in service
to the poor and suffering. In a letter dated January 16, 1921, to George A.
Simons during the hardest of times in Petrograd her hope of what people
might one day say of her was simply, "she died with great love for the poor,
seeking souls, who needed spiritual aid."

Even though when she came to St. Petersburg she did not speak Russian
well at all, we have learned from one of the parishioners that she was able to
communicate immediately with the poor and suffering. A. K. said of her:[15]

> She had a hard time at first in this strange place, not knowing even the
> Russian language, which is not easy for foreigners to learn. But Sister
> Anna possessed another language – the language of love for suffering
> mankind. The poor, sick, and distressed understood her well. Nationality
> and creed make no difference. She is one and the same to everybody. Eve-
> rywhere she goes she wins the hearts of the people through her patience,
> love, and good temperament. Who does not know Sister Anna? How
> many poor has she visited, how many sick has she helped, how many
> unhappy has she comforted and how many tears has she dried?
>   . . .
> How will she keep up the church, how will she help the poor and
> sick of our congregation, and how will she herself exist? She does not
> get anything from anybody. Without hesitation she sacrifices her own
> things and tries to help others who have less than she has.

In Sister Anna hope reigned supreme. As she concluded a letter of October 13, 1926, to Bishop Nuelsen, she stated the constant hope with which
she imbued all that she undertook in the name of Christ and the church,
"we hope to extend our work with new energy and new means." It is not
surprising that when Bishop Nuelsen wrote about Sister Anna three years
later in his book on Methodism, *Kurzgefasste Geschichte des Methodismus
von seinen Anfängen bis zur Gegenwart*, he wrote the following passage[16]
that expresses the hope she constantly brought to the mission in Russia.

> In spite of the complicated situation of the church in Russia and the par-
> ticularly difficult financial conditions, Sister Anna has succeeded with

God's help to sustain the work and the church and to bring the outreach of the church forward, which is underscored by some forty preaching stations today in Russia. As the leader of the Methodist Church in Russia, Sister Anna is a wise and dear mother of young pastors and deaconesses, who are working effectively in our congregations among the Russian people and who are the sons and daughters of Russia. At the same time under Sister Anna's leadership the blessed assistance for children has gone forward and in the course of this entire year has had particularly joyful success.

If one learns anything from the life of Sister Anna Eklund, it should be that there is a language, which transcends all barriers of tongues, cultures, and ethnicity – the language of love. This is the language we learn, as did Sister Anna, from the life of Jesus Christ. His self-emptying, self-giving love, translated into human behavior and action creates an international language that can be understood by all people in all places. Sister Anna is a model of Christian speech/language for the twenty-first century, namely, the language of love. You speak this language by giving of yourself and all that you have to the poor and suffering. How do you learn the vocabulary of this language? By simply doing what Sister Anna did and the Christ before her, whom she served. You give and give and give again to those who are in need.

In conclusion I turn to a poem George Albert Simons wrote about Sister Anna Eklund to whom he refers as "Phoebe" with resonances of the New Testament woman of this name.

"Deaconess Phoebe"
Dedicated to Sister Anna of Petrograd
Paul, when writing his epistle to the Christian church at Rome,
An epistle truly weighty like a classic, learned tome,
Closes with a tender tribute to beloved Phoebe's name,
Who by humble courier-service stept into immortal fame.
"I commend to you our sister Phoebe," fondly writes Saint Paul,
Deaconess, yea servant, of the Church Cenchrea, serving all;
And receive her in the Lord and worthy of the saints, I plead,
In such matters do assist her as of you she may need:
For she's helped so many helpless and myself among them too.
Romans sixteen, first two verses, gives this testimony true;
Then a score of fellow-workers – none could Paul forget –
Who in diverse manners labored throwing out the Gospel net.
Soul-illumined Phoebe's portrait never fadeth from our view,
For her Christlike spirit liveth in a thousand Phoebes new!
Yea, there's one in starving Russia, faithful, fearless at her post,
Helping "Paul" who's absent: Sister Anna is a conquering host!
Written at Helsingfors, Finland
Sunday, December 11, 1921

Notes

1 In 2001 this author published a volume, *Sister Anna Eklund 1867–1949: A Methodist Saint in Russia – Her Words and Witness • St. Petersburg 1908–1931* (New York: GBGM Books, 2001). In preparation for that volume the author translated the large number of German-language letters of Anna Eklund, which were found in the Archive of Bishop John L. Nuelsen in Zürich, Switzerland. She wrote to Bishop Nuelsen and Dr. George A. Simons, the superintendent of the Russia Mission in German, as the former was a first-generation indigenous German who immigrated with his family to the USA and the latter was a second generation German-American. Both men spoke and wrote fluent German. German was Anna Eklund's second language as she had done her diaconal training in Hamburg and in Frankfurt am Main, Germany. Her letters are wonderful narratives and tell her "Russian" story and that of the growth and development of early Methodism in Russia. The 2001 volume included most of her letters in full. While this chapter is a more limited space to tell her story, the excerpts from her letters are invaluable in learning who this woman was and how she lived out her faith and ministry in some of the darkest days of Russian and European history.

2 Kimbrough, *Sister Anna Eklund*, 10–12. All of the letters and excerpts of Sister Anna Eklund and others that appear in this chapter are from the Archive of Bishop John L. Nuelsen. The one exception is the first letter of George A. Simons cited here, which is found in the Methodist Archives of Drew University, Madison, NJ.

3 Ibid., 24–25; letter dated October 21, 1920; translated from German by the author.

4 Ibid., 26; letter dated December 4, 1920; translated from German by the author.

5 Ibid., 28; letter dated December 9, 1920; translated from German by the author.

6 Ibid., 30.

7 Ibid., 32–33, letter dated January 20, 1921; translated from German by the author.

8 Ibid., 35–36, English-language letter.

9 Ibid., 42, English-language letter.

10 Ibid., 52, English-language letter dated March 22, 1921.

11 Ibid., 55–57, English-language letter.

12 Ibid., 58–59, English-language letter dated April 7, 1922.

13 Ibid., 65.

14 John D. Nuelsen, Theophil Mann, and J. J. Sommer, eds., *Kurzgefasste Geschichte des Methodismus*, trans. S T Kimbrough, Jr. (Bremen: Verlagshaus der Methodistenkirche GmbH, 1929), 769–770. See Kimbrough, *Sister Anna Eklund*, 107–8.

15 Kimbrough, *Sister Anna Eklund*, 52, English-language letter dated March 22, 1921.

16 Nuelsen, *Kurtzgefasste Geschichte des Methodismus*, 770.

Sources

Archive of Bishop John L. Nuelsen. *United Methodist Conference Office*, Zürich, Switzerland.

Kimbrough, Jr., S T. *Sister Anna Eklund 1867–1949: A Methodist Saint in Russia – Her Words and Witness • St. Petersburg 1908–1931*. New York: GBGM Books, 2001.

"Methodist Archives." Madison, NJ: Drew University. Russia, and Baltics Mission Materials.

Nuelsen, John L., Theophil Mann, and J. J. Sommer, eds. *Kurzgefasste Geschichte des Methodismus*. Translated by S T Kinbrough, Jr. Bremen: Verlagshaus der Methodistenkirche GmbH, 1929.

9 Ines Piacentini Ferreri

Pioneer of "Wholesome Feminism" in Italy

Andrea Annese

Evaline Odgers, Methodist Missionary in Italy

Ines Piacentini Ferreri (1875–1961) was an important figure among the Italian Methodist women of the late nineteenth and early twentieth centuries. The wife of an Italian Methodist Episcopal Church (MEC) minister and superintendent, Carlo Maria Ferreri, she had important appointments in that Church including the editorship, for about forty years, of the magazine for children *Vita Gioconda* (1906–1943).[1] She taught in schools managed by the Woman's Foreign Missionary Society (WFMS) of the MEC, and also played a role in the *Unione Cristiana delle Giovani* (UCDG), the Italian branch of the Young Women's Christian Association (YWCA), an interdenominational organization of ecumenical character.[2] In addition to all of this, she provided organizational support to her husband. Most particularly, she authored articles in which she discussed the condition and role of women. The life and ministry of Ines Piacentini Ferreri affords a unique "case study" of a European Methodist pioneer who reflected in significant ways on the "wholesome feminism of Jesus." An examination of her life and writings enables us to understand Methodist women pioneers and "Bible Women" in Italy more fully – to comprehend what they *did*, but also what they *thought* and *wrote*.[3]

The early life of Ines Piacentini Ferreri

The life of Ines Piacentini Ferreri intersected some key events in modern Italian history: the very first years following Italian unification, the two World Wars, the Fascist period, and the birth of the Republic. Born in Rome as Ines Piacentini, daughter of Ermenegildo Piacentini and Marianna (or Anna) Giannoni, her actual birth date remains somewhat elusive.[4] One of the registers of the Methodist Episcopal community in Rome (the community to which Ines's family belonged) reports that she was baptized there on March 14, 1875.[5] Another register of the same church, however, states that she was born on February 1, 1877.[6] Other registers record her birth as both 1875[7] and 1877.[8] A definitive birth date of February 1, 1875, however, can be proved from two important pieces of evidence. Firstly, pastor Vincenzo Ravì (who signed the baptism certificate dated 1877) was appointed to Naples at that time, and was not in Rome. The date of his appointment to Rome, and his pastoral ministry there, supports the 1875 birth date.[9] Secondly, and more significantly, in an autobiographical article, Ines states that on February 1, 1960 she celebrated her 85th birthday, confirming that she was born in 1875.[10]

This autobiographical article, in fact, is part of a series written by Ferreri during the last months of her life. While revealing much about her life, it also serves as a window into the history of Methodism (and Protestantism) in post-unitary Italy. Ines intertwines her autobiographical memories with comments and pieces of information about some key figures, communities, and events related to Methodism.[11] These memoirs reveal that Ferreri attended the Methodist Church in Rome from early childhood. As a precocious teenager, in the late 1880s and early 1890s, she was entrusted with leadership of a Sunday school class.[12] A gifted teacher, she attended the "scuola normale," an Italian school that conferred teaching diplomas. At that time, the Methodist Episcopal community in Rome was located near the Trevi Fountain in what was known as the piazza Poli, the first regular Protestant church opened in Rome.[13] On September 20, 1895, a large structure with a new and spacious sanctuary in the via Firenze/via Venti Settembrewas was dedicated and the theological faculty commissioned by superintendent William Burt (1852–1936).[14] Mrs. Ferreri described these developments in detail in her account.

By the turn of the century, the evidence documents the fact that Ines had earned her diploma, and some sources demonstrate that she practiced her skills as a teacher.[15] Her name appears in the Conference Minutes of the Italian MEC and acknowledges her teaching ministry at the Methodist female school of via Garibaldi in Rome during the 1896–1897 school year.[16] It also celebrates the fact that she had won a competitive state exam, perhaps in relation to her teaching at the *Asilo Isabella Clark*.[17] But even after having begun her career in public schools, she continued working in the Methodist institutions. In 1898–1899 she taught again in the *Asilo*,[18] and later collaborated with the Crandon Institute, a highly regarded international school for upper classes girls.[19] These schools were managed by the WFMS and constituted a major part of its work in Italy. Pedagogical activity remained a central aspect of Ferreri's ministry – teaching, writing, and editing books for children – and she even developed a special magazine for them.

Pastor's wife and magazine editor

In 1902 Ines Piacentini married Carlo Maria Ferreri (1878–1942), later a minister of the MEC, at that time Secretary of the *Associazioni Cristiane dei Giovani* (ACDG), Young Men's Christian Association (YMCA), of Rome (and National Secretary until 1909).[20] He was editor of the official weekly magazine of the Church, *L'Evangelista* (from April 1924 to September 1925), and held crucial administrative tasks: superintendent of the (Italian) Southern District from 1914 to 1919, then of the Central District from 1920, and of the so-called unified "Italy District" created in 1926. In 1939 he became superintendent of the *Chiesa Metodista Episcopale d'Italia* (Methodist Church of Italy – CME), just constituted, which gained independence from the American Church in 1940. The MEC Board of Missions had been forced to withdraw its financial support for the Italian Church (definitively from January 1, 1936), which created a crisis in the life of the Church. But Carlo Maria Ferreri was able to manage the situation and to keep the Church viable by selling many of its properties to retire its outstanding debts. Because of his efforts in this regard, and the fact that he was the first Italian superintendent of the MEC, he is considered a key figure in the history of Italian Methodism. Unfortunately, he died from injuries sustained in a street accident on September 22, 1942.[21] Carlo and Ines had five children, born between 1903 and 1913: Raoul, Ilaria, Nada, Bruno, and Mario.

In the early years of the twentieth century Ferreri performed a critical leadership role in the MEC. An article published after her death acknowledged that she "was one of the first who felt the beauty and usefulness of women's organized service in the Evangelical communities, and to this service she gave large contribution."[22] From its establishment in 1906 to its discontinuation in 1943, she managed the Methodist magazine for children, *Vita Gioconda*, which replaced the analogous *L'Aurora* (1893–1905). According to the historian Giorgio Spini, this magazine was valuable and shared the innovative perspective of the Italian (not only Protestant) journals of the beginning of twentieth century.[23]

Vita Gioconda was a monthly periodical, the first issue of which was published in January 1906. The editorial board was deliberate in its choice of the name for this renewed publication: "Knowing that your child's existence is made of smiles and joy, [this magazine] wanted to symbolize this in its name and named itself – *Vita Gioconda* [Joyous Life]."[24] This illustrated magazine included a broad range of material, including short stories, poems, dialogs, games, historical and scientific curiosities, and information. As editor, Ferreri drew up each issue primarily on her own. In the October 1906 issue she introduced columns inspired by religious experience in an effort to reach out to different segments of the Italian society.[25]

In these new columns she included brief Bible meditations, short stories of religious inspiration, and a "Dictionary of Bible Names," conceived as a support for Sunday School lessons.[26] *Vita Gioconda*, however, was not exclusively religious in its orientation. She dedicated the July 1907 issue, for example, almost entirely to Giuseppe Garibaldi, a beloved founding father of modern Italy, the centenary of whose birth occurred on July 4 of that year. That issue contained stories inspired by Garibaldi's life, biographical and historical information, and a list of Garibaldi's "virtues" the editor hoped others might emulate.[27] In subsequent issues of *Vita Gioconda*, Ferreri featured excerpts drawn from the classics of Italian (and other) literature, including the works of Dante, Leopardi, and Virgil. She also collaborated with significant religious figures and artists, publishing the biblical commentaries of the noted pastor/scholar, Eduardo Taglialatela (1875–1937),[28] and the artwork of Paolo Paschetto (1885–1963),[29] who – especially in the early years – designed the cover layout.

Ferreri also published a number of books with the Italian Methodist Episcopal publishing house (*Casa Editrice Metodista*, later *La Speranza*), including translations, hymns, and narratives (see the bibliography at the conclusion of this chapter). She translated the prose work of the American writer, Felicia Buttz Clark (1862–1931), *The Cripple of Nuremberg* (1900),[30] with the title *Il gobbo di Norimberga: Racconto dell'epoca della Riforma in Germania* (1907, new edition 1911).[31] She also translated a book by the renowned Harriette Emilie Cady (1848–1941), *Lessons in*

Truth: A Course of Twelve Lessons in Practical Christianity (1896), with the title *Verità* (1920).[32] She published a novella, *Sulla via del Maestro* (On the Master's Path) and some of her hymns in 1912. She produced "religious courses" in translation: *Racconti biblici ad uso delle scuole domenicali e delle famiglie*, vol. I: *Libro di testo per gli alunni*, and vol. II: *Libro di testo pei Maestri* (the "first course" was edited in 1922, the second in 1923, for a total of four books). These consisted of her own adaptations of "Bible Stories for Sunday Schools and Families," and included manuals for both teachers and students.

She also collaborated frequently with other Italian Methodist and Protestant magazine editors during her lifetime, such as those who published the Methodist *L'Evangelista* and *Voce Metodista*, the interdenominational, Waldensian *Gioventù Cristiana*, and the journal of the ACDG's Italian Federation.[33] Ornella Grassi once observed that Ferreri's favorite activity was that of Christian writer (*scrittrice cristiana*):

> She intended to educate and instruct, but above all to make young people – to whom she addressed most of her work – aware of all the good and beautiful things that one can – that one should – look for, with all one's strength, in this wonderful world created by God.[34]

Ferreri cooperated closely with the UCDG, the Italian equivalent of the YWCA, an interdenominational organization with evangelical aspirations, but with an ecumenical character. She served as President of the Rome branch and member of the National Committee of the UCDGs' Italian Federation.[35] During World War One she held important leadership roles, with other Italian Methodist women, in organizations that supported soldiers (e.g. shipping packages with woolen socks and undergarments, consumables, and other needed items).[36] In this regard she also employed her talent as a writer, composing quite a number of patriotic poems.[37] In the last months of her life, in fact, Ferreri renewed her vocation as a "Christian writer," with the publication of her autobiographical articles of 1960–1961. As their title, *Un ritorno che è forse un addio* (A Return that is, perhaps, a Farewell), demonstrates, these functioned as a literary last will and testament. Ines Ferreri died in Rome on August 26, 1961, the year in which Italian Methodists celebrated the arrival of the first Wesleyan Methodist missionaries and the centennial of their Church.[38]

An analysis of Ferreri's "Feminist" writings

Ferreri authored a number of articles related to the status and role of women. Of particular interest are a number of articles from the 1920s in which she explicitly reflects upon "feminism." In *Femminismo o mascolinizzazione?* (Feminism or Masculinization?), she indicates that her primary concern is to remove misconceptions about "feminism" that seem to have been embraced by "the majority of women."[39] She seeks to define "feminism" and what it truly means to be a "feminist." "I am a feminist," she writes, "inasmuch I rebel against the idea of the woman as a knick-knack, an instrument of pleasure, an automated machine for reproduction or household chores." She makes the claim that the law actually protects "the vices and the medieval conception of men's arrogance." The majority of contemporary women, she continues, misconceive genuine feminism. In their minds, feminists are women who "stroll at all hours with an arrogant and ungraceful look. . . . attend cafés by themselves, smoking cigarettes and blowing smoke – the only thing that fills their head. Moreover, they have crew cuts [*portano i capelli a spazzola*] in their effort to be like men." Ferreri observes that some women may be like this, but they exemplify "masculinization" and are not feminists. True feminism does not take "from men their worst flaws, vices, and bad habits, which they themselves reproach." Rather, for Ferreri, the feminist claims her most sacred rights and the elevation of her dignity; authentic feminism consists in the "elevation of all gifts that God gave us as women. . . . liberation through intellectual and moral elevation, so that love, intelligence, goodness, motherhood, become factors of a redemptive power for modern society."

In this article Ferreri reflects a common attitude about women at that time, namely, that women had the potential – even the responsibility – to elevate society. Rather than being relegated to a legal and social condition of "inferiority," she argues for a "gender equality" that entailed equal rights and a celebration of the "gifts" that women contribute to society. The feminism she espouses compares favorably to what some scholars have described as "difference feminism" or "relational feminism." "With deep roots in late eighteenth century authors such as Mary Wollstonecraft, and very common in continental Europe during the late eighteenth and early twentieth centuries, this view advocated the eradication of legal and social injustice related to gender inequality. It sought an 'equality in difference,' i.e., maintaining and emphasizing the complementary distinctiveness of each sex."[40]

In rapid succession – just one week later – Ferreri published a second article entitled *Femminismo sano* (Wholesome Feminism).[41] She insists on a definition of feminism which she describes as "true, good, and wholesome" feminism. In her articulation of this view she includes allusions to Jesus and citations of the Gospels; she offers something approaching a "feminist exegesis" of the Bible. She discusses the episode of Jesus at the home of Martha and Mary (Luke 10:38–42) and uses this to demonstrate "good feminism." With particular reference to Jesus' words: "Martha, Martha, you are worried and distracted by many things. . . . Mary has chosen the better part" (vv. 41–42), she argues that Jesus saw woman as she was intended to be. God intended her to deal with "noble and spiritual things;" her "mission" and "right" is "to know, to deal with spiritual matters, that are social matters, and elevate herself," to reach "the place for which God created her." As is well-known, this biblical passage is one of the most investigated in feminist exegesis and theology.[42] In the short space of this essay it is not possible, nor the proper place to evaluate the compatibility of Ferreri's reading and contemporary feminist hermeneutics. Even current feminist scholars represent a diversity of interpretations related to this pericope.[43] While her interpretation falls short with regard to modern critical method, her attempt to propose a "feminist" reading of this text deserves acknowledgment and attention. She also correlates this passage with other biblical texts that address the place and role of women.

She evokes Genesis 2:18–25, for example, deviating from standard androcentric interpretations of the language:

> In the *Book of Genesis* is written that God created woman as *a helper* (Gen 2:18.20) for man. A *helper*, please note, therefore a cooperator, therefore a human being capable of understanding all the life issues and to walk hand in hand with him on the path of progress and achievement of civil rights.

God decrees this validation of women, she argues, and confirms it through his Son. She explicitly rejects the "traditional" exegetical thesis according to which God created woman *inferior* to man.[44] She advocates that all women pursue "the wholesome feminism of Jesus" (*il sano femminismo di Gesù*). For her, as one might well expect, educational concerns remain paramount. Leaving aside all economic and political claims "for the moment," she admonishes all Christian leaders to "educate women who can worthily be considered men's partners in the battle for the moral and spiritual elevation of society."

As in the previous article, Ines insists on the "moral and spiritual elevation of society." She maintains that, while other social concerns are not without validity – namely economic and political claims – the task of social moral reconstruction remains the primary task of women. She was painfully aware of the fact that Italian women, in 1924, were not allowed to vote (that injustice would not be removed until 1946), but her primary concern was the role that women could and should play for the sake of *humanity* – for its progress and elevation. She warns that if women do not cultivate their spiritual and intellectual faculties, they condemn themselves to "a position of great inferiority compared to men."[45]

On the one hand, one can easily read a "conservative" perspective into Ferreri's position – there is no appeal for women to battle for the right to vote, for example – and the main role of woman seems to be that of wife and mother. She even defines "family" and "house" as "our first duties." On the other hand, her advocacy of gender equity and her vision of men and women as "partners in the battle for the moral and spiritual elevation of society" reveal her intention to subvert traditional attitudes. Undoubtedly, these perspectives were not contradictory in her own mind. Her position can be understood in light of the emerging "feminism" of her own time, and a brief comparative study of her view with that of a contemporary feminist illustrates this possibility. In 1908 (Anita) Italia Garibaldi (1878–1962) – granddaughter of Giuseppe Garibaldi, member of the Methodist Episcopal community of Rome, graduate of Crandon Institute, collaborator with the WFMS, and director of the Methodist girls' school in Rome from 1908 to 1912 – published her own article on the topic of feminism, "Femminismo Cristiano" (Christian Feminism).[46] Like Ferreri, she states that the right to vote is not what will "eliminate the problems complained by the suffragettes." She even contends that the extreme actions of some women "have brought their cause into discredit." She celebrates the ACDG/YWCA as a women's organization involved in the "moral and social enhancement" of women.[47] In the same vein as Ferreri's arguments, she insists on the importance of women's education and an alternative reading of scripture along the lines of a "feminist-oriented" exegesis.

A final article demonstrates the way in which World War One continued to cast its long shadow on European society long after the Treaty of Versailles. In *La donna e il problema della pace* (The Woman and the Issue of Peace), published in 1924, she laments the fact that the "demon of war" remains on the horizon of humanity.[48] She reports her participation in a women's meeting where they discussed the issue of peace and war, especially questions about "how to avoid the risk of war." Characteristically, she sides, in these discussion, with those who emphasize education, and particularly the pedagogical role of women. Quoting one of the other participants, she claims that "Modern society was educated for war, its conscience is war-oriented; let's educate the new generation for peace, let's give it a peace-oriented conscience." She advocates the role of women in promoting the cause of peace, concluding with this visionary statement: "We mothers, sisters, educators have the task of building the new generations."

The continuing labors of Ferreri

In 1944 Ines Ferreri had a brief correspondence with Ralph Eugene Diffendorfer (1879–1951), then Executive Secretary of the Division of Foreign Missions of the MEC's Board of Missions, and a pivotal figure of twentieth-century Methodism.[49] On July 15, 1944, after postal service had been restored between the United States and Italy, Diffendorfer wrote Mrs. Ferreri a touching letter, asking for updates on the continuing work of the church.[50] He also wanted to tell her how all the American Methodists were "affected by Dr. Ferreri's death" in September 1942. He commended Ferreri on the way he had guided the Italian Church through the difficult waters after the Great Depression and through the opening years of World War Two. During the 1930s he had managed the transfer of properties from the American to the Italian Church, having worked closely with the American Board. These connections with the Ferreri family had been particularly cordial. But the letter also demonstrates Diffendorfer's personal concern for

Ines – now a widow with five children following the tragic accident that deprived her of her husband. He implores:

> How I long for a letter from you or some of your family, giving us in your own words how you have fared in recent months, where you are living, and what has happened to all of the people and the churches and institutions so dear to us.

Ferreri drafted a three-page manuscript letter in English, which she posted to Diffendorfer on September 4, 1944.[51] She opens the epistle with an apology for her "bad English," explaining her decision to abandon her mother-tongue: "I think that is better to make you laugh a little at my gross errors, than to send you a cold, official letter, thought and written by others." This statement provides some insight into Ines's character. She then recalls her husband's death, and explains how he had organized all the administrative matters concerning the Italian MEC, leaving "everything in perfect order." "Perhaps, our lovely Father has called him to rest," she observes, "before other dreadful events came under his so loved Church and the poor Italy." She turns her attention, then, to matters of the family, writing about her sons and daughters. Since they had all moved out of her home by that point in time, she claims, it was not easy even to get news from them. But she did have news of the extended family through her son, Bruno, "who is in Madrid's Italian Embassy." She reports some news from various Methodist communities scattered across Italy with which she had continued correspondence. In a postscript Ines expresses her happiness for the possibility of a Diffendorfer visit to Rome. She also informs him that the Italian Church was experiencing a very difficult period. They "need help," she explained, "not only material but above all moral." This brief correspondence demonstrates the close connections that Ferreri had with important leaders within early twentieth century Methodism. It also provides some insight into the ways in which she sought to manage some of the organizational issues in the difficult situation of Italian Methodism at that time. Apparently, it was her deep desire to be able to pick up the baton from her husband and build upon the foundations that he had set in place. Ines Ferreri's closing years were filled with "intellectual inactivity."[52]

In the last months of her life, in particular, she reflected on the meaning of her life and used her autobiographical articles to draw her narrative to a close. Since her favorite activity, as Ornella Grassi had observed, was that of "Christian writer," nothing could have been more fitting. For this Methodist woman, the writing and the teaching, as well as her leadership within the life of the church, all resonated with a way of life inspired by religious experience and her Methodist beliefs. The "feminism" of this Methodist pioneer was inextricably connected to her evangelicalism. Her Methodist way of life led her to practice a form of "Christian feminism" that was deeply rooted in the scriptures – the "wholesome feminism of Jesus."

Selected works of Ines Piacentini Ferreri
(a chronological listing)

Vita Gioconda (the Methodist magazine edited by I. Piacentini Ferreri, 1906–1943).

"Rapporto della 'Vita Gioconda'." In CME, *XXV Sessione della Conferenza Annuale d'Italia, tenuta a Pavia dal 9 al 13 Maggio 1906*. Pp. 111–12. Roma: La Speranza, 1906.

"Alla Conferenza Annuale della Chiesa Metodista Episcopale Anno Eccl. 1906–07." In *CME, XXVI Sessione della Conferenza Annuale d'Italia, tenuta a Roma dal 14 al 18 Maggio 1907*. Pp. 96–97. Roma: La Speranza, 1907.

Clark, F. Buttz. *Il gobbo di Norimberga. Racconto dell'epoca della Riforma in Germania* [*The Cripple of Nuremberg*]. Translated by I. Piacentini Ferreri. Roma: La Speranza, 1907. (2nd ed., 1911).

Sulla via del Maestro. Novella. Roma: Casa Editrice Metodista, 1912.

Cady, H. E. *Verità* [*Lessons in Truth: A Course of Twelve Lessons in Practical Christianity*]. Translated by I. Piacentini Ferreri. Roma: La Speranza, 1920.

Racconti biblici ad uso delle scuole domenicali e delle famiglie. Vol. 1: *Libro di testo per gli alunni*. Translated by I. Ferreri Roma: La Speranza, 1922.

Racconti biblici ad uso delle scuole domenicali e delle famiglie. Vol. 2: *Libro di testo pei Maestri*. Translated by I. Ferreri Roma: La Speranza, 1922.

Racconti biblici per uso delle Scuole Domenicali e delle famiglie. Secondo corso. 2 volumes. Translated and adapted by I. Ferreri. Roma: La Speranza, 1923.

Vita Gioconda. Novelle per bambini. Roma: La Speranza, 1923.

Per le feste dei nostri fanciulli. Raccolta di poesie, monologhi e dialoghi. Roma: La Speranza, 1924.

"Femminismo o mascolinizzazione?" *L'Evangelista* (April 23, 1924): 4–5.

"Femminismo sano." *L'Evangelista* (April 30, 1924): 7.

"La donna e il problema della pace." *L'Evangelista* (May 7, 1924): 4.

"La nostra anima lontana." *L'Evangelista* (May 21, 1924): 5.

"Rapporto della Direttrice di 'Vita Gioconda.'" In *Chiesa Metodista Episcopale d'Italia, XLVII Sessione della Conferenza Annuale. Tenuta a Torino dal 19 al 22 Giugno 1930*. Pp. 163–65. Roma: Casa Editrice Metodista, 1930.

"Curiosità natalizie." *Gioventù Cristiana* (December 1930): 330–333.

"Spigolature nel campo delle leggende natalizie." *Gioventù Cristiana* (December 1931): 102–104.

"Un ritorno che è forse un addio" [article series]. *Voce Metodista*. (June 1960): 3; (July 1960): 3; (August–September 1960): 3; (October 1960): 3; (December 1960): 3; (February 1961): 6; (March 1961): 4; (April 1961): 4; (June–July 1961): 6; (August 1961): 2.

[These works have not been repeated in the Sources listed below.]

Notes

1 In Italy there were two Methodist Churches: the WMC, organized along the lines of a Presbyterian synodal polity with its origins in the British mission, which began in 1861, and the MEC, with its origins in the American mission (which began in 1871). In 1946 these two traditions merged, giving birth to the CME. On the history of Methodism in Italy, see F. Chiarini, ed., *Storia delle Chiese metodiste in Italia: 1859–1915* (Torino: Claudiana, 1999) and

Il metodismo italiano: 1861–1991 (Torino: Claudiana), 1997; P. Naso, ed., *Il metodismo nell'Italia contemporanea: Cultura e politica di una minoranza tra Ottocento e Novecento* (Roma: Carocci, 2012); Andrea Annese, "Il metodismo in Italia dall'Unità al 'caso Buonaiuti:' Profilo storico-religioso," PhD dissertation, Sapienza University of Rome, 2017; G. Spini, *Risorgimento e protestanti* (Torino: Claudiana, 1998), *Italia liberale e protestanti* (Torino: Claudiana, 2003), and *Italia di Mussolini e protestanti* (Torino: Claudiana, 2007); and L. Vogel, "Comunità e pastori del protestantesimo italiano," in *Cristiani d'Italia. Chiese, società, Stato, 1861–2011*, 2 vols., edited by A. Melloni, 1025–1042 (Roma: Istituto della Enciclopedia Italiana, 2011).

2 On the history of the WFMS, see Frances J. Baker, *The Story of the Woman's Foreign Missionary Society of the Methodist Episcopal Church, 1869–1895* (Cincinnati: Curts & Jennings/New York: Eaton & Mains, 1898; M. Isham, *Valorous Ventures: A Record of Sixty and Six Years of the Woman's Foreign Missionary Society, Methodist Episcopal Church* (Boston: WFMS, 1936); Dana L. Robert, *American Women in Mission: A Social History of Their Thought and Practice* (Macon: Mercer University Press, 1997) and "Holiness and the Missionary Vision of the Woman's Foreign Missionary Society of the Methodist Episcopal Church, 1869–1894," *Methodist History* 39, 1 (October 2000): 15–27.

3 It is not easy to categorize Ines Ferreri: strictly speaking, she was not an "official" Bible woman, though she shared many characteristics with them, and her work began a couple of years after that of the earliest pioneers. Certainly, she was a significant figure among the early Italian Methodist women (whether pioneers or second generation) who worked within the nascent Church and played an important leadership role.

4 See Archivio Storico delle Chiese Metodiste (hereafter ASCM), Fondi comunità locali, Roma folders, series Chiesa episcopale, folder 1: Registro unico 1895–1896 and f. 7: Membri di chiesa 1916?-1945. I would like to express my gratitude to Luca Pilone (Archivio della Tavola Valdese) for his invaluable help in retrieving data from these folders.

5 Ibid., f. 1: Registro unico 1895–1896.

6 Ibid., f. 7: Membri di chiesa 1916?-1945.

7 Ibid., f. 3: Membri di chiesa sec. XX terzo quarto-1979.

8 Ibid., f. 1: Membri di chiesa post 1946–1956.

9 See L. Pilone, "Vincenzo Ravì," in Dizionario Biografico dei Protestanti in Italia, <www.studivaldesi.org/dizionario/evan_det.php?evan_id=436> (accessed June 2017).

10 Ines Piacentini Ferreri, "Un ritorno che forse è un addio," Voce Metodista (June 1960): 3 (the very first installment of this series has a slightly different title from those which follow).

11 Ibid., (July 1960): 3; (August–September 1960): 3; (October 1960): 3; (December 1960): 3; (February 1961): 6; (March 1961): 4; (April 1961): 4; (June–July 1961): 6; (August 1961): 2. Ines died before she was able to complete the series. Her reflections conclude with events in the 1890s.

12 Ibid., (August 1961): 2. We are not told the exact date of this event, but it is possible to infer the terminus post quem and the terminus ante quem: here she is describing a period that immediately follows superintendent Leroy Vernon's resignation (1888), and that predates the establishment of the Methodist Episcopal Boys' School in Rome (1892).

13 St. Paul's Methodist Church, dedicated on Christmas Day 1875 (*Fifty-Seventh Annual Report of the Missionary Society of the Methodist Episcopal Church for the Year 1875* (New York: MEC, 1876), 126–129). The Methodist Episcopal

Church of St. Paul's Within the Walls, usually considered the first Protestant church in Rome, was actually dedicated on March 25, 1876.

14 For a biographical sketch of this important churchman, see E. T. Clark, "William Burt," in., *The Encyclopedia of World Methodism*, edited by Nolan B. Harmon, 2 vols. (Nashville: The United Methodist Publishing House, 1974), 1:362.

15 ASCM, Fondi comunità locali, fonds Roma, series Chiesa episcopale, f. 2: Stato d'anime 1897–1898.

16 The MEC had one school for boys in Rome (from 1892 to 1935) and two for girls: the Collegio metodista femminile (in some WFMS Reports, The Girls' Home School) established in 1889, moved to the new building of via Garibaldi in 1894, and closed in 1915 (when it merged with Crandon) and the International Crandon Institute, established in 1896 (the name "Crandon" was added in 1900) and closed in 1935, which was a renowned college for upper class students of various nationalities and faiths. For further information, see the Annual Reports of the WFMS and the Minutes of Conference of the Italian Methodist Episcopal Church.

17 M. E. Vickery, "Rapporto della Società Femminile per le Missioni Estere [WFMS]," in *Chiesa Metodista Episcopale [CME], XVI Sessione della Conferenza Annuale d'Italia. Tenuta in Venezia dal 12 al 17 Maggio 1897* (Roma: Tipografia Metodista, 1897), 27–30. The Asilo Isabella Clark (Isabel Clark Crèche) was another Methodist Episcopal educational work in Rome, operational from 1896 to 1912. It was a nursery school for needy children.

18 F. Clark, "Rapporto dell'Asilo Isabella," in *CME, XVIII Sessione della Conferenza* (Roma: Tipografia Metodista, 1899), 87–8.

19 Although the official Reports do not contain explicit statements about the teaching activities of Ferreri at Crandon Institute, it is more than probable that she was engaged in this way, or at least that she collaborated in some manner with the director. In some of the published Italian Minutes, for example, she is mentioned and thanked for her assistance in this respect. See M. J. Eaton, "Rapporto per l'Istituto Crandon," in *Chiesa Metodista Episcopale d'Italia, XLVI Sessione della Conferenza* (Roma: Casa Editrice Metodista, 1929), 66. M. J. Eaton, the director of the Crandon Institute, after thanking "all the teachers," mentions "Mrs. and Mr. Ferreri," stating that she considers them "as belonging to the 'family' of Crandon Institute," and that she thanks both "with heart deeply touched." She adds that the students greatly appreciate and love the two (in the present article, English translations of the Italian sources are always mine). See also the Minutes of Conference for 1930 (Mrs. Ferreri "gave help" to the Institute, p. 152) and 1931 (p. 247). It should be remembered, as well, that the Reports did not always mention all the teachers of the schools, so it is not easy to get a precise and complete picture of the teaching staff.

20 The ACDG was the Italian equivalent of the interdenominational YMCA, i.e., the Italian branch of the international YMCA Federation. In Italy there were many local ACDGs, the first founded in 1851. In 1887 they all came under the umbrella of the Italian National Federation of ACDGs. After World War One, American agents founded two "American" YMCAs in Rome and Turin. They received American funding and management and were less religious in their orientation than the original ACDGs that were directly connected with local evangelical churches, all "ecumenical" in their orientation as well. But even these YMCAs were federated with the ACDGs, and all of them were often indifferently named YMCA/ACDG. The same scenario obtained for the women's parallel organization, the UCDG/YWCA, established in Italy in 1894. See Spini, Italia di Mussolini e protestanti, 195–209; M. Introvigne and P. Zoccatelli, eds, Le religioni in Italia, "Opere rivolte alla gioventù," <www.cesnur.com/

opere-rivolte-alla-gioventu/> (accessed June 2017); and M. Gay Meynier, Breve storia della Y.W.C.A. italiana dalleorigini ad oggi (1894–1981), n.p., [1981].

21 See L. Pilone, "Carlo Maria Ferreri," in *Dizionario Biografico dei Protestanti in Italia*, <www.studivaldesi.org/dizionario/evan_det.php?evan_id=487> (accessed June 2017) and A. Scorsonelli, "Carlo Maria Ferreri," in *Harmon, Encyclopedia of World Methodism*, 1: 838–839.

22 Ornella Grassi, "In memoria di Ines Piacentini Ferreri," *Voce Metodista* (August 1961): 2.

23 Cf. Spini, Italia liberale e protestanti, 316. Vita Gioconda was "redatto da Ines Piacentini Ferreri con molta intelligenza e modernità di spirito."

24 "Piccoli Lettori," Vita Gioconda (January 1906): 1. The name Vita Gioconda was suggested by the Methodist Episcopal minister, Vittorio Bani. See Ines Piacentini Ferreri, "Rapporto della Direttrice di 'Vita Gioconda,'" in *Chiesa Metodista Episcopale d'Italia, XLVII Sessione della Conferenza Annuale. Tenuta a Torino dal 19 al 22 Giugno 1930* (Roma: Casa Editrice Metodista, 1930), 163.

25 Ferreri, "Rapporto della 'Vita Gioconda,'" 111. This periodical "attempted reaching diverse constituencies without appearing to be too openly Protestant. . . . I have been working to make the journal effective with regard to moral influence, without overly emphasizing the religious tone that distinguishes us." Ines reports there are families whose "heads" are atheists and even "schools managed by nuns."

26 On this new style of the magazine, see Ines Piacentini Ferreri, "Alla Conferenza Annuale," in *CME, XXVI Sessione della Conferenza Annuale d'Italia, tenuta a Roma dal 14 al 18 Maggio 1907* (Roma: La Speranza, 1907), 96–7. On the general development of Vita Gioconda, see Ferreri's reports in the Conference Minutes for 1906, 1907, and 1930) and the reports of the Press Committee each year.

27 Vita Gioconda (July 1907).

28 He was university professor of pedagogy, philosophy, and literature and translated the works of R. Tagore into Italian; see Pilone, "Eduardo Taglialatela."

29 This artist of evangelical faith (Baptist, while of Waldensian origin) was a significant figure of Italian Art Nouveau and Art Deco. He designed the Emblem of Italy (Emblema della Repubblica Italiana).

30 Felicia Buttz Clark was herself a Methodist, wife of Nathaniel Walling Clark (1859–1918), Methodist minister who was a professor in the Martin Mission Institute (Frankfurt am Main, Germany) 1889–1893 and then President of the Methodist Episcopal Theological School in Rome, where they lived for several years. Many of Felicia Clark's writings, including *The Sword of Garibaldi* (1903), *The Jesuit* (1908), *The City of Mystery* (1914), *Virgilia* (1917), were translated into many languages, including German, Swedish, and Danish, as well as Italian.

31 According to Ferreri's recollections, it was not a real translation: "[F. Clark] told me that she wanted to create a novel that she had already conceived when she lived in Germany with her husband, and proposed that we write it together, she in English and me in Italian. . . . both of us drew up a chapter at a time, subsequently checking them carefully, to avoid misunderstandings" (Ferreri, "Un ritorno," (June–July 1961): 6).

32 Lessons in Truth was one of the fundamental texts for the United Church.

33 See Ines Piacentini Ferreri, "Spigolature nel campo delle leggende natalizie" (A Collection of Tales and Legends Concerning Christmas), *Gioventù Cristiana* (December 1931): 102–104. In this same issue she also published an original poem, Natale (p. 95) and her translation of a French short story (pp. 112–116). See also Ines Ferreri, "Curiosità natalizie," *Gioventù Cristiana* (December 1930): 330–333.

34 Grassi, "In memoria di Ines Piacentini Ferreri."
35 See I. Zilli Gay, "Ines Ferreri," *Ali* (July–August 1961): 127; cf. Meynier, *Breve storia della Y.W.C.A. italiana*, esp. 316–321, 328–342.
36 It is not possible to obtain sufficient or definitive data about World War One because of the scarcity of sources.
37 These poems were published in *L'Evangelista* in 1915–1918. See "Maggio (1915)," *L'Evangelista* (May 25, 1916): 1. The work of Italian women during the war is documented by the same Methodist periodical and in the CME Minutes of Conference for 1918. Generally speaking, the Italian Methodist (like the other Italian Protestants) were pacifists and remained neutral until May 1915 when they gradually began accepting the perspective of "democratic interventionism" and supported Italian intervention. Increasingly they perceived this action as inevitable and as a "(defensive) war against war." They embraced this view fully after Italy entered the war on May 24, 1915, joining the Entente. Cf. Andrea Annese, "Le Chiese metodiste e la Grande Guerra: Il dibattito ideologico e l'impegno pratico," in *La Grande Guerra e le Chiese evangeliche in Italia (1915–1918)*, edited by S. Peyronel Rambaldi, G. Ballesio, and M. Rivoira (Torino: Claudiana, 2016), 105–143.
38 ASCM, Fondi comunità locali, fonds Roma, series Chiesa evangelica metodista, f. 3: Membri di chiesa sec. XX terzo quarto.1979.
39 Ines Piacentini Ferreri, "Femminismo o mascolinizzazione?" *L'Evangelista* (April 23, 1924): 4–5.
40 Offen describes this kind of feminism as "relational" as opposed to "individualist feminism." See K. Offen, "Defining Feminism: A Comparative Historical Approach," *Signs* 14, 1 (Autumn 1988): 119–157. See also D. Riley, *Am I That Name? Feminism and the Category of "Woman" in History* (Minneapolis: University of Minnesota, 1988), esp. 77–78, 81–82 and W. Walters, *Feminism: A Very Short Introduction* (Oxford: Oxford University Press, 2005), 88 and 90.
41 Ines Piacentini Ferreri, "Femminismo sano," *L'Evangelista* (April 30, 1924): 7
42 For a basic examination of various feminist theologies and their main topics, see F. Ferrario, *La teologia del Novecento* (Roma: Carocci, 2011), 187–195 and A. Valerio, *Donne e Chiesa: Una storia di genere* (Roma: Carocci, 2016), 196–200.
43 This narrative has elicited a number of interpretations with regard to the place and role of women. Destro and Pesce, for example, have proposed that Jesus, in this episode, opens the possibility for an autonomous action of women: A. Destro and M. Pesce, "Dentro e fuori le case. Mutamenti del ruolo delle donne dal movimento di Gesù alle prime chiese," in *I Vangeli. Narrazioni e storia*, edited by Navarro Puerto and M. Perroni (Roma: Carocci, 2012), 290–309.

"Gesù . . . crea la possibilità di un'azione femminile autonoma," they write, "ad esempio quando si reca, forse da solo, nella casa di due donne, Marta e Maria (Lc 10, 38–42)" (p. 301). Other studies caution against identifying in Luke too positive a view of women's role, arguing that this author tended to diminish women's leadership and to subordinate their discipleship. Elizabeth Schüssler Fiorenza argues in this direction (*But She Said: Feminist Practices of Biblical Interpretation* (Boston: Beacon Press, 1992), 52–76). Cf. W. Carter W., "Getting Martha Out of the Kitchen: Luke 10:38–42 Again," in *A Feminist Companion to Luke*, edited by Amy Jill Levine and M. Blickenstaff (London/New York: Sheffield, 2002), 214–231. For the possibility of a feminist reading of that periscope, consult the work of S. F. Wemple who argues that "Christianity initiated a new era. . . . Accepted as fully equal to men in their spiritual potential, Christian women could transcend biological and sexual roles and seek fulfillment in religious life . . . [Luke 10:38–42] proclaimed this revolutionary doctrine" (*Women in Frankish Society: Marriage and the Cloister, 500 to 900* (Philadelphia: University of Pennsylvania Press, 1981), 149).

44 It is not possible, obviously, to include an extensive treatment of this issue. See M. Navarro Puerto, "Ad immagine e somiglianza divina. Donna e uomo in Gen 1–3 come sistema aperto," in *La Torah*, edited by I. Fischer and M. Navarro Puerto (Trapani: Il Pozzo di Giacobbe, 2009), 189–239 and H. Schüngel-Straumann, "Dall'esegesi androcentrica a quella femminista di Genesi 1–3," in *L'esegesi femminista del XX secolo*, edited by E. Schüssler Fiorenza (Trapani: Il Pozzo di Giacobbe, 2016), 123–139.

45 On the theme of cultivating these faculties – cultivating the "soul," see Ines Piacentini Ferreri, "La nostra anima lontana," *L'Evangelista* (May 21, 1924): 5, where there is also an allusion to the episode of Jesus, Martha, and Mary.

46 About her, see the Minutes of Conference of the Italian Methodist Episcopal Church, especially for 1908–1912, and the anonymous article, "La nipote di Giuseppe Garibaldi," *L'Evangelista* (April 3, 1908): 5.

47 Italia Garibaldi, "Femminismo Cristiano," *L'Evangelista* (November 6, 1908): 3. For more information on the history of the relationship between women and Christianity, women and the church, see Valerio, *Donne e Chiesa Donne e Chiesa*, 147–203.

48 Ines Piacentini Ferreri, "La donna e il problema della pace," *L'Evangelista* (May 7, 1924): 4.

49 See "Ralph Eugene Diffendorfer," in *The Encyclopedia of World Methodism*, ed. Harmon, 1: 684. After holding other executive positions, "in 1924 he became corresponding secretary of the Board of Foreign Missions and remained in this, or a comparable position, until Church union in 1939, when he became executive secretary of the Division of Foreign Missions of the Board of Missions of The Methodist Church." He held this position until retirement in 1949.

50 Methodist Archives, Drew University, Missionary Files (Microfilm Edition), f. Ferreri, Carlo M. (Rev. & Mrs.), July 1940–December 1946, 9–10. "When I saw this announcement this morning," he wrote, "I said, 'My first letter will be to Mrs. Ferreri'" (p. 9).

51 Ibid., 4–8. In this folder there are both the manuscript and the typewritten transcription (but this contains some misreadings).

52 In her autobiographical memoirs she tells of her return to writing after "Fifteen years of intellectual inactivity" Ferreri, *"Un ritorno"* (June 1960): 3.

Sources

Annese, Andrea. "Le Chiese metodiste e la Grande Guerra: Il Dibattito Ideologico e l'impegno pratico." In *La Grande Guerra e le Chiese evangeliche in Italia* (1915–1918). Edited by S. Peyronel Rambaldi, G. Ballesio, and M. Rivoira. Torino: Claudiana, 2016.

Annese, Andrea. "Il metodismo in Italia dall'Unità al "caso Buonaiuti:" Profilo storico religioso." PhD dissertation, Sapienza University of Rome, 2017.

Baker, Frances J. *The Story of the Woman's Foreign Missionary Society of the Methodist Episcopal Church* 1869–1895. Cincinnati: Curts & Jennings/New York: Eaton & Mains, 1898.

Carter, W. "Getting Martha out of the Kitchen: Luke 10:38–42 Again." In *A Feminist Companion to Luke*. Edited by Amy Jill Levine and M. Blickenstaff. London/New York: Sheffield, 2002.

Chiarini, F. *Il metodismo italiano*: 1861–1991. Torino: Claudiana, 1997.

Chiarini, F., ed. *Storia delle Chiese metodiste in Italia*: 1859–1915. Torino: Claudiana, 1999.

Clark, F. "Rapporto dell'Asilo Isabella." In *CME, XVIII Sessione della Conferenza*. Roma: Tipografia Metodista, 1899.

Destro, A., and M. Pesce. "Dentro e fuori le case. Mutamenti del ruolo delle donne dal movimento di Gesù alle prime Chiese." In *I Vangeli. Narrazioni e storia*. Edited by Navarro Puerto, and M. Perroni. Roma: Carocci, 2012.

Eaton, M. J. "Rapporto per l'Istituto Crandon." In *Chiesa Metodista Episcopale d'Italia*, XLVI *Sessione della Conferenza*. Roma: Casa Editrice Metodista, 1929.

Ferrario, F. *La teologia del Novecento*. Roma: Carocci, 2011.

Fifty-Seventh Annual Report of the Missionary Society of the Methodist Episcopal Church for the Year 1875. New York: MEC, 1876.

Fiorenza, Elizabeth Schüssler. *But She Said: Feminist Practices of Biblical Interpretation*. Boston: Beacon Press, 1992.

Garibaldi, Italia. "Femminismo Cristiano." *L'Evangelista* (November 6, 1908): 3.

Gay, I. Zilla. "Ines Ferreri." *Ali* (July–August 1961): 127.

Grassi, Ornella. "In memoria di Ines Piacentini Ferreri." *Voce Metodista* (August 1961): 2.

Harmon, Nolan B., ed. *The Encyclopedia of World Methodism*. 2 volumes. Nashville: The United Methodist Publishing House, 1974.

Introvigne, M., and P. Zoccatelli, eds. *Le religioni in Italia*, "Opere rivolte alla gioventù." <www.cesnur.com/opere-rivolte-alla-gioventu/> (accessed June 2017).

Isham, M. *Valorous Ventures: A Record of Sixty and Six Years of the Woman's Foreign Missionary Society, Methodist Episcopal Church*. Boston: WFMS, 1936.

Meynier, M. Gay. *Breve storia della Y.W.C.A. italiana dalleorigini ad oggi (1894–1981)*. np, 1981.

Naso, P., ed. *Il metodismo nell'Italia contemporanea: Cultura e politica di una minoranza tra Ottocento e Novecento*. Roma: Carocci, 2012.

"La nipote di Giuseppe Garibaldi." *L'Evangelista* (April 3, 1908): 5.

Offen, K. "Defining Feminism: A Comparative Historical Approach." *Signs* 14, 1 (Autumn 1988): 119–57.

Pilone, L. "Carlo Maria Ferreri." In *Dizionario Biografico dei Protestanti in Italia*, <www.studivaldesi.org/dizionario/evan_det.php?evan_id=487> (accessed June 2017).

Pilone, L. "Vincenzo Ravì." In *Dizionario Biografico dei Protestanti in Italia*. <www.studivaldesi.org/dizionario/evan_det.php?evan_id=436> (accessed June 2017).

Puerto, M. Navarro. "Ad immagine e somiglianza divina. Donna e uomo in Gen 1–3 come sistema aperto." In *La Torah*. Edited by I. Fischer, and M. Navarro Puerto. Trapani: Il Pozzo di Giacobbe, 2009.

Riley, D. *Am I That Name? Feminism and the Category of "Woman" in History*. Minneapolis: University of Minnesota, 1988.

Robert, Dana L. Robert. *American Women in Mission: A Social History of Their Thought and Practice*. Macon: Mercer University Press, 1997.

Robert, Dana L. "Holiness and the Missionary Vision of the Woman's Foreign Missionary Society of the Methodist Episcopal Church, 1869–1894." *Methodist History* 39, 1 (October 2000): 15–27.

Schüngel-Straumann, H. "Dall'esegesi androcentrica a quella femminista di Genesi 1–3." In *L'esegesi femminista del XX secolo*. Edited by E. Schüssler Fiorenza. Trapani: Il Pozzo di Giacobbe, 2016.

Spini, G. *Italia liberale e protestanti*. Torino: Claudiana, 2003.

Spini, G. *Italia di Mussolini e protestanti*. Torino: Claudiana, 2007.

Spini, G. *Risorgimento e protestanti*. Torino: Claudiana, 1998.

Valerio, A. *Donne e Chiesa: Una storia di genere*. Roma: Carocci, 2016.

Vogel, L. "Comunità e pastori del protestantesimo italiano." In *Cristiani d'Italia. Chiese, società, Stato, 1861–2011*. 2 volumes. Edited by A. Melloni, pp. 1025–42. Roma: Istituto della Enciclopedia Italiana, 2011.

Vickery, M. E. "Rapporto della Società Femminile per le Missioni Estere [WFMS]." In *Chiesa Metodista Episcopale [CME], XVI Sessione della Conferenza Annuale d'Italia. Tenuta in Venezia dal 12 al 17 Maggio 1897*. Roma: Tipografia Metodista, 1897.

Walters, W. *Feminism: A Very Short Introduction*. Oxford: Oxford University Press, 2005.

Wemple, S. F. *Women in Frankish Society: Marriage and the Cloister, 500 to 900*. Philadelphia: University of Pennsylvania Press, 1981.

10 Sketches of Methodist women pioneers

Paul W. Chilcote, compiler

Mary Matthews & Macedonian Women

Most of the Methodist women pioneers in the European context remain hidden behind the veil of the past. Their names were never recorded. Their witness and influence will never be known – part and parcel of the lost history of women. The dearth of sources for women in Methodist history (like most history) precludes the composition of a portrait that is little less than cryptic – a sketch more than a portrait. Some are remembered, however, despite the fact that little is known about their lives and labor for the Lord. On the other hand, some more famous women, who are remembered generally for their place in history, have not been recognized for the pioneering role they played in Methodism. In this concluding chapter we present vignettes of women about whom some things are known and about whom we wish we knew more, particularly with regard to their pioneering work within Methodism in their several contexts.

Maria Charlotta Hydén: Finnish Methodist pioneer

Lars-Erik Nordby

In the first half of the nineteenth century we can observe a growing British influence in the, until then, almost completely Lutheran Nordic Countries.[1] For example, the British and Foreign Bible Society (BFBS) inspired and supported establishing Bible Societies throughout Europe, the Norwegian Bible Society in 1816.[2] In 1830, George Scott, an English Methodist minister, was sent by the Wesleyan Methodist Mission Society (WMMS) to Sweden. This was on the initiative of Samuel Owen, an English steamboat builder and pioneer in Swedish industrial entrepreneurship, to labor among Owen's own English workers. Scott soon learned Swedish and started a Methodist Society within the Church of Sweden, took the initiative to establish the Swedish Missionary Society, was one of the founders of the Swedish Temperance Movement, founded a Society for young children's schools, and built the English Church in Stockholm. In 1842 he had to leave the country because of growing resistance against his influence in society. Scott has been regarded as the most influential foreigner in Swedish church life since the sixteenth century reforms in the church.[3]

In Finland a Scottish Quaker James Finlayson (1772–1852) visited Tampere in 1819 to sell Bibles. He had earlier founded a textile factory in St. Petersburg with support from Tsar Alexander I and saw now the possibility of using water power from the river to build a factory. That was the beginning of the largest cotton mill in the Nordic countries. In 1836 the company under the name Finlayson and Compagnie was sold to a consortium and the German Ferdinand Uhde become its manager. He had connections with Johannes Gossner in Berlin and was a friend of George Scott.[4] The company started an orphanage, library, school, church, and hospital.[5]

On Scott's recommendation, Maria Charlotta Hydén was invited by Uhde to Tampere in 1840 to teach at the company's school.[6] Hydén was born in 1805 in Lochteå in Ôsterbotten, Finland. At age 14 she came to Stock-holm where she lived until 1840. During her stay in Stockholm she came into contact with Scott and became a member of his Methodist congregation.[7] She was among the first 28 members when the congregation was founded in 1939.[8] As an extremely gifted teacher, she had a strong influence on her pupils. According to Björklund, quoting Torsten Ekholm, more than 60 years after her death in 1929, her former students celebrated her life and commemorated her legacy in a special Christmas celebration in memory of their beloved teacher.[9] Jussi Hietala, in his *Pro Gradu* (Master) thesis, provides evidence of her work as a teacher in the Finlayson school from 1840–1868. This school was among the earliest to cater to the needs of the youngest children in Finland, and it introduced the so-called Lancaster system or mutual instruction where the children were divided in groups and the best of them taught the others. In Maria Charlotta's time, hundreds, maybe even more than a thousand children, most of them seven to ten years of age, learned reading, writing, mathematics, and handicraft skills. The school was free and open to everyone.[10]

Bjorn Elfving describes her work this way: "As a teacher for young children she had a great influence on her pupil's spiritual life. The first Monday each month she spoke intensely to the children about mission work and collected money for it, probably for the Methodist mission."[11] Maria Charlotta became a pioneer for mission work in Finland, and Tampere became a center for mission interest. In the local markets she came in contact with farmers from central Finland and Savolax and raised money for the Swedish Mission Society that Scott, among others, had founded.[12] She even used the Christmas holidays to travel to Vyborg and Sordavala in east Finland to tell about the work of the Mission Society.[13]

When the Methodist Episcopal Church (MEC) began to exert its influence on Finland through the efforts of sailors converted on the Bethel Ship in New York harbor as part of the Scandinavian Seaman's mission in the 1850s and 1860s, there is no indication that Maria Charlotta showed interest in the new movement. In fact it is more probable that she followed her spiritual father George Scott.[14] When he was back in Sweden in 1859 preaching at a pastors' meeting, he advised the believers not to leave the State Church but to work from inside it.[15] In that way Maria Charlotta and Scott both followed the example of Wesley himself.

Fredrikke Nielsen: Norwegian Methodist pioneer

Thor Bernhard Tobiassen

Fredrikke Nielsen was a well-known Norwegian actress from Bergen. She was born in 1837 on a small farm close to Haugesund.[16] Her mother was not married and her father emigrated to the USA shortly after her birth. At eight years of age she went to Bergen, but it was not until she was 15 that she discovered the true facts about her mother and who she was. She grew up among poor people and went to school only sporadically.[17] Despite her lack of education, Fredrikke seemed to be able to draw exceptional insight from literary works she encountered. Around the time of her confirmation, she was captivated by a local theater group. The theater in which they performed had been founded actually by Ole Bull, an internationally recognized violinist from Bergen who had given concerts all over Europe and in the USA. Bull was keen to establish institutions that could strengthen the identity of Norway as a sovereign nation shortly after their separation from Denmark.[18] Fredrikke was swept into this world of theater and became part of this Norwegian wave in the life of the culture.

She played a lot of characters created by new and young writers like Henrik Ibsen. She also became a close friend to Ibsen who was an instructor at the Theater in Bergen for six years, from 1851 until 1857. Some scholars who have scrutinized the relation between Fredrikke Nielsen and Henrik Ibsen speculate that it may have been more intimate than friendship.[19] Ibsen represented a new style in the world of drama influenced by trends in Denmark and Germany which stressed the contrast between the idealistic and the diabolic. Fredrikke resonated strongly with his ideas and his influence endured in her life long after he moved from the city.[20] In reciprocal fashion, some have noted that Fredrikke inspired Ibsen in many ways, and stories from her life became part of the narratives in his dramatic productions. He probably disapproved of her conversion, and in one of his last productions he describes two women, one dressed in white, the other in black, and both representing Fredrikke – the white as he had met her as a young actress; the black as the revival preacher she had become.[21] Fredrikke made appearances on other stages in Norway, Trondheim and Oslo in particular, and is mentioned in a book about theater history in Norway.[22]

Fredrikke married Harald Nielsen, an actor as well, who found it necessary to change his profession as the consequence of a serious illness, making his living in later years as a photographer. Fredrikke gave birth to eight children. Six of these lived to adulthood.[23] Her oldest son, Hagbart, moved to Halden where he worked as a pharmacist. In Halden, it was Hagbart who first encountered the Methodist movement. He became a member of the Methodist Church there. In a letter to his mother, he bore testimony to his experiences in this community and highly recommended that she seek out the Methodists as well, but no congregation existed in Bergen at that time.[24] In 1879 a young preacher from Hønefoss arrived in Bergen, however, and after a few months he established a new choir and a Sunday school. Later, the Methodist church recorded its first members. While Fredrikke Nielsen was not one of these, through these connections she eventually met Lars Petersen, who engaged her in conversations about her spiritual life and sought to penetrate her skepticism. At some point in 1880 she changed her attitude and embraced her new-found faith among the Methodists.[25]

Despite the fact that Fredrikke prepared a draft of an autobiography, only a small part of it remains extant. She had planned to publish the book, but died just before her plans could be executed. Her children opposed this plan and burned many of the original papers. Nevertheless, the primary story which she had wanted to tell, about how God had told her to leave the theater and start preaching, soon became well-known. Circumstances inside the theater also played a role in this transition in her life. New management had refused to permit her to maintain the privileges to which she had become accustomed. Disputes arose between them, including matters pertaining to her salary, and they seemed to be at an impasse. Regardless, her decision to leave the world of the theater must have been a very difficult one. Her income from acting supported her family in which four children were under the age of 15. Because of her husband's disabilities, he had been unable to provide for the family and died soon after all these events. So she entered her new world at great sacrifice.

Fredrikke's first thought, in fact, was simply to make preaching her new way of life. Before fully abandoning her acting, however, she explored the possibility of public reading to see if she might be able to support her family through this arena. A market, in fact, soon materialized around her reading of literary texts and carried her into a tour from Finnmark to Bergen. She traveled along the coast of Norway and visited different towns and communities in which her lectures were held in schools and public halls. She sent the remuneration she received from ticket sales to her family in Bergen, and this provided for their subsistence.[26] Wherever she was able to secure a chapel or small church, she generally provided a lecture, but the audiences also sang hymns, which provided her an opportunity to read prayers and perhaps a sermon written by someone like Dwight L. Moody or John Wesley. Under these circumstances, she never sold tickets, but requested that people provide a "love offering" to help support her work.

After she had engaged in these kinds of activities for a while, she started writing her own materials for presentation. Her gatherings began increasingly to take on the character of revival meetings. Her life as an actress, of course, prepared her well to express herself through the use of her voice, her body, and by the way she engaged her audience. All these techniques she made use of as a preacher. Some of the Methodist pastors in Norway allowed her to use their churches, but some of them would not permit a woman to preach.[27] Eventually, these revival-style meetings carried her all across Norway, Sweden, and Denmark. She even traveled to the USA to receive what she thought would be part of an inheritance from her father. The meetings she initiated there, however, became so popular that she stayed for five years. Some of her revival meetings among the Methodists were held with Swedish immigrants. For some years she continued in this practice, visiting the USA on a number of occasions.[28] Fredrikke Nielsen died in Bergen, Norway, in 1912 and the pastor of the Methodist Church officiated at her funeral and burial.[29]

Mary Ellen Piggott: Methodist missionary wife in Italy

Jacqui Horton

Born in 1840, Mary Ellen Brown was the third child of Samuel Brown, a substantial farmer, and his wife Mary (née Dearlove). Mary's mother died in childbirth with her fourth child when Mary Ellen was just a toddler. Samuel owned a large farm in Finedon, Northamptonshire and was a prominent member of the village Methodist community, his brother, John, being a minister of the Wesleyan Methodist Church. The church where Samuel's children attended Sunday school and services is now a house.

At the time of Mary Ellen's birth, the Methodist minister in nearby Wellingborough was one William Piggott. Having come from St. Ives, in Cornwall, he and his wife, Catherine, who had been raised on a farm in Buckinghamshire, had five children. Their eldest, Henry (b. 1831), would have been a nine-year-old schoolboy when Mary Ellen was born and ten when her mother died. Wellingborough is only four miles from Finedon and they were part of the same Methodist Circuit. The Piggotts and Browns would certainly have known one another and the tragedy of the Brown children losing their mother would have been felt in the Piggott household where there were children of similar age.

When Mary Ellen was 16, Henry Piggott – who had become a Wesleyan minister himself by that time – came back to the area to help out as a result of another minister's sickness. Henry was 25 and the two must have formed an attachment because, three years later, they were married in Wellingborough Wesleyan Church by Mary's Uncle, Rev. John Brown. The couple's first posting together was in Ealing, Brentford. We know something of their life together from snippets in Henry's many letters to his parents. For instance, this description of Mary Ellen's management of the household accounts:

> You would be amused at our experiences in house-keeping. Pollie (Mary Ellen) is a most rigorous housewife. She exacts from me a scrupulous account of every penny of expenditure, and there exists a certain pocket-book for the receipt of these items, of which I can assure you I stand in very salutary dread. Every now and then comes a day of balancing accounts, and if a few pence happen to be missing, of which no account can be rendered, my good wife's careful soul is in a state of fearful tribulation. With all this, we shall find thrifty management necessary to make ends meet.[30]

Henry and Mary Ellen's first two children (Mary Dearlove – after Mary Ellen's maternal grandmother – b. 1860, and Ralph Henry, b. 1861) were born in Brentford. Then came a testing time – was God calling them to go to Italy? We know something of Mary Ellen's struggle because Henry wrote this in a letter to his parents:

Pollie (Mary Ellen) feels the matter a great trial. Her mind is in considerable conflict about it. Yet she does not, and will not say: "Do not go." As with myself, so with her, the great point is: "Does the cloud move or stay?"[31]

But move to Italy they did at the end of 1861 and both Henry and Mary Ellen learned the language before their departure. We can only imagine what it was like for Mary Ellen, with a baby (who was not in good health) and a toddler, in a strange country where home comforts were not readily at hand.

We can get an idea, however, from this letter extract which describes the day after their arrival:

A true and faithful account of our conditions would startle you not a little . . . within, the floors of all the apartments are covered with cement – not a bit of carpet anywhere. They have now and then had a dry brush over within the last twelve months, but they do not appear to have known the effect of water at any stage of their existence. The furniture is scanty and poor. In the bedroom are no jugs for water, no glass for the teeth – just a white basin which is supposed to be replenished over night for common use next morning. Our experience the morning after our arrival will give you a fair idea of the pickle we are in. Wife and I had an all-but-sleepless night with the baby, so that when morning came she was utterly prostrated with headache and weariness. . . . Well, we have begun our missionary life. But we can often laugh and joke at our discomfort.[32]

Theodore Piggott comments: "For the devoted wife and mother the time must have been one of a severe trial."[33]

The Piggotts had gone into an uncertain, and unknown, mission field. There was no ready manse or church building or obvious area in which to settle. They moved house several times in the next few years. Henry was establishing churches and schools and bases for mission. Mary Ellen was in support as well as doing her own work of bearing, and bringing up children. In August 1862, William Arthur was born, but his short life ended in March 1863. Another boy, Arnold Wycliffe, arrived in September 1864, but he too did not see his first year. Things seemed more hopeful for Helen Brown (born May 1866) who made it into her second year. In 1866, the family moved from Milan to Padua. It was not just the family that had to transfer, as the following account shows:

Our family, will be a large one when all the pupils arrive. We shall have seven boarders, a French young lady from the Waldensian valleys, a certain Miss Rollier, as pupil teacher. Miss Hay, Margherita Delia Pina, myself, wife, three children, two lads who are studying with me for Evangelical work, and three servants – twenty persons in all – and we may have more. You will see that my wife will have her hands full.[34]

We can only imagine how Mary Ellen coped with the move and all these people! She had a six-year-old, a five-year-old, and a five-month-old baby. A further child was born in late 1867 and named Theodore Caro – the latter name given to him by his sister Helen who refused to give up the label "baby" and called him "Caro" instead. Very sadly, the spirited Helen caught scarlet fever in February 1868 and died after an illness of just two days. Mary Ellen had now lost three infants in quick succession; her second child (Ralph) continued to suffer ill-health and the latest baby now became seriously ill. Henry wrote home: "We hardly see our way clearly yet; but it cannot surely be God's will that we should stay in Italy at the cost of all our children's lives."[35]

The editor of the *Life and Letters*, Theodore Piggott, comments:

> Of the mother's thoughts and feelings we have no written record before us; but we know how her indomitable spirit rose to face her troubles. In no event could she have permitted considerations personal to herself to weigh down the balance against the claims of her husband's work, and that work was just in the condition in which it could least bear interruption or change of management.[36]

No other passage in Theodore's book shows Mary Ellen's absolute support and commitment to her husband's work as this one does.

In June 1868, Mary Ellen was able to get a break as she took the children on a visit back to England. When she returned to Italy, she was able to leave baby Theodore with Henry's parents and, in fact, it was Henry's sister Ellen (the child's aunt) who took on the care of the delicate baby. It perhaps seems strange that Mary Ellen should leave a baby behind, but the situation becomes clearer when we read a letter that Henry wrote to his parents in which he suggests that it may not be right to continue in his role as leader of the Methodist mission to Italy. After talking about the complexities of the Italian religious scene and the lack of time to think about them – because he is always rushing from one thing to another – he continues:

> There is another motive which I did not mention: that is the state of my wife's health. If we remain here she will fall, of a general wasting and decay of vital powers which will leave her the ready prey of any attack of illness. She never in her life passed such a year as this, nor was she ever in such a state of bodily debility as at present. . . . After these ten years' experience and training, I would rather work for Italy during the rest of my life than in any other sphere; but not under present conditions.[37]

Mary Ellen had obviously suffered as a result of six pregnancies, the loss of three children, and the worry of the possibility of losing the latest baby. Of course, there was an inevitable effect on Henry, as well, no matter how much his grown-up son thought that the mission work was being entirely prioritized. Happily, the subsequent children all survived to adulthood, along with their three elder siblings. Beatrice Itala was born in December 1869 and Henry Howard in September 1871. Anne Romola was born in September 1874.

In 1873 the Piggott family and the center of operations for the WMC mission in Italy moved to Rome. Their building in Via della Scrofa was consecrated in 1876. As the story in *Life and Letters* progresses, we hear little of Mary Ellen. We are told that the family withdrew to a village in the Alban hills each summer and so we can imagine Mary Ellen enjoying the change of scene and, probably, a let-up in her involvement in the mission and work, although it carried on for her husband. We get a glimpse of her normal life from a letter at the end of 1879: "Our doors are daily besieged by beggars, and my wife's work among the poor women brings before us most heart-rending cases of distress. We tax ourselves to the utmost, but after all it is so little we can do."[38]

The uncertainty in 1868, as to whether it was right for the Piggotts to stay in Italy, seems to have continued, for in May 1882 we read:

> I suppose it is definitely decided that we remain in Italy. Every exit seemed hedged up. . . . To some extent it is a submission of my own judgement to that of others. I have sincerely thought that a change of direction would be good for the work. . . . But I feel that I must consider that God has expressed His will by means of the barriers that have arisen on every hand.[39]

The next record of interest with regard to Mary Ellen relates to the departure of "our children" to India in December 1888. The surviving Piggott children at this time were 28, 27, 21, 19, 17, and 14. Theodore (here the 21-year-old) reports that Mary Ellen bore her husband 11 children of whom eight survived beyond infancy. This means that there were two other children whose names and years of birth are not mentioned. We can deduce that Romola (14) and, possibly her elder brother, were sent to school in India because Indian schools are later mentioned in this account. Also later, Theodore mentions two younger sisters at school in England, so it seems that the tenth and eleventh children were both girls (perhaps the Winifred and Maud later mentioned in the account).

From all this, we can surmise, perhaps, that their financial situation permitted the younger children to be educated abroad; Mary Ellen's health may have also meant that it was best for everyone if the youngest ones were not at home. Indeed, her state of health is also mentioned in the letter about the departure for India:

> The one dark shadow is my dear wife's health. I begin to fear that no permanent cure is now to be hoped for. By great care she may stave off

those terrible spasmodic attacks, which are like passing through the dark valley to return again: but she will be, I fear, an invalid to the end.[40]

Eleven years later, Henry reports:

The doctor thinks that my wife ought not to stay in Wolverhampton through the latter half of September. I propose that she and Winnie follow you to Lucerne. . . . you would come on all to Como (in Lombardy). Of course all this must depend on Pollie's health. If she does not gather strength the next fortnight, the whole plan will have to be reconsidered.[41]

Theodore, son and editor of the *Letters*, continues:

The sad circumstances immediately following this letter may perhaps be told by reproducing a communication sent to the Methodist Recorder of the current date. "It is pretty generally known that Mrs. Piggott has, for many years, suffered much from spasmodic asthma; an occasional summer's visit to England has usually given temporary relief. It has been a disappointment to all that this year the usual benefit has not accrued. Medical help gave some alleviation, but the invalid was counselled to return to Italy before the English summer closed. Arrangements were immediately made for the journey. Day by day her condition gave increasing anxiety. On arrival at Bellinzona her husband was greatly shocked by the change which he immediately detected. It was hoped that a little rest at Como would enable her to get to her loved home by easy stages, but on Sunday morning Mrs. Piggott passed way. . . . On Friday she was laid under the shade of the cypresses in the Cimetero Testaccio in Rome – the new Protestant cemetery – a spot very sacred to hundreds of English homes. The service at the cemetery was conducted by the Rev. T. W. S. Jones, and every Evangelical Church in Rome was represented."[42]

The inscription on Mary Ellen's gravestone reads:

In loving memory
of
Mary Ellen Piggott
wife of
Rev. James Henry Piggott
born at Finedon January 26th 1840
died at Como September 24th 1899
Her children rise up and call her blessed
Proverbs 31 verse 28

At the graveside ceremony marking the 100th anniversary of Henry Piggott's death, I provided a presentation on the lives of Henry and Mary Ellen in England and Rev. Tim Macquiban addressed the topic of Henry's mission and ministry in Italy. As I reflect on this occasion, I only now realize that this Cemetery Chapel witnessed the funeral services of Henry and (probably) of Mary Ellen. The Chapel was built in 1898 so would have been very new. The "new" cemetery referred to in the extract above was, in fact, in use from 1821, the Pope having forbidden any further burials in the adjacent "old" Cemetery. According to Theodore, his father was devastated by the loss of his life's partner, but this is only mentioned in passing. At the end of 1900 we read in a letter extract: "It is a great pleasure, as you may suppose, to have our visitors with us, and in spite of sad recognition of one vacant place, I can even take some part myself in the merriment of the rest."[43]

The remainder of the *Life and Letters*, of course, focuses on the continuing story of Henry, his missionary, ecclesial, and theological activities. The last chapter provides extracts of tributes from those attending his funeral; there is no mention of Mary Ellen. She can be remembered, however, by us for her partnership in the gospel with Henry, her bearing and mothering of their 11 children, and her own mission and ministry to the poor and needy of Italy in the nineteenth century. We can thank God for her and for her witness; the remaining fragments of her pioneer ministry stand as a legacy for all those missionary partners whose sacrificial endeavors have faded away into obscurity.

Marie Bagger: Scandinavian pioneer nurse and deaconess

Lars-Erik Nordby

Inger Furseth compares the women's position in early Methodism in Norway with their position in the Socialist Thrane movement and writes:

> Only the Methodists developed roles for women within the movement organization; a fact that helped the mobilization of women for religious collective action. Women were active in the public and the private spheres of the movement's activities. They became crucial for the survival of early Methodism, because they were the most active fundraisers. . . . Women became, then, a significant resource for Methodism, a resource from which the labor movement omitted to draw.[44]

A good example of these women is Marie Bagger, a Danish nurse who played an important role in the creation of the deaconess work at the *Betaniaforeningen* (Bethany Association) in Norway. She was born in Kullerup, near Nyborg, in Denmark on 18 August 1860. Her father was a Danish Lutheran parish priest.[45]

When she was 22 years old she traveled to the USA. There she worked with mentally ill patients.[46] After returning to Denmark she took nursing courses at the Municipal Hospital in Copenhagen. She had contact with the MEC and a possibility emerged for her to work as a slum sister. As soon as she was approved for the position, she went to England and studied the care of the poor and learned skills related to work in economically deprived communities. Once her studies were completed she was sent to Norway.

In 1891 she described the nursing profession as "a bright and glorious deed" in an article she published in the MEC newspaper *Kristelig Tidende*. She actively recruited other young women to this ministry of service and emphasized the importance of education.[47] In 1894 Marie wrote a letter to the Norwegian Annual Conference in order to provide input with regard to a potential plan to create a Deaconess Home. This correspondence proved to be extremely significant in relation to the Annual Conference and with regard to the later development of the deaconess work in the MEC. She included clear suggestions concerning how the work could be undertaken and, among other things, she suggested using the term nursing instead of deaconess work "because that is what the doctors call it." She also emphasized the fact that, since many doctors had become wealthy from the income of their own clinics, the sisters also ought to be able to secure a stable income from this work.[48]

When the MEC Society for Nursing and Deaconess Work in Norway was established in Oslo in 1897, Marie Bagger was one of the three original deaconesses engaged for this new work. The other two women, Hanna Thoresen and Marie Kristoffersen, were trained as nurses in 1896 at the *Bethanienverein* in Hamburg.[49] The following year Bagger left the *Bethanienverein*. It has been speculated that the reason for her departure may have been the fact that Hanna Thoresen was named matron instead of Marie, but it was more likely the consequence of the connection between her first "call" to be a slum sister and her subsequent ministry. After a few years working in private care, Marie initiated a ministry among the poorest of the poor in Oslo. In January 1903 she settled in the worst area in Oslo, known as *Vaterland*, noted for its brothels, licentiousness, and alcohol abuse.[50] Together with Olafia Johannesdottir, a woman from Iceland, they soon became famous for their work in the so-called White Ribbon, where they cared for the most vulnerable children and their mothers in the district.

They organized excursions and protected children from violence. Inga Bjørnson, in the women's magazine, *Urd*, wrote an article about Marie Bagger in 1911. Bjørnson describes how Bagger was walking down *Smalgangen*, a slum street in *Vaterland*, with "gray looking" children playing around and shabby girls in the windows looking for customers. She commented:

> The prison is a paradise compared with these! Suddenly she came to a gate in a fence upon which the name "The Hope Mission" was inscribed. She went inside and found a wonderful little garden with

oriental lamps. And in here the two ladies ran a children's mission with the name the Pearl of Hope. They also organized an association for the children's mothers, mothers who were doing their best while living with alcoholic husbands. She had even made drawings for housing for workers in the area.[51]

In 1917 Marie traveled back to Denmark. In conjunction with this trip, her friends in Oslo – representing all the strata of society from working class women to the wife of Norway's prime minister – celebrated her work among the poorest of the poor in Oslo. They presented her with a gift of 1,000 Norwegian Crowns, a significant amount of money, wrapped in a Danish and Norwegian flag.[52] In her *Memoirs*, Laura Barratt, the wife of T. B. Barratt, a leading Methodist and the first director of the *Betaniaforeningen*, described a close connection between Marie Bagger and the Barratt family. She makes the claim that Bagger followed Barratt when he left the Methodist Church to become a founding leader of the Pentecostal movement in Norway at the beginning of the twentieth century.[53] While in Denmark, however, she moved in with her family and then, during a horrendous outbreak of the Spanish flu, established a center for the care of the poor and sick at the Jerusalem Church, the country's largest Methodist Church, which served as a temporary hospital under her leadership. In her later years she moved into the *Betaniaforeningen* in Copenhagen and stayed with the deaconesses there. It was here that her life of service to the poorest of the poor and the needy came to its end on September 27, 1935.

Mary Matthews: pioneer of Methodism in Macedonia

Christina Cekov

Mary Louisa Matthews was born in Ohio on August 28, 1864. She attended Mount Holyoke Seminary for Women in South Hadley, Massachusetts from 1880 until 1883. There Mary joined a secret society of girls who had decided to become missionaries. In September 1888, after several years of teaching, Mary got her appointment from the American Board of Commissioners of Foreign Mission (ABCFM) and departed for Monastir, then European Turkey, (now Bitola in the Republic of Macedonia) to teach at the American School for Girls. The Monastir station was established by the ABCFM in 1873 because of its strategically important location, in a town of consuls and with a railway connection to Thessaloniki and other parts of Macedonia. The girls' school was opened as a day school in 1878, and served from 1880 on also as a boarding school. In 1920 it was taken over by the Methodist Mission because the ABCFM resigned from this area. Mary's associates were the principal of the school, Harriet Cole until 1909, and from 1911 to 1916, Delpha Davis. Mary became the principal of the school and served as such from 1909 until her departure in 1920. The teaching staff were aided by native teachers, mostly graduates from Monastir and Samokov Girls' Schools. Outstanding was Rada Pavlova who served the Monastir school for over 30 years.

Mary was in Monastir during the last years of the Ottoman Empire (European Turkey). There were brigands in the mountains and increased oppression by the Turks, who had stationed 50,000 soldiers in Monastir. During all these years of running a school for girls and much more, she acted heroically through one crisis after another: unrest at the end of the Ottoman Empire; the Young Turk Revolution (1906–1908); a cholera epidemic (1911), outbreaks of typhus and scarlet fever (1912 and 1913), the Balkan War I (1912) and II (1913), earthquakes and the bombardments of her school and city by airplanes, gas bombs (1917) and shells during World War One (1914–1918), and with the partial occupation of the school property by German, French and British troops. Governments changed frequently and laws concerning the school also changed. In 1903 the Mission urged all missionaries from Macedonia to withdraw. The four missionaries in Monastir signed a petition to the Mission Board, asking to stay:

> It is possible, of course, that we may be massacred, but we indulge strong hope that for a while, at least, we may comfort and strengthen the hearts of many native friends, our school girls from our two boarding schools, 50,000 starving, homeless refugees – which forbids the thought of flight. We would rather perish in Macedonia, if it be the Lord's will, than to prolong our days outside somewhere else and be ashamed of ourselves.[54]

During these times the mission station was caring for refugees and orphans. Girls and teachers of the school helped in a newly opened hospital for civilian wounded. They did relief services in all wars, giving flour and bread to people in need, without making a difference between Turks, Macedonians, Serbs, Bulgarians or Jews. In 1903, after the Macedonian Uprising against the Turks, a bloody rebellion which left many children without one or both parents, the Essery Memorial Orphanage was added to the Mission. Mary collected orphans from the streets and took them in, along with frightened Turkish refugees. She was for two and a half years the only American in town, left with 17 orphan girls, who had nowhere else to go and three families of refugees under her care. She found foster families for ten girls in England and led them on the dangerous, life-threatening journey to Thessaloniki and sent them off, rescuing them. How ironic was the admonition from the foreign secretary of the Women's Board of Mission, Kate Lamson, who in a letter dated April 22, 1913, warned Mary not to spend her furlough in England because of the terror of militant suffragettes active there.[55]

Under Serbian occupation all other schools had to close, but since the Serbs felt the Macedonian language was "Southern Serbian language" and because most of the students and native teachers were Macedonians, the school was allowed to continue.[56] Mary had over 100 students now and wrote,

> I think our class of 1913 will be able to say what no other class could ever say. They began the year in Turkey, continued most of the year in Serbia and may finish their course in a third country and yet they have lived in the same building all the time.[57]

She collected in the house and dug out of the walls more than 100 pounds of fragments of shells and shrapnel. One afternoon, while having tea at the home of her friend Mrs. Hartley, a piece of shrapnel struck her hostess, killing her.[58] From 1917 to 1918 she did relief work helping more than 900 women to get the money their husbands and sons had sent back home. This was very appreciated, and it broke down the prejudice against the Protestants which had existed for many years. "It was the most satisfactory relief work possible," stated Mary.[59]

Mary was appreciated by female and male coworkers and it was she who got the Board of Mission to sign a paper affirming the equality of male and female missionaries.[60] She did not always appreciate her conservative missionary colleagues, described by her as those "who are so conservative as to object to any new enterprises, and so often block the works for those who would accomplish much!"[61] A glimpse of her progressive view of things can be seen in letters, written in her very own, diplomatic style, like this comment she made in a letter she wrote in 1936 to the president of Mt. Holyoke College, Mary E. Woolley: "I cannot say I am glad that you will be succeeded by a man!"[62] At the end of 1920, after many lonely years serving in the Mission, Mary went on a furlough – but with the intention of going back. She wrote to friends in a letter, 1920, "If you ever hear of my going on strike, you may know it is for fifty hours a day, not eight."[63]

Unfortunately, Mary Matthews never went back to Monastir. It is assumed that the Serbian government did not allow her come back, suspecting her to be an American spy. Mary Matthews worked as diligently and effectively as her colleague Ellen Stone, but she did not receive the attention and prominence of Miss Stone who was kidnapped by freedom fighters and held for ransom, events which won her a celebrated place in Macedonian history. Dr. J. L. Barton, the foreign secretary for the ABCFM, said in a letter of July 21, 1919: "Mary Matthews is one of the heroines of this war and deserves the Victoria Cross or something better." In 1937 her Alma Mater, Mt. Holyoke, awarded her a medal for unusual service to humanity.

Mary L. Matthews died on the last day of 1950 at her sister's home in Lancaster, Wisconsin, not knowing all that she had accomplished by her work. I am convinced that her unselfish work under terrible conditions at the girls' school in Monastir, which produced generations of educated, brave, and capable women, who went back to their home village churches and taught many children and their mothers to read and write, teaching them at the same time about their faith, is one important reason that the Methodist Church in Macedonia is still alive.[64] Even though she did so much for the people of Bitola and the Methodist Church in Macedonia, in her later years, looking back at her missionary work, she stated: "Missionaries are not less human than others. They never know what they may be called upon to do next. I would like to do my missionary work again and do it better."[65]

Notes

1 A special word of thanks to Hans Växby for his help in identifying and locating resources for the preparation of this article.

2 See Andreas Aarflot, *Norsk Kirkehistorie, Bind II* (Oslo: Lutherstiftelsen, 1967), 476–505.

3 Gunnar Westin was a well-known expert on the life and ministry of George Scott. See his monumental two-volume study, published in successive years: Georg Scott och hans verksamhet i Sverige, 2 vols. (Stockholm: Svenska Kyrkans Diakonistyrelses Bokforlag, 1928, 1929).

4 Westin, *Georg Scott*, 1: 519–520; 2: 292–295, 302–303.

5 For more information on this interesting circle of Christian missioners and colleagues, see the Letter of Ferdinand Uhde to Georg Scott in Westin, *Georg Scott*, 2: 292–295.

6 Westin, *Georg Scott*, 1: 519.

7 Ibid.

8 Leif-Göte Björklund, *Rikssvenska metodistpredikanters betydelse för metodist-kyrkans framväxt och utveckling i Finland 1880–1923* (Åbo: Åbo akademis förlag, 2005), 116.

9 Ibid., 116, fn 309; cf. Torsten Ekholm, *Gamla Karleby: metodistforsamling 50 år* (Ekenäs: Metodistforsamling, 1933), 6–7.

10 Jussi Hietala, "Maria Charlotta Hydén Finllaysonin pikkulastenkoulun opettaja ja lāhetyksen suuri persona," *Pro gradu Thesis*, University of Tempare, 2015.

11 Björn Elfving, *Metodistkyrkan i Finland 100 år* (Helsingfors: Metodistkyrkan i Finland, 1984); 13.

12 Westin, *Georg Scott*, 1: 520.

13 Björklund, *Rikssvenska metodististpredikanter*, 117

14 See evidence of her deep affection for Scott in her letter to him of March/April 1842; Westin, *George Scott*, 2: 302–303.

15 Westin, *Den kristna friförsamlingen i Norden* (Stockholm: Enst Westerbergs Boktr. och Förlags, 1956), 73.

16 Fredrikke Nielsen et al., *Minnen från min barndom och mina forsta ungdomsår* (Oslo: Novus, 1998), 16.

17 Ibid., 43, 64.

18 Ibid., 76–78.

19 Ibid., 116.

20 Ibid., 84.

21 Ibid., 121.

22 H. Wiers-Jenssen and J. Nordahl-Olsen, *Den Nationale scene: de første 25 aar* (Bergen: John Griegs forlag, 1926), 101.

23 Willy Heggøy, *Om Fredrikke Nielsen* (Oslo: Nasjonalbiblioteket, 1998), 113.

24 Ibid., 205.

25 Ibid., 221–222.

26 Ibid., 268.

27 Ibid., 351.
28 Ibid., 415–417.
29 Ibid., 454.
30 Theodore Caro Piggott, ed. *Life and Letters of Henry James Piggott, B.A., of Rome* (S.I.: Forgotten Books, 2016), 34–5.
31 Ibid., 47.
32 Ibid., 53.
33 Ibid.
34 Ibid., 67.
35 Ibid., 71.
36 Ibid.
37 Ibid., 73.
38 Ibid., 129.
39 Ibid., 130–131.
40 Ibid., 137.
41 Ibid., 146.
42 Ibid., 147. One hundred eighteen years later, I stood by the graveside (and under the cypresses) as we marked the centenary of Henry's death in November 1917.
43 Ibid., 151.
44 Inger Furseth, "People, Faith, and Transition: A Comparative Study of Social and Religious Movement in Norway, 1780s–1905," Dr. Polit. *Thesis*, University of Oslo, 1999, 258.
45 Robert Nielsen, *Betaniaforeningen og dens diakonisser* (Aarhus: En arbeidsgren i Metodistkirken, 1998), 42–44.
46 Inga Bjørnson, *Vaterland* (Oslo: Urd, 1911), 201.
47 Kristelig Tidende (1891): 32.
48 Betty-Ann Solvoll and Kjerstin Winge, *Betanien Oslo 1897–1987: 90 år* (Oslo: C. Hanssens Trykkeri og Bokbinderi, 1987), 9–10.
49 Ibid., 12.
50 Nielsen, *Betaniaforeningen og dens diakonisser*, 43.
51 Bjørnson, *Vaterland*, 200–201.
52 Nielsen, *Betaniaforeningen og dens diakonisser*, 43.
53 Laura Barratt, *Minner: Utgitt I anledning Laura Barratts 80 års dag* (Oslo: Filadelfiaforlaget A/S, 1946), 58.
54 "Letter of Lewis Bond," *Missionary Herald* (December 1903): 543–544.
55 Letter of April 2, 1913; Mount Holyoke College Archives, Special Collections, South Hadley, Massachusetts.
56 Mary L. Matthews, MS Report of the Girls' Boarding School, 1914; Mount Holyoke College Archives, Special Collections, South Hadley, Massachusetts, np.
57 Letter to friends, April 22, 1913; Mount Holyoke College Archives, Special Collections, South Hadley, Massachusetts. Cf. Matthews, MS Report of the Girls' Boarding School, 1913 and Turan Omer, "American Missionaries and Monastir 1912–17," *Middle East Studies* 36, 4 (October 2000), 129.
58 Mary L. Matthews, MS Diary; Mount Holyoke College Archives, Special Collections, South Hadley, Massachusetts, Wed., March 7, 1917.
59 Mary L. Matthews: MS Summary of Monastir Years; Mount Holyoke College Archives, Special Collections, South Hadley, Massachusetts, np.
60 Letter to Dr. Barton, March 26, 1903; Mount Holyoke College Archives, Special Collections, South Hadley, Massachusetts.
61 Ibid.
62 Letter to Mary E. Woolley, President of Mt. Holyoke College, June 21, 1936; Mount Holyoke College Archives, Special Collections, South Hadley, Massachusetts.
63 Mary L. Matthews, "Report from MLM," *Missionary Herald* (1920): 47

64　Matthews, *MS Report of the Girls' Boarding School*, 1914.
65　Matthews, *MS Summary of Monastir Years*, np.

Sources

Aarflot, Andreas. *Norsk Kirkehistorie, Bind II*. Oslo: Lutherstiftelsen, 1967.

Barratt, Laura. *Minner: Utgitt I anledning Laura Barratts 80 års dag*. Oslo: Filadelfiaforlaget A/S, 1946.

Björklund, Leif-Göte. Rikssvenska metodistpredikanters betydelse för metodistkyrkans framväxt och utveckling i Finland 1880–1923. Åbo: Åbo akademis förlag, 2005.

Bjørnson, Inga. *Vaterland*. Oslo: Urd, 1911.

Ekholm, Torsten. *Gamla Karleby: Metodistforsamling 50 år*. Ekenäs: Metodistforsamling, 1933.

Elfving, Björn. *Metodistkyrkan i Finland: 100 år*. Helsingfors: Metodistkyrkan i Finland, 1984.

Furseth, Inger. "People, Faith, and Transition: A Comparative Study of Social and Religious Movement in Norway, 1780s-1905." Dr. Polit. *Thesis*. University of Oslo, 1999.

Heggøy, Willy. *Om Fredrikke Nielsen*. Oslo: Nasjonalbiblioteket, 1998.

Hietala, Jussi. "Maria Charlotta Hydén Finllaysonin pikkulastenkoulun opettaja ja lähetyksen suuri persona." *Pro gradu Thesis*. University of Tempare, 2015.

Kristelig Tidende (1891). "Letter of Lewis Bond." *Missionary Herald* (December 1903): 543–544.

Matthews, Mary L. "*MS Diary, 1917, Mount Holyoke College Archives, Special Collections*." South Hadley, MA.

Matthews, Mary L. "*MS Report of the Girls' Boarding School, 1913–1914, Mount Holyoke College Archives, Special Collections*." South Hadley, MA.

Matthews, Mary L. "*MS Summary of Monastir Years, Mount Holyoke College Archives, Special Collections*." South Hadley, MA.

Matthews, Mary L. "Report from MLM." *Missionary Herald* (1920): 47.

Nielsen, Fredrikke et al. *Minnen från min barndom och mina forsta ungdomsår*. Oslo: Novus, 1998.

Nielsen, Robert. *Betaniaforeningen og dens diakonisser*. Aarhus: En arbeidsgren i Metodistkirken, 1998.

Piggott, Theodore Caro, ed. *Life and Letters of Henry James Piggott, B.A., of Rome*. S.I.: Forgotten Books, 2016.

Solvoll, Betty-Ann, and Kjerstin Winge. *Betanien Oslo 1897–1987: 90 år*. Oslo: C. Hanssens Trykkeri og Bokbinderi, 1987.

Westin, Gunnar. *Den kristna friförsamlingen i Norden*. Stockholm: Enst Westerbergs Boktr. och Förlags, 1956.

Westin, Gunnar. *Georg Scott och hans verksamhet i Sverige*. 2 volumes. Stockholm: Svenska Kyrkans Diakonistyrelses Bokforlag, 1928, 1929.

Wiers-Jenssen, H., and J. Nordahl-Olsen. *Den Nationale scene: De første 25 aar*. Bergen: John Griegs forlag, 1926.

Index